SOUTHERN COLORADO STATE COLLEGE LIBRARY.

DISCARDED BY
COLORADO LIBRARY

D0428633

F 1410
A 32

80355

Southern Colorado State College
Pueblo, Colorado

NATIONALISTS WITHOUT NATIONS

OTHER BOOKS BY VICTOR ALBA AVAILABLE IN ENGLISH:

Alliance Without Allies
The Mexicans

Nationalists Without Nations

The Oligarchy Versus the People in Latin America

Víctor Alba

FREDERICK A. PRAEGER, *Publishers*

New York • Washington • London

FREDERICK A. PRAEGER, PUBLISHERS
111 Fourth Avenue, New York, N.Y. 10003, U.S.A.
5, Cromwell Place, London S.W.7, England

Published in the United States of America in 1968
by Frederick A. Praeger, Inc., Publishers

© 1968 by Frederick A. Praeger, Inc.

All rights reserved

Library of Congress Catalog Card Number: 68–13325

Printed in the United States of America

F 1410
A 32

80355
SOUTHERN COLORADO STATE COLLEGE LIBRARY

Author's Note

This is a political book. Its purpose is to interpret some facts that I assume the reader already knows—at least in outline.

People in Europe and the United States talk less and less about nationalism, but they talk more and more about it in Africa, Asia, and Latin America—that is to say, in places where conditions are quite unlike those in Europe when the concept of nationalism began to take shape there.

Indeed, we use the same word to describe two distinct attitudes. Just as Communists, for example, call themselves socialists, revolutionaries, or democrats whenever those terms will serve to enhance their prestige, many who today call themselves nationalists do so in order to reap some benefit from the term, or at least from its emotional appeal. But such self-styling is a misuse of language. Today's nationalists are like girls who, although their society no longer places any value on virginity, proclaim their purity from the housetops.

It is interesting to find what is behind this term "nationalism," for, if the word itself has little significance, what it is used to cover up has plenty. Because I know the countries of Latin America and since they are my concern, I shall limit my discussion to them. What *is* Latin American nationalism? Are we dealing with a single nationalism, or does the word cloak different actualities? Is there really any such thing as Latin American nationalism (rather than merely a different one for each country)?

These are the questions I shall try to answer. In this attempt, I shall fall back on my own experience rather than on libraries, on political intuition rather than on the conventional recherché terminology of most specialists.

This book in a way complements an earlier book of mine—*Alliances Without Allies,* written in 1964. In it, I discussed the social and economic consequences of the division of Latin American society into two great blocs: a sector that forms public opinion—the oligarchy, the middle class, the intellectuals, and the skilled workers—which grows and improves its condition at the expense of the second sector, the vast, submerged mass of people (60–90 per cent of the total population, according to the country in question), who have no part in economic developments, political life, or social progress. In this book, I shall discuss the consequences of this division for Latin American politics (both domestic and international), and, to avoid the charge of partiality, I shall frequently quote Latin American writers, even at the risks of appearing monotonous and of being accused of writing with a pair of scissors.

If I have escaped those risks, the reader has Elisabeth Sifton, my editor, to thank. Her sense of humor, patience, and ability to make clear what in my manuscripts (and in politics too) is obscure is a pleasant source of continual astonishment to me.

V. A.

Contents

NATIONALISTS WITHOUT NATIONS

1

Definition and Confusion

In a Century and a Half

In 1819, Simón Bolívar told his country's lawmakers, "My vision is fixed on the centuries to come, and from that vantage point, as I observe with wonder and awe the prosperity, the splendor, and the life that have been granted this vast region, I am enraptured, and it seems to me that I really see it as the center of the universe." At about the same time, Hegel remarked, in *The Philosophy of History,* "America is . . . the land of the future. . . . It is a land of desire for all those who are weary of the historical lumber-room of old Europe." And Adam Smith, writing of lands where colonists were settling not in order to exploit the natives but to spend their lives there (Argentina and the United States, for example), considered that such settlements would advance "more rapidly to wealth and greatness than any other human society," not only as a result of the discipline and skilled techniques the settlers brought with them but also because in other places "rent and profit eat up wages, and the . . . superior orders of people oppress the inferior one. But in new colonies, the interest

3

of the . . . superior orders obliges them to treat the inferior one with more generosity and humanity." He added that abundance of land and scarcity of labor would ensure a high level of wages, and that the workers would be able to become landowners.[1]

Events in the United States have borne out Smith's dictum, but they have proved him a poor prophet in the case of Argentina. Between 1864 and 1894, Argentina received British capital —investments and government loans—in the amount of £125 million, £30 million more than Canada received during the same period. Uruguay, another country that fits Smith's description, received £16 million in the same period, while New Zealand, a larger country, was receiving £40 million.[2] Yet, according to U.N. statistics on national per-capita income, Canada and New Zealand today rank second and third, respectively; Argentina, nineteenth; and Uruguay, twentieth—although Uruguay and Argentina are not unlike Canada and New Zealand. The populations of all four countries were largely immigrant in origin; all four began as independent or autonomous countries, with economies based on agriculture and cattle breeding.

What will explain the difference in outcome? Why have the Latin American countries fallen so far behind in the race for prosperity and well-being?

When the Spanish American countries won their independence, they were wealthier and had better administrations, and their supply of cheap labor was even greater than that of the thirteen North American colonies. Nonetheless, we find that, in 1964, a century and a half later, "Latin America, whose principal source of income was agriculture, was buying agricultural products of North America in the amount of $536 million. . . . Of the $536 million worth of farm products exported by the United States, $343 million represented sales by private business, and the remaining $193 million sales of surplus products in accordance with Public Law 480 empowering the United States Government to dispose of its surpluses abroad."[3]

How was this possible? A century and a half ago, Latin American agricultural production far surpassed that of the United States. Even a century ago, when the United States already possessed almost all the area it covers today, Latin America was still ahead.

Are the Latin Americans lazy, stupid, or self-denying? Have the soil and subsoil of Latin America suddenly been exhausted? Were the people in the Latin America of yesterday more capable than those of today? And were those in the United States, Canada, or New Zealand less so? Or are the Americans, Canadians, and New Zealanders economic geniuses?

None of these explanations settle anything, because they have no connection with reality. The Latin Americans are neither better nor worse than Americans or Canadians, and the soil and subsoil of Latin America have not lost their productive capacity. The true answer must be sought on other, less elementary grounds—precisely my intention in this book—for this answer is essential to any effort to speed up Latin America's progress. We shall seek the answer along the only paths of history that can explain economic and social phenomena: the paths of politics, which is to say, those of the exercise of power.

The Love of Those Far Away

If the basic element is the exercise of political power, we must ask ourselves who wields that power in Latin America. The immediate answer will be "the nation." This, in turn, leads us to ask ourselves, "What is a nation?" Books upon books have attempted to define *nation* and to trace the history of the concept.

The sense of belonging to human groups has always existed. According to Hans Kohn, it corresponds

. . . to certain facts—territory, language, common descent—which we also find in nationalism. But here they are entirely transformed, charged with new and different emotions, and embedded in a broader context. They are the natural elements out of which nationalism is formed; but nationalism is not a natural phenomenon, not a product of "eternal" or "natural" laws; it is a product of the growth of social and intellectual factors at a certain period of history.[4]

Nationalism, in fact, is a product of bourgeois society; it first took shape and found political expression in the French Revolu-

tion and later developed in other countries out of their commitment to the French experience or from their reaction against it
or against Bonaparte. At that stage, said Saint-Simon, the "national party comprise[d] all those who cultivate the land, the
craftsmen, manufacturers, and all those whose work serves production directly or indirectly [as well as] the scholars and
artists," while the antinational party was made up of "the nobil-
ity, the property owners who live without doing anything . . .
the judges who support the arbitrary systems . . . all those who
oppose the establishment of a system more favorable to the economy and to freedom."

Nationalism does not issue forth by spontaneous generation.
"Nation" is an abstraction; the sense of it must be taught. Nationalism always, in one way or another, is due to propaganda.
"Three factors enter into the propaganda of nationalism: the
elaboration of a doctrine by a group of intellectuals . . . ; the
fact that the doctrine finds as its champions citizens who discover
in it a balm for the soul, sometimes a boon to the purse . . . ;
and the implantation of the doctrine in the popular mind by the
new methods of mass education."[5]

While the nations of nineteenth-century Europe were in process
of formation, the idea of nationhood was taken over by the nationalists as a means, not as an end, and nationalism became
something else—liberal, conservative, or radical—besides nationalistic. In the opinion of Mazzini, the nationalist revolution was to
serve to organize humanity. According to Count Szechenyi, a
Hungarian nationalist leader, the unity and independence of the
Magyar people had to bring forth "finer blossoms" that all humanity could enjoy. Bishop Grundtvig, of Denmark, believed
that love of country and nationalistic fervor would inevitably
lead to a higher Christian morality. For Matthew Arnold, the
individual would find in patriotism "the sense of self-esteem gen-
erated by knowing the figure which his nation makes in history;
by considering the achievements of his nation in war, government, arts, literature, or industry." To Veblen, patriotism was a
"sense of partisan solidarity in respect of prestige." Clearly, then,
nationalism could lead almost anywhere.[6]

Only later—when nationalism had established itself as an accepted value no longer in need of propaganda, when the European nations had begun to take shape and become stabilized—did nationalism per se emerge, finding its most amusingly reactionary manifestation in the works of the Frenchman Paul Déroulède and its most tragic with a Hitler or a Stalin. "What characterizes the development of a reactionary nationalism, with all its aggressive traits of a neurotic obsession, is its proliferation of outward form at the expense of content: The symbol, the parade, fetishism take on a greater importance than reality."[7]

However, a nation of such "nationalists" per se is still unformed, is distinct from a true nation; this kind of nationalist would have a nation without classes, all its citizens comprising an elite of gentlemen or an idyllic "socialist" society, or some other ideal. Since such a nation does not really exist, the "nationalists" are forced to replace it with symbols. Their unreal nationalism, which emerges just when reality is pushing forward toward a victory of genuine nationalism, is an isolationist reaction on the part of those who do not feel capable, individually or as a group, of surviving in a society broader than the nation itself.

The French Communist Paul Nizan (who later broke with the Party) has shrewdly observed that, after the French Revolution, a problem arose—"that of discovering how the abstract individual [envisaged] by the rights of man could become the universal man. One means for bringing about this evolution was, precisely, the nation."[8] But the reactionary nationalist has no desire to reach universality. On the contrary, he would like to destroy the universal, and, in his dreams of global dominion, he sees the world not as a unity of harmonious and coordinated nations but as an extension of his own nation, as an enormous colony.

Nationalism, then, is a bourgeois product that manifests itself in industrial societies as a means to higher ends. And, when nations have taken their final shape—when they are completed, so to speak—this nationalism leads to the search for supranational organizations. Or, where local circumstances create a new image of the nation that does not correspond to reality, a new type of nationalism emerges as an end in itself, one that eventually leads to racist aberrations and to a totalitarianism ready to use brute force in order to make the dream of a nation come true.

Thus far, we have talked about nationalism without defining it. Fundamentally, it is a sentiment, and all who share it know what it is without needing a definition. But here we are concerned not with feeling it but with understanding it. Renan offered a memorable formula in a famous lecture at the Sorbonne in 1882: "A nation is a soul, a spiritual principle. Two things that actually are only one come together to build this soul or spiritual principle. One of them lies in the past, the other in the present. One is the common possession of a rich heritage of memories; the other is a present accord, the desire to live together, and the will to continue to accumulate and build the common heritage."[9]

Mazzini, who took the making of a nation for his life's work, doubtless knew what he was talking about when he said, "Nationality comprises common thought, a common law, a common aim. These are its essential elements. . . . Wherever men do not recognize a common principle and accept it with all its consequences, wherever there is no unanimity of mind, the nation does not exist; there is only a multitude, a fortuitous agglomeration that any crisis can dissolve."[10]

The Communists have a more rigid and circumscribed idea of the nation. According to Stalin, who was a specialist (as People's Commissar for Nationalities under Lenin):

A nation is a historically evolved stable community of people, formed on the basis of a common language, territory, economic life, and psychological make-up manifested in a common culture.

It goes without saying that a nation, like every other historical phenomenon, is subject to the law of change, has its history, its beginning and end.

It must be emphasized that none of the above characteristics is by itself sufficient to define a nation. On the other hand, it is sufficient for a single one of these characteristics to be absent and the nation ceases to be a nation.[11]

Political scientists have never been chary of definitions. Karl Deutsch has argued that the proof of a nation consists not in conventional cultural, political, or economic factors but in the capacity of the members of the nation to communicate more, and more effectively, among themselves than with those who are not

members. The Spaniard Carretero Nieva, who lived in a wasps'
nest of nationalities and, therefore, had first-hand knowledge of
the subject, said:

> The most acceptable definition of a nation that we can find is that it is a
> matter of stable (though not everlasting) community, historically formed
> by lasting residence together on the same territory, which is commonly
> sensed and accepted, and which gives birth to habits and modes of
> thinking and feeling reflected in a community of culture, and sometimes
> in a special language. The concept determining this definition is one not
> of things but of the community of things.[12]

Professor Kohn considers that "the nationality feels that it has
been chosen for some special mission, and that the realization of
this mission is essential to the march of history, and even to the
salvation of mankind."[13]

If the more tangible ingredients of nationhood (territory, language, religion, culture, and the like) vary in these definitions,
they nevertheless all contain a common denominator, an idea
that we must consider fundamental: that people feel, believe,
think, or know that they are members of a nation. This means
that the word "nation" must ultimately be defined as something
subjective, as some awareness by the people of a nation that they
are part of the nation.

Although we can more or less identify a nation through its
members, we do not yet know the characteristics of the nationalism that constitutes the theme of this book. No doubt, it would
be amusing for an author to write a book on a subject he himself
cannot define, but the results would be less than scholarly, and
no editor would accept the manuscript. Perhaps, then, we ought
to clutch anew at the specialists' coattails.

Nationalism is "an ideological commitment to the pursuit of
the unity, independence, and interests of a people who conceive
of themselves as forming a community," according to a definition
offered by Lloyd Fallers.[14] Carlton Hayes maintained that "when
the cultural bases of nationality become by some process of education . . . the object of popular emotional patriotism, the result is nationalism."[15]

Kohn said:

The modern period of history, starting with the French Revolution, is characterized by the fact that in this period, and in this period alone, the nation demands the supreme loyalty of man, that all men, not only certain individuals or classes, are drawn into this common loyalty, and that all civilizations (which up to this modern period followed their own, and frequently widely different, ways) are now dominated more and more by this one supreme group-consciousness, nationalism.[16]

Doob, who defines patriotism as the "more or less conscious conviction of a person that his own welfare and that of the significant groups to which he belongs are dependent upon the preservation or expansion (or both) of the power and culture of his society," has defined nationalism as the "set of more or less uniform demands (1) which people in a society share, (2) which arise from their patriotism, (3) for which justifications exist and can be readily expressed, (4) which incline them to make personal sacrifices in behalf of their government's aims, and (5) which may or may not lead to appropriate action."[17]

For Marxists, nationalism is justified only among oppressed people, for whom it is the only hope for progress. Alexander Manor, an Israeli, wrote in this vein more lucidly than most postwar Marxists. He said:

The conditions for production are abnormal . . . when territory and the means for protecting it—political independence, freedom of speech, and cultural development—are restricted or lacking. . . . Class antagonisms become abnormally diffused, and national solidarity gains constantly in strength. . . . Language, for example, then takes on a value far beyond that of a simple medium for protecting the market; when freedom of speech is curtailed, the oppressed feel still more closely bound to their language.[18]

Again, we see that the common denominator of all these definitions is the consciousness of belonging to a nation. But nationalism has certain ideological requirements. Montesquieu wrote, "What we call virtue in the republic is love of country, that is, love of equality," and Rousseau said, "The fatherland cannot endure without freedom." Lassalle argued, with all his energy and passion:

The principle of free independent nationalities is the basis, the source, the mother, and the root of the concept of democracy in general. Democracy cannot tread the principle of nationalities under foot without raising a suicidal hand against its own existence, without depriving itself of the support of every theoretical justification, without basically and on principle betraying itself. We repeat, the principle of democracy has its foundation and life source in the principle of free nationalities. Without this it stands on air."[19]

Today, Kohn affirms that "nationalism is inconceivable without the ideas of popular sovereignty preceding—without a complete revision of the position of ruler and ruled, of classes and castes."[20]

So not only does nationalism insist that the people be conscious of belonging to a nation, but this awareness must shape the nation's desire for freedom, equality, and democracy. Two men expressed this well, both of them fiery polemicists, neither of them greatly concerned with social questions but interested in these issues because they considered them basic. Miguel de Unamuno, obsessed as he was with death and God, was moved to write this about nationalism:

In the ocean there are islands established upon immense deposits of coral that grow from the depths of invisible abysses. A storm may lay waste the island, may even cause it to disappear, but, thanks to its foundation, it will rise again. Social life and its history are based on the silent, slow work of obscure social coral polyps buried in the deeps. . . . Although the patriotic concept of the villager who has never seen beyond the horizon of his hamlet may be narrow, poor, rachitic, it is deeply rooted in history, it is a historic fact, not a more or less durable chance event. The living, sensitive, strong roots of patriotism are alive in him. Historically, the feeling that is drawn from the primitive agrarian community is more mature than the chauvinism of the great property owner who exploits the land through a manager but who, perhaps, has never seen it and is incapable of distinguishing barley from rye.[21]

And Nietzsche struck another keynote. As Kohn has said, "Nationalism—our self-identification with the life and aspirations of uncounted millions whom we shall never know, with a territory which we shall never visit in its entirety—is qualitatively different from the love of family or home surroundings. It is qualitatively akin to the love of humanity or of the whole earth. Both belong to what Nietzsche called . . . *Fernstenliebe,* love of those far away, and which he distinguished from *Nächstenliebe,* love of those near by."[22]

The "love of those far away" sums it all up: the consciousness of belonging to a nation, the desire that in it there may be freedom, equality, and democracy. Without it, there may be a common land, language, culture, history, or religion (as there were in the thirteenth and seventeenth centuries), but not a nation.

Now, then, what relation do those concepts of nation and nationalism have to Latin America?

Latin American Witnesses

The patches on the map that represent the Latin American countries are no different, on the whole, from those that marked off the territories of the Spanish viceroyalties and captaincies general. The countries of today were formed on the basis of decisions made by Spanish administrators.

In the century and a half of their independence, the ex-colonies have had ample time to become nations. To be sure, they had to deal with at least two distinct races (three, in countries with a large Negro population). But, in many European countries, invasions and conquests superimposed two or three new peoples on the original inhabitants, and they mingled. Spain itself is a mixture of Iberians, Celts, Carthaginians, Greeks, Romans, Goths, Visigoths, Arabs, and Jews. Yet Europe and the United States needed less time for the old kingdoms, provinces within kingdoms, or colonies to emerge as modern nations.

Indeed, has Latin America seen the emergence of nations at all? This question is basic. Many Latin Americans have asked it themselves during the past 150 years. No one with any degree of intellectual responsibility has answered it affirmatively.

"Are we Europeans?" asked the Argentinian Faustino Sarmiento (1811–88). "So many things contradict it. Are we natives? A scornful smile from our blonde women is probably the only answer. Are we mixed? No one wants to be that, and there are thousands who would not care to be called either Americans or Argentinians. Are we a nation? A nation without an amalgam of materials or a proper foundation."[23]

Antonio Caso (1883–1946), a Mexican philosopher, believed that three *European* events had decisively influenced Latin

America: the Discovery, a Spanish accomplishment; the Renaissance, an Italian one, which shaped the culture that was soon to be transplanted to the New World; and the Revolution, a French one, which was the forerunner of the Latin American wars of independence.[24] And the Colombian historian Luis López de Mesa wrote, "We are simultaneously America, Africa, and Europe, all without serious spiritual confusion."[25] Pedro Henríquez Ureña (1884–1946), from the Caribbean region, maintained that, in the cultural field, one must accept

. . . frankly as inevitable this complex situation: that, when we express ourselves, there will be, conjointly with something that is ours alone—the product of our own life, sometimes of native origin—another substantial component (though it may constitute only a skeleton), which we have received from Spain. I shall go even further: Not only do we write the language of Castile, but we belong to the Romance family, which still constitutes a community, a unity of culture, descended from the one that Rome organized under her power. To use the oft-repeated phrase of Sarmiento, we belong to the Roman Empire.[26]

With his characteristically poetic touch, the Cuban José Martí (1853–95) described the divisions existing in Latin American society:

We were a sight to behold, with the chest of the athlete, the hands of a dandy, and the brow of a child. We were in masquerade, with breeches from England, waistcoat from Paris, jacket from the United States, and cap from Spain. The silent Indian gave us a wide berth and went to the mountains, to the tops of the mountains, to baptize his children. . . . It would have been a stroke of genius to harmonize, in charity, and with the boldness of the founding fathers, the Indian headband and the robe; to open up to the Indian; to make room for the able Negro; to shape freedom to the form of those who rose up and won it. But we are left with the judge, the general, the scribe, and the prebendary.[27]

Another Mexican philosopher, Leopoldo Zea (1912–   ), explained the same situation on the level of personality, where

. . . the problem is posed of the man who finds that he has an existence or way of life that he does not consider his own, that he sees as something lent to or, worse, imposed on him. . . . Thus is laid bare the disarticulation of the Spanish American: He is split in two, with no fusion possible, given the tremendous contradictions apparent among the separate parts. We still seem to find ourselves in a transitional stage in spite of all the efforts already made.

For, he adds, "The Spanish Americans still carry under their skin the conqueror and the conquered, the colonial, the romantic liberal, and all the other figures of our past. Moreover, in spite of our claims to having been all of those, we go on without being any of them completely. We go on assuming their attitudes only as a matter of form."[28] Another Mexican, the economist Antonio Carrillo Flores, agreed: "In a certain sense, we are still in the process of formation."[29]

Let us continue our review of Latin American witnesses. A Uruguayan sociologist, Roberto Fabregat Cúneo, pointed to the uncertainty of the present situation:

When the time came for us to form a separate continent, we were able neither to be another Europe nor to create a new form of culture. We cannot manage to be either a copy of the old continent or a new world in a new reality. The former would be geographically and anthropologically impossible; the latter is too much of an undertaking for a half-empty continent, left to itself, torn by internal struggles and personal conflicts as arbitrary as they are sterile. The sketch was left unfinished almost as soon as the first lines were drawn.[30]

Manuel Ugarte (1878–1951), a vigorous anti-imperialist Argentinian, held that "All our efforts must be directed toward raising up an integral nationality and rebuilding to some degree, while respecting every autonomy, the immense empire that Spain and Portugal founded in the New World."[31]

The Latin American nations in which these witnesses lived or live are not new. Yet,

We must proceed with much greater caution before affirming the existence of nations *à la* Renan in the various Latin American countries. I am aware of the clearly unique qualities deriving from such objective facts as demographic structure and the high proportion of native blood in several of these countries, but I have an idea, based on brief experience as an open-eyed traveler, that it is hard indeed seriously to proclaim "Mexicanity," "Peruvianity," or "Argentinity," as some try to do now and then.[32]

All the witnesses called so far have been intellectuals and political figures. Now, let us come closer to popular opinion. Two American sociologists made a study of the degree of "national identification" among various social groups of Latin America,[33]

and their findings (see table below) revealed some interesting things.

Degrees of National Identification (Percentages)

County and Population Group	Degree of Identification		
	High	Medium	Low
Brazil			
Managerial personnel and technicians	30	43	27
Skilled workers	20	41	39
Slum dwellers	17	45	38
Argentina			
Medical students, first year	37	42	21
Medical students, last year	46	30	24
Doctors	26	39	24
Mathematics and physics students, first year	36	40	24
Mathematics and physics students, last year	41	34	25
Graduate mathematics and physics students	41	36	23
Economics students, first year	28	37	35
Economics students, last year	38	28	34
Graduate economics students	15	33	53
Chile			
Elementary-school teachers	62	33	5
High-school teachers	55	33	12
Professors, University of Chile	56	28	16
Professors, Catholic University	15	32	53
Mexico			
Members of Congress	15	32	53

Where Is Hell?

As can be seen from the table, the percentage of persons in Latin America with a high degree of national identification is low. Subsequent chapters dealing with the political and social situation in Latin America since the time of independence permit only one conclusion: The nation-state does not exist in Latin

America. None of the definitions of the word "nation" apply to any Latin American country; in other words, none of those countries are nations. As I said, for a country to be a nation, there must be a common awareness of belonging to a nation, as well as a common desire for freedom, equality, and democracy. Neither of these two prerequisites is to be found in any Latin American country (except, perhaps, in Mexico, for reasons I shall give further on).*

Latin American society is a traditional one; it is a society opposed to being transformed into a nation. The Latin American states are not nation-states but oligarchies. Therein lies the key to the whole problem. The Latin American countries are not nations, because the oligarchies have always systematically opposed any move toward nationhood, any evolution that would be conducive to the emergence of national characteristics. For any development of those characteristics would mean the end of oligarchy.

But, as we live in an era in which nationalism is the rule and in which mass means of communication rule out intellectual or ideological isolation, the oligarchies have encouraged a special type of nationalism, one that will serve as a substitute for nationhood. This type of nationalism, in its successive manifestations, forms the theme of this book.

This ersatz nationalism fostered by the oligarchies is anti–North American. Many people in the United States, out of either simplicity, shortsightedness, or adherence to outmoded formulas, have reacted to this by setting up a false syllogism:

Nationalism = anti-Americanism
Anti-Americanism = Communism
Ergo, Nationalism = Communism

* When I say that the Latin American countries are not nations, I do *not* say that they are all alike, that each is lacking in individuality. England, France, and Castile were not nations in the Middle Ages, but they were countries with their own personalities. An Argentine and a Guatemalan are not alike, but this does not mean that Argentina and Guatemala are finished, complete nations. Naturally, the degree of *not* being a nation varies. Some countries have advanced farther than others along the road to real nationhood. Of all the Latin American countries, Mexico probably comes closest to being a true nation. Thus, when I speak in this book of the countries of Latin America, it should be understood that, unless I indicate otherwise, I am excluding Mexico.

This logic is mirrored in a syllogism devised by many Latin American "nationalists":

> Anti-Communism $=$ pro-Americanism
> Pro-Americanism $=$ Imperialism
> *Ergo,* Anti-Communism $=$ Imperialism

I shall try to dissect the psychological and social mechanisms that produce this false logic.

Sartre has said, "Hell is other people." Someone else modified the definition to read, "Hell is one's own self." Latin America is committed to a version of the first definition: "Hell is the United States." I shall try to prove that the political and, especially, the social hell of Latin America can best be explained by a version of the second formula: "Hell is Latin America itself."

The mission of Latin American nationalism is, precisely, to keep Latin Americans from becoming aware of this truth.

2

Independence Without Nationalism

The Creoles and the Common Man

The Roman and Spanish empires probably were the only two that truly acted as civilizing forces. That is, they were the only colonial empires that, when they were forced to withdraw, left their colonies in a situation almost identical with that prevailing in the motherland. When the hour of independence struck for Spanish America, the colonies were not very different from Spain; their social structure and administrative apparatus were identical with those in the Peninsula. During the reign of Charles III, from 1759 to 1788, proposals had been made to create a commonwealth embracing Spain and her colonies by putting each colony under the rule of a son of the Spanish monarch. The viceroyalties and captaincies general sent representatives to the Cortes at Cadiz. The main difference between Spain and Spanish America lay in the composition of the two populations: The colonial populations contained a high percentage of Indians, Negroes, mestizos, and mulattoes. But in neither the colonies nor the motherland did the common people themselves play any political role.

A popular saying aptly described the situation: "The conquest was the work of the Indians; independence was the work of the Spaniards." The conquistadors relied on the help of some Indian groups to subdue other hostile Indians whom they were determined to dominate. Later, in 1810, a great many Indians fought in the armies of the King of Spain because the monarch was their protector whereas, generally speaking, the Creoles (American-born Spaniards) fighting for independence were their exploiters. The Creoles started, led, and capitalized on the war for independence. In the beginning, the purpose of the struggle was not so much to separate from Spain as to refuse obedience to the King, whom Napoleon had placed on the Spanish throne, a man too liberal for the Creoles' taste. Independence was, at first, a reactionary social movement.

During the colonial era, the two strongest affirmations of the American personality were made by Spaniards. Soon after the conquest, the Dominican monk Francisco de Vitoria (1480–1548) proclaimed, in Spain:

Before the arrival of the Spaniards, the Indians were in peaceful possession of their goods, publicly and privately, and, therefore, they must be held to be owners, and their possession cannot be disturbed. . . . The Emperor is not the owner of the globe; it is doubtful that Jesus Christ himself would have been Lord over the world for exclusively material and tangible ends, but, even if He had been, to hold that Christ would delegate this function to the Emperor is sheer invention.[1]

Later, in the jungles of the Orinoco, the extraordinary Lope de Aguirre (1508–61), leading a group of Indians and a handful of Spaniards, rebelled after a quarrel with the Pizarro brothers and proclaimed his independence. In an astounding letter to the King of Spain, he wrote, "Now truly we have come to realize in these realms how cruel you are and how you have broken your faith and word. But you, King and Lord, if you lay claim to being a just king, cannot maintain any claim to these lands where you have never risked a thing unless you first satisfy those who have toiled and sweated on this soil."

Clearly, Ortega y Gasset was not simply stating a paradox when he claimed that the independence of the American people began with the conquest.

The Creole Jesuits expelled from Mexico by Charles III in 1767 did more to lay the theoretical foundations of the movement for independence than even the French Encyclopedists. Francisco Javier Clavijero (1731–87) and Andrés Cavo (1739–1803) spoke out in ringing tones for a union of Spaniards and Indians to form a single nation. "There can be no doubt," Clavijero said, "that the Spaniards would have been wiser if, instead of taking women from Europe and slaves from Africa to Mexico, they had striven to create one nation of themselves and the Mexicans by inter-marriage."[2]

During the colonial era, some Negroes fled to the mountains and established short-lived kingdoms of their own. Indians mutinied, but only sporadically. Canek led an insurrection in Yucatán; Tupac Amaru, in Peru; and other men rose up elsewhere. But the Creoles lived in a state of constant protest, and, although the sons of Spaniards, they had no assurance of getting off lightly if they fell into the hands of the law. The tenor of the *comunero* (common man) movements was Spanish and social, especially that of 1721 in Asunción, led by José Antequera, and later, in 1730, by Fernando Mompó; and that of 1781 in Socorro, New Granada, under the leadership of José Antonio Galán. The rebels were not fighting for independence; they were trying to create conditions under which social mobility would become possible. Except for Galán, none of them gave a thought to the Indians and Negroes. Galán's view was broader. He went so far as to demand differential taxes for the Indians and the poor Creoles. When the leaders of the Socorro movement signed the articles of surrender, at Zapaquirá, in 1781, the people and popular rule were not even mentioned, except that the document used the ancient Castilian terms *común* (the people) and *comunidad* (the community of common people). The surrender was drawn up in accordance with the democratic spirit of ancient Iberian juridical and political traditions. One of the most important of these was the ancient Castilian and Aragonese custom of barring the king from imposing taxes without the consent of his subjects as represented through the institution of the town hall (*cabildo*). This tradition was invoked in order to suppress certain imposts "in perpetuity, so that [their] name may never be heard again."[3]

In what is now Venezuela, Juan Francisco de León, a Canary Islander, led a rebellion that lasted from 1749 to 1751. The rebels, who were Creoles, seized Caracas. But de León's son Nicolás, when he took over leadership from his father, sought the aid of Negroes and mulattoes and was one of the first to show signs of national feeling by declaring that he was acting in defense "of our country, for if we do not do it, we may lose it in the end."⁴

During this time, Spaniards themselves were criticizing the economic system and backwardness of the mother country, and the Creoles likewise applied these criticisms to the American territories. Logically enough, the very Spanish institution of the *cabildo* became an important instrument of protest—the site at which independence was later proclaimed and the first emancipated local power was established. Some of the leaders of the independence movements followed the teachings of the French Encyclopedists; others followed the example of the United States. But most of the Creoles saw fit to voice their protest through the agency of town government. In 1809, Camilo Torres (1766–1815), a Colombian who was later to be shot by the Spaniards, presented to the Cortes at Cadiz a Memorandum of Grievances in which he championed the interests of the Creoles with arguments drawn from Spanish history and legislation:

It has been decided by a fundamental law of the kingdom that taxes may not be imposed or apportioned, nor services, nor contributions, nor coinage, nor any other new tributes, particularly or generally, in any of the realms of the monarchy unless the representatives of all the towns and cities [of the realm] are summoned and consent is given by the said representatives who may come to the Cortes. How, then, can contributions not assented to by deputies who constitute a true representation be demanded of the Americans?⁵

As the English historian Cecil Jane has said, the representative organs of Spanish America were not sprung from the "Mother of Parliaments"; they were born of the "public town meeting [*cabildo abierto*]. . . . The Spanish Americans during the colonial period had lived a vigorous political life in their cities and towns; they had become used to the working of local institutions and to a particular machinery of local government."⁶

At the time of the outbreak of the wars for Latin American independence, the people in the principal cities in each province came together and proclaimed open town meetings to decide what to do about the anomalous situation that had arisen in Spain. Most of the assemblies set up juntas to take charge of the government. The juntas appointed leaders with executive power, and draft constitutions were drawn up and approved in public meetings. The juntas performed more or less the same functions as the Continental Congress in the North American colonies, or as the National Assembly and the Convention in France.

Before long, however, the root of municipal popular government began to wither. The poor Creoles (whom we would now call middle-class Creoles) who headed mutinies and tried to win support from the Indians and mulattoes were displaced. The Creoles from the great families became the leaders in the wars for independence. An attempt to unite all the people—the Creoles, Indians, Negroes, mestizos, and mulattoes—might have laid the foundations of a nation, and, indeed, some pioneers did speak about a nation. For them, independence had a special as well as a political meaning. But, to the wealthy Creoles, the movement was solely political, and its objectives were economic. Their idea was not to reform society but to hand it over to other political administrators.[7] A Chilean Social Democrat put it very well:

The movement for independence was a rebellion of the great Creole landholders against Spanish despotism, because [Spain] did not favor their interests as it should have by permitting the free expansion of latifundist production and trade. . . . [They wanted to] destroy the colonial monopoly and institute economic freedom. The Creole aristocracy and the city dwellers constituted the revolutionary class, because agricultural and industrial production and trade, which could be developed only by breaking down the walls of monopoly, were in their hands. Their own economic needs provided the incentive that forced the landholding aristocracy and the incipient urban bourgeoisie to seek their economic emancipation through political independence.[8]

Agustín de Iturbide (1783–1824), Simón Bolívar (1783–1830), and José de San Martín (1778–1850), all wanted to preserve the old order insofar as that was possible. "The War of Independence was the most conservative revolution which has ever occurred."[9] Bolívar went so far as to say that "the Army and the Church were the most efficacious, if not the only supports for an authority that could save us and a stable government."[10] And yet, Bolívar was the most democratic of the liberators; he tried to be close to the people. José María Morelos (1765–1815), of Mexico, was perhaps the only leader who could give a popular ring to his words. His humble origin, and that of some of those who rebelled with him and later joined the armies of Iturbide, in the long run, were largely responsible for endowing the Mexican political experience with a character completely unlike that of the other Latin American countries and for giving it a greater *national* quality.

The men of action were not the only ones with a conservative outlook. The theorists of independence shared their view. In Colombia, Antonio Nariño (1765–1823), championing an equal poll tax on every citizen, declared, "It is an error to believe that to levy the same amount, shared equally by all contributors, would mean an inequality that harms the poor and favors the rich. . . . No man, class, guild, or association of men may or should be more burdened by the law than any other."[11]

The Transfer of Property

It would be a mistake, though, to think that the Liberators were inflexible oligarchs. That was left to their descendants. The Liberators tried to satisfy the common people, to attract to their cause, if not the masses, at least the majority of the whites and even mestizos. (It is worth remembering that, in many places, class lines then followed—as they still do—color lines and divisions, and that racism, although it is disguised and not legal, has never been wholly absent from Latin American society. Racism there is hypocritical and paternalistic but no less discriminatory than in countries where it is overt. Even today, racism influences Latin American life, though everyone denies that it exists.[12])

While the Creoles tried to satisfy other social groups, they never intended to give them the slightest chance to gain political power. "In general, the Creole leaders try to attract to their cause the free dark-skinned groups and the free mestizos and to mitigate, by legislative action and decree (inspired by political fore-

sight or philanthropic sentiment), the most shocking social inequalities while proclaiming that public office is filled according
to merit, without regard to title, fortune, or birth."[13] What happened in Bolivia is typical of what happened in other countries:

The 20 per-cent royal duty [tribute] paid to the Crown for the exploitation of the mines was replaced by taxes paid to the new state. But the
situation of the peasants and the Indians remained unchanged. Either
the same Spanish owners remained or Creoles took their place. And
the Indians continued to be serfs. . . . With the vision of a genius,
Bolívar recognized the problem and believed it his duty to decree certain measures to help the Indians. These were the decrees of Trujillo
[Peru] ordaining that land be given to the Indians, that the property
of which they had been despoiled be returned to them, and introducing
modifications in the system of personal taxation. But he had not probed
to the root of the problem, which was the economic power of the landholders. . . . Marshal Andrés de Santa Cruz (1792–1865), one of the
great figures of the war for independence, became president of the republic. He was a man with a national concept, the organizer of the
Bolivian state. He introduced legal codes and established schools. But
Marshal Santa Cruz was interested in land. He was a great landholder,
and he nullified Bolívar's decrees.[14]

The insurrection of 1814 in Peru, led by Mateo García Puma-
cahua (1734–1815) and soon crushed by the royalist authorities,
was motivated by social aspirations. The colored groups and the
mestizos who followed the Asturian leader José Tomás Boves
([?]–1814) and the Canary Islander Francisco Tomás Morales
(1781–1844) into Venezuela after 1813, and who brought about
the overthrow of the second republic, were also united in a movement of predominantly social character.[15]

There can be no doubt that the people saw the war for independence as their chance to obtain land and to destroy the caste
system. This lent their participation a social purpose that the
Creoles deliberately glossed over or stifled. Miguel Hidalgo
(1753–1811), of Mexico, promulgated a law that ordained the
distribution of land to the mutinous peasants. Bolívar, despite
his social conformism, realized that, if he were to recruit armies
and stabilize the new countries, the masses had to be placated,
and he had been the first to raise the question of land reform in
Venezuela. But, in 1830, military bonds were issued instead of
parcels of land, a move that served to line the pockets of specula-

tors and some of the *caudillos*. Hidalgo and Bolívar were, in fact, exceptions. Hidalgo was executed and Bolívar was exiled from Venezuela by the Creole oligarchy. In the end, the war strengthened and consolidated latifundism instead of destroying it.

Nevertheless, the landowners changed, although the ownership structure did not. Many Spanish landowners returned to Spain or were exiled for their loyalty to Spanish authority. Their lands passed into the hands of Creoles, who thus grew rich from the war for independence. In some countries of Latin America, several decades were to pass before foreigners, individually or as members of business organizations, would begin to acquire land. At that time, the foreigners who were most successful in obtaining land were the English in Argentina and the Spaniards in Mexico.

"This transfer of large territorial holdings from a few hands to a few other hands coincided with a definite step backward in the process of social liberation."[16] Bolívar, in 1816, at the time of his expedition from Haiti, had promised to free all slaves who enlisted under the revolutionary flag, and he emancipated his own slaves at Aragua and Barlovento. But, in 1830, the landholding slave owners persuaded the Venezuelan Congress not to abolish slavery, and that theoretically liberal and democratic republic did not emancipate until 1865. Other countries followed much the same pattern.

The flood of optimism felt by the masses during the war dried up. Except for the political change, everything remained as before. Existing privileges were augmented by new ones. A flaw in the new order of things—the oligarchic system—kept the countries from following the road taken by the peoples of Europe and the United States; the old colonies had won political freedom, but they retained the landholding system of Spain, and its injustices were aggravated by the absence of the safeguards and protection that the Spanish monarch traditionally tried to give his people. While industry in Europe and the United States in the wake of the French Revolution and the Napoleonic Wars was becoming mechanized under the rule of capitalism, Latin America still clung to an obsolete, uneconomic social system. The maintenance of this system demanded the oligarchy's total control of political life and the exclusion of the people. The first generation of government officials after independence met both requirements and managed to conceal their basic objectives, including the manipulation of their countries' constitutions—a favorite sport of Latin American politicians—beneath a constant flow of rhetoric in praise of democracy.

In this society, in which there still were no political parties, or in which parties took the form of rival Masonic lodges—for example, the Scottish rite and the York rite in Mexico, the conservatives issuing from the one and liberals from the other—the people were without a voice. From those elements of the masses who had distinguished themselves and won promotion in the war came the *caudillos,* who expressed the social aspirations of the people. That is, for want of a better way, the people tried to make their aspirations felt through these popular military figures. But the *caudillos* were by definition bad politicians; if they had been good, they would never have reached *caudillo* status. The oligarchies tamed them easily, now with sweet talk, now with social embarrassment, now simply by bribery. Yet, if the *caudillos* were not much good as representatives of the people, they played a very important historical role by becoming the pioneers of militarism. That is, they made it an accepted, or at least an acceptable, fact that the armed forces would have a voice in politics. After the officers who had taken part in the war for independence had died, the only desires of the second generation of militarists were for power and booty. Naturally, they let themselves be led by whomever could fulfill their wishes, and that meant the Creole oligarchs. Consequently, the common people remained disfranchised, and the oligarchs acquired a supplementary police force to protect their social system.

The Failure To Unite

The war brought little change in the social structure and no modification of territorial boundaries—the other fundamental phase in the formation of a nation.

The prime movers of independence viewed the various Spanish viceroyalties and captaincies general as parts of a whole. San

Martín marched across the Andes to help free the lands on the Pacific, and Bolívar and Antonio José de Sucre (1795–1830) came down from the north for the same purpose. But the enthusiasm with which the people acclaimed the Liberators in Bolivia began to cool as soon as they realized that the independence of their "country" might soon be circumscribed. In Ecuador, the veterans of Colombia were regarded with aversion.

During the colonial period, localism had been at once encouraged and satisfied by the granting of broad autonomy to the various parts of the Empire. When independence was proclaimed, that autonomy remained intact and was even enlarged. Areas that had had autonomous colonial governments became independent states. The old colonial administrative lines were converted into the boundaries of new states. As time passed, the dividing lines served as pretexts for a series of ridiculous little wars, which, in turn, became a source of geopolitical injustices that still incite demagogic outbursts by "patriotic" governments, politicians, and military men.

As in Spain—which to this day has not come up with a structure that will permit the various nations on the Peninsula to live together successfully—the men of the independence era in Latin America, although they made efforts to rise above local interests (quickly aborted), did not succeed in creating anything more than a group of scattered states. San Martín planned a state that would comprise all the lands south of Panama; Iturbide established a short-lived empire that embraced all the Spanish lands north of Panama; Bolívar managed temporarily to unite most of the territories that had made up the viceroyalties of Peru and New Granada. The goal of an abortive Pan-American Congress in Panama in 1826 was to form a federation that would comprise the entire old Spanish Empire in America. But each group of Creoles preferred a state, an army, and a flag of its own. The Creoles still thought like colonials.

The survival of any oligarchy depends on a control that is virtually impossible to establish over huge territories, particularly under the technological conditions that prevailed at the beginning of the last century; hence the rise of disjunctive tendencies in each state. For decades, these tendencies determined a political life in which only the oligarchs and the military took part. The provinces of the new states were granted local autonomy like that of the colonial period. "Bolívar left Sucre as his lieutenant in Bolivia; he intended to administer Ecuador, Peru, Colombia, and Venezuela by similar means. [But he detested] federalism, which he characterized as 'regulated anarchy,' 'a law which implicitly prescribes the necessity of dissociating and ruining the state and all its members.'" San Martín championed the immediate amalgamation of all provinces but "felt that the force of localism was too strong to be overcome in a moment. After Maipú [where, in 1818, the patriots completed the liberation of Chile by defeating the royalists], he assented to the practical independence of Chile under [Bernardo] O'Higgins [1778–1842]."[17]

The desire for separation won out over the idea of union. Bolivia and Peru separated; Greater Colombia broke into its three component parts. Both Colombia and Venezuela wanted to carry division still further. For a time, Colombia was little more than a feeble alliance of independent states; Venezuela worked out a compromise—federalism. Central America soon broke its bonds with Mexico, and Mexico seemed for a time to be on the verge of greater fragmentation as Texas briefly enjoyed the life of an independent republic before the United States annexed it. The only practicable way of coping with localism was the federal system. But, in Central America, even that failed, for the single republic was replaced by the five tiny nations that still decorate the varicolored map of the isthmus.

Plowing the Sea

Thus, independence destroyed those features of the Spanish heritage that might have led to the creation of nationalities: the spirit of the *cabildo*, which gave the people an opportunity to take part in political life, and the idea of integration, which might have united small territories into a major state or federation of states. Militarism came into being because the people ceased to participate in the life of the state. Localism came into being because no real federations or confederations existed.

The men who won independence belonged to the Creole aristocracy and the oligarchies, and, though certainly not revolutionaries, they were endowed by the magnitude of the task they had undertaken with a certain breadth of vision. The oligarchies supported them as a necessary evil. Later, they apotheosized them into overblown figures of a gilded myth that served to distract attention from what was going on. No wonder, then, that, by the time their work was done, the *caudillos* of independence felt disillusioned. San Martín, Bolívar, José Gervasio Artigas (1774–1850), Bernardino Rivadavia (1780–1845), and many others died ostracized or in exile. Sucre was assassinated. Bolívar, embittered, wrote shortly before his death, "In South America there is neither trust nor faith neither among men nor among the various states. Every treaty is here but a scrap of paper and what are here called constitutions are but a collection of such scraps."[18] If, in moments of optimism that come with the flush of victory, he predicted a brilliant future, in others, he showed a pessimistic side: "Inevitably, America will fall into the hands of the unleashed rabble, only to pass gradually into those of petty tyrants of every color and race."

When he saw what was happening all around him, Bolívar came to the heartbreaking conclusion, seldom mentioned in Latin America, that "we who have struggled for the independence of America have plowed the sea." He was right. The Latin American countries did not achieve independence. They proclaimed themselves independent, but they remained dependent on the landholding Creole oligarchs who monopolized economic power and permanently dominated those who exercised political power. A Chilean positivist, José Victorino Lastarria (1817–88), later made a pronouncement that still provides the key to Latin American nationalism: "Independence was the work not of the people but of armies, armies that might more rightly have been called the armies of the *caudillos*."[19]

For a country to be a nation, all its inhabitants and all its social groups must share in its government, its aspirations, and its achievements. In such a nation, some people may play a small role and others a big one, but, in one way or another, to one degree or another, all participate. They have something in common. Without that something, which all feel, there can be no

nation. But an oligarchic system cannot tolerate general participation, nor can it allow a community of feeling. Everything must
rest in the hands of the privileged groups.

The struggle for Latin American independence was won by
men who were not and never could be nationalists. The task of
making nations out of the countries and their people was left to
succeeding generations.

3

The Colony Lives on in the Republic

Being and Seeming

According to an old Spanish tale, a horseman came to an inn one day and, addressing himself to a ragged youth whom he met at the door, asked the boy to look after his horse. "Allow me to inform Your Grace," the youth answered haughtily, "that you are speaking to a gentleman, Don Francisco de Cienfuegos and Albuquerque." To which the horseman replied, "Then let Your Grace seem what he is, or else be what he seems."

The new countries of Latin America were not what they seemed to be—democratic nations—nor did they seem what they were—oligarchic states. Since power invariably was held by the oligarchs, politics necessarily dwindled until it had become nothing more than an exercise in rhetoric to keep up a convincing front and to conceal what was behind it.

Bolívar's teacher Simón Rodríguez (1771–1854) wrote, "Europeans who write on social themes dream of the empty spaces of America, where, with a handful of people, they would carry out their plans for a new social order. American social writers are ashamed of not finding themselves in urban districts of a hundred thousand inhabitants."[1] Rodríguez thus highlighted the basic characteristic of Latin American political life: no desire for a new social order or for change from the European model. Possibly the Latin American countries are the only ones in history that made no attempt to build their own new society, distinct from the colonial society, after winning independence. When Martí looked back many years later, he felt prompted to write, "The colony lived on in the republic."[2]

What might be called the second generation of leaders were men without illusions. Juan Bautista Alberdi (1810–84) remarked that "Everyone feels that things are not as they should be. A vague need for a better order of things makes itself felt in everyone's spirit."[3] Another Argentinian, Bartolomé Mitre (1821–1906), put it this way: "[We are] a nation out of joint, a revolution without a government, an embryonic democracy without organic principles, a public organization without any clear notions of constitutional policy, a society enervated by sorrow, without the institutions to safeguard individual rights."[4]

After a century and a half of independence, the Uruguayan sociologist Roberto Fabregat Cúneo felt that the situation had not changed:

America finally holds her fate in her hands. And she is making a miserable wreck of it. This is a long period in our history about which no one can read without shame or horror. The mistakes of the colonial regime live on and are aggravated. Isolation, violence, and absolutism make America a conglomeration of chaotic bits that only enhance by contrast the resplendent constitutional texts. The despoliation of the indigenous masses continues beneath the bureaucratic disputes and the altercations of the generals.[5]

Again, I have let the witnesses speak. Now, the questions are: What made the reality that is depicted in these despairing words? What made the countries of Latin America lose their chance, while the United States prospered and grew? Why do their thinkers consider them to be possessed by some evil? Why do they seem out of joint?

In the United States, European immigrants worked the land with their own hands. Small landholdings were the base of the social and political structure. But the base of the Latin American social structure, and consequently of its political structure, was the ownership of large tracts. The common people of Latin America did not own land. The active municipal life of the old colonies was not preserved, and, with its loss, the people could not make their voices heard. Yet in spite of the people's silence and submissiveness, the Creole oligarchs did not feel secure. They feared a republic so much that they considered engaging European monarchs to rule over them. Iturbide had himself crowned in Mexico, and other *caudillos* were quick to seize political power as payment for their participation in the struggle for independence. The seizure of Montevideo by the Portuguese in 1817, and the ten-year-long foreign occupation of the Banda Oriental (now Uruguay) "was encouraged by Buenos Aires in order to annihilate the *caudillo* Artigas and his followers along the coast, abetting the Portuguese monarch in his plan and hope of crowning a European prince on the Río de la Plata, the only solution the Buenos Aires oligarchy could come up with."[6]

None of those devices worked. But they did serve to keep the peasants fettered, accomplishing a task at which the oligarchs were always active and highly proficient.

The abolition of the system of property ownership established by the Spanish Empire led to a truly cruel and inhuman form of feudal serfdom for the peasants: the system of land tenancy, or sharecropping, set by our liberal codes of law. The farm worker, or sharecropper, is a tenant on the land that he cultivates on his own account and at his own risk, suffering all the losses and hazards of weather, while the landowner receives the lion's share of the crops and earnings. The system lends itself to such a heap of abuses on the part of the landowner that it turns him into a true feudal lord. . . . Furthermore, the system encourages absentee landlordism. The owner loses contact with the soil. . . . He goes off to live in the city or abroad, leaving his land to the rascals and thieves who are his managers and foremen.[7]

City and Country

Of course, this state of affairs did not evolve smoothly. There were also cities, and the city dwellers had a somewhat (but only somewhat) more open-minded attitude. Small groups of them hoped for a change. During the early years of independence, how-

ever, most of them could not quite imagine a social transformation; they contented themselves with demanding what we would
call a more representative democracy.

The desire for change showed up most clearly in two areas:
that of relations between church (a major landholder in many
countries) and state, and that of national political organization.
The struggle was a long and, at times, a bloody one, involving,
with regard to the church, liberals and conservatives and, with
regard to the constitutions, federalists and centralists. The landholders supported federalism because they believed it would help
them retain their large estates; the big businessmen in the cities,
particularly those engaged in international trade, championed
centralism. So the civil wars in Argentina, Venezuela, Ecuador,
Colombia, and, to a degree, Mexico were the outgrowth of the
antagonism between country and city.

The country had been kept in a deplorable state of servitude, poverty,
and ignorance. The cities were the seats of power, wealth, and knowledge. Sarmiento coined the saying that the city was civilization and the
country barbarity. . . . Federalism was not a democratic doctrine, although its strength, represented by the *caudillos* of the interior who
carried the rural population along with them, might lead one to believe
that it represented a movement for the liberation of the dispossessed
classes.[8]

Now the oligarchs were interested in selling raw materials
abroad. In exchange for the freedom to do this, the oligarchs
agreed to protect the few urban industries, by means of a ban
on the importation of manufactured products and permission to
import raw materials. The result was that the rich lived better
and the poor worse. And, in spite of the political rivalry between
the oligarchs and the infant industries, both acted like accomplices in the maintenance of the social structure, for the emerg-
ing manufacturing bourgeoisie failed to see that its interests
would be furthered by social change and never demanded it.

The struggle between the centralists and the federalists is of
considerable importance to a study of Latin American nationalism. For it throws light on the means by which the oligarchs, with
demagoguery and sentimentalism, managed to make the people
forget their real interests and become cannon fodder (or election

fodder, as the case might be) in behalf of the oligarchic cause—a cause disguised (unconsciously, of course) sometimes as anti-clericalism, sometimes as traditionalism, and sometimes even as equalitarianism. We have seen that the peasants, who should have particularly wanted the victory of the centralist cities—a source of strength that could free them from the landholders—nonetheless leaned toward the federalists. The oligarchs knew how to blind those they meant to exploit.

They were adept at several methods of blinding. One was to arrange matters so that the cities placed obstacles in the way of a town-hall democracy, fearing the power it might give the rural districts. In the end, the gainers were the oligarchies, which thus kept alive the rivalry between the vaguely reformist city and the countryside and did away with the danger that the country people might gain recognition for their interests and defeat the oligarchies. The ideological influence of Europe and the United States was felt by only a few of the oligarchs; the majority clung to their feudal ideas. As Julio Ycaza Tigerino (1919–   ), the conservative Nicaraguan author whose description of sharecropping was quoted earlier, said, "The provincial demarcations within the federal government became the boundaries of fiefs ruled by *caciques;* parties became the political fiefs of a handful of gentlemen; and the state itself became a party fief. Democratic institutions were feudalized."[9]

Caudillos and Wars

In the Anglo-Saxon countries, one of the principal functions of the legislative branch is to act as a check on the executive. In the Latin American countries, the chief executive is given an almost completely free hand. The functions of an Anglo-Saxon parliament are broad and permanent; those of a Latin American congress are intermittent and narrow.

To be sure, political parties took shape in the course of time. But they were parties in name only: they did not represent ideologies so much as small interest groups—"Masonic lodges, the ecclesiastical conventicles, and the barracks cabals."[10] Parties of this type never probed beneath the surface of things, because they were composed of members of the oligarchies or the middle-class bureaucracies that served the oligarchies (however grudgingly). None of these wanted to change the social structure; consequently, none tried to help the people to participate in government. Their excuse was that the people were not ready. One Argentine political figure, Joaquín V. González (1863–1923), was ultimately forced to this admission: "How many bloody tragedies, how many painful vicissitudes and vacillations our country might have been spared if we had left intact those town halls that passed judgment on the authorities. With their precious treasures of freedom and law, they seemed like perfect republics, even within an ironclad monarchy!"[11]

What happened to political life when neither real parties nor the town halls existed and the people counted for nothing? What was it like?

Political life was manifested mainly through the activities of the *caudillos*. If their rise had depended upon the masses, they might be thought to have possessed charisma, but the *caudillos* waxed and waned within the very narrow confines of the social groups linked to the oligarchies. The two issues, already mentioned, around which political life revolved—church-state relations and the constitutions—were posed and solved more often through action of the *caudillos* than through popular movements. The *caudillos* moved within the orbit of the oligarchic society but did not attempt to change it; it was all in the family.[12]

The *caudillo* identified his interests with what he called the national interests, but these were really the interests of the oligarchs. The land, the public treasury, and the administration were his private preserve, his huge ranch. His followers, he liked to say, were "unconditionally" his men; that is, they clung closely to the man himself rather than to his nonexistent or feigned ideology. The *caudillo* wanted approbation, but he would settle for paid praise and let the neutrals be neutral. "He who is not against me is for me," he could say. This slogan set the *caudillos* apart from the modern totalitarian dictator, who holds that "He who is not for me is against me."

With minor variations, the career of the *caudillo* conformed to a pattern prevalent throughout Latin America: first, the *cau-dillo* fascinated the people; then, he established his political dom-ination over them by force; and, finally, he consolidated his rule and enjoyed unlimited power.

Everything about the *caudillo* reveals first of all his instinct for per-sonal prepotency: his tragic sense of civic duty, his worship of the hero cult, his vanity and authoritarianism, his stormy anxiety over opposition, combined with the passionate gestures by which he succeeds in moving the masses. He takes possession of the [people] until finally the power is his. Then, the nation becomes the state; the state, the government; the government, the party; and the party is the *caudillo,* who denounces his personal enemies as enemies of the country. To keep himself in power, the *caudillo* will do whatever he needs to, and more besides. "I must shoot anyone who steps in my way to oppose me, be he archbishop, gen-eral, magistrate, or anything else," fulminated Mariano Paredes y Arrillaga [1797–1849], the traitorous Mexican petty chieftain. Once he is sure of his victory, he discards the vague doctrines and the constitu-tional formulas with which his legal experts rallied support during the struggle. . . . "Never have I followed the thinking of anyone but my-self," writes the Venezuelan Antonio Guzmán Blanco [1829–99]. By vio-lence, shrewdness, or cajolery he conquers or wins over, one by one, all those in the nation who might be in his way—budding *caudillos,* bril-liant scholars, ambitious plutocrats. "I had to choose between the peni-tentiary and the cabinet," declared a collaborator of Manuel Estrada Cabrera [1857–1924], the Guatemalan political leader. At last he begins his reign, which will end nobody knows when. Peace and material prog-ress are his greatest conquests. The dictator now has in his hands the sum total of power, an invisible, all-powerful network by which he dominates whatever his hands can reach—courts and prisons, the press, schools, and drawing rooms. The *caudillo* appoints deputies and gover-nors; his will is law. He may sometimes designate his heir, like Francisco Solano López [1827–70], in Paraguay, or José Tadeo Monagas [1784–1868] and his brother José Gregorio [1795–1858], in Venezuela, who shared power for a long time, until José Ruperto, son of the former, fi-nally inherited it. . . . Politics? For what? It is a dangerous noise. Perhaps it is enough to administer well. As the Mexican general Porfirio Díaz [1830–1915] used to say, "Don't stampede the horses."

During this period, the vanity of the glorious *caudillo* is rewarded but never satisfied. He calls himself "Most Serene Highness," "Hero," "Re-storer of the Law," "Father of his Country," "Son of God," "Hero of the Desert," *"Caudillo* of Peace and Labor," "Defender of America," "Supreme Leader of the Revolution." . . . If the Pope is reluctant to make him a bishop, as in the case of José Matías Delgado [1768–1833], of Central America, he may make him a papal nobleman. All the *caudillos* are, moreover, generals. Europe covers them with resplendent medals. United States ambassadors introduce them as creatures of providence. Tolstoy called Díaz a modern Cromwell.[13]

The behavior of the *caudillos* was ruinous to the people and to Latin America's future. In 1838, at the height of the United States' federal growth, the five Central American republics dissolved their federation merely as a result of petty quarrels and personal ambitions. José Gaspar Rodríguez de Francia (1776–1840) closed Paraguay off from the world and even forbade foreign trade; he suspended the export of yerba maté and lumber, both of which were basic in the national economy. After a few years, Paraguay was so impoverished that Francia was forced to close all the schools and abolish all the commissioned ranks in the army. Prisoners had to beg for food from their guards.

Not even the memory of Bolívar could improve matters in his own country. "Our history thus begins with a republic of socially insensitive philosophers and theorists who are able to reconcile their republican ideas with slavery. This contradiction created the ferment that gave rise to the Federal War [1858–63], that extraordinary uprising of the popular masses that lasted five years. . . . The liberal side won, but the people's aspirations were lost. The leaders of both sides reached an understanding, and everything was settled within the family.[14]

The *caudillos* seldom hesitated to go to war. In some countries, war gives the people, who furnish the cannon fodder, the right to be heard. Not so in Latin America. The common people are killed in war, but it is the *caudillos,* who wear the "plumes of victory" or the "crape of defeat"—as one of them might say, in reciting a speech written by some shoddy, turncoat intellectual—who keep on blinding the people to their own interests.

No sooner was the Peruvian-Bolivian federation established than armed conflict with the Republic of Chile broke out. . . .

A period of anarchy in Peru; a reformist rebellion in Bolivia; passages at arms between Peru and Bolivia; the dictatorship of Manuel Isidoro Belzú [1808–65] in Bolivia; mutiny against the President of Peru in Arequipa; invasion of Peru by Belzú's troops; civil war; the revolution of 1857 against Belzú's son-in-law, General Jorge Córdova [1822–61]; rebellion and civil war against President Ramón Castilla [1797–1867]; war against Ecuador by Peru. . . . Civil conflict in Bolivia in 1861; dictatorship in 1868; military mutiny in 1873; war with Chile in 1879; mutiny in 1899. . . . Things went no better in Ecuador, where, after a similar series of conflicts and revolutions, the theocratic dictator Gabriel García Moreno [1821–75] seized power.

For many long years, Uruguay was at war with the Argentine General Rosas; intervened in the bloody alliance against Paraguay; went through military presidencies and revolutions lasting into the twentieth century. Colombia suffered through a civil war from 1839 to 1841, a dictatorship in 1854, civil clashes in 1859. The revolution of 1879 cost 80,000 casualties; and the one that broke out at the end of the century, almost 100,000. On the other hand, Venezuela started off by enjoying almost twenty years of peace, and its fortunes might have been considered secure. But the lack of a constructive policy was a foregone conclusion in the virtually hereditary administrations of Presidents Tadeo and Gregorio Monagas, who alternately succeeded each other. In 1858, there was a revolution, with centralist overtones. Then came an insurrection, in 1863, against President Juan Crisóstomo Falcón [1820–70]; in 1864, the state of Guayana declared its independence, and civil war followed. In 1865, insurrection; in 1867, mutinies in Caracas; in 1868, revolution. The president left the country and ex-President Monagas returned. . . .

That was our history during the period in which the United States was growing—annexing territories, organizing them, linking them socially and economically by the rail network. When that country was faced with a critical civil war, it was for essentially economic reasons arising out of the problem of slavery. Meanwhile, South America's population continued to decline and its lonely silent reaches were shattered by endless petty personal feuds and territorial conflicts.[15]

The question that repeatedly emerges from these quotations from our witnesses is: What is the reason for all this? The answer is simple. The great landholder does not try to achieve the greatest possible productivity of his land; he produces only what he considers necessary for himself. By the same token, in the realm of politics, he seeks not the greatest good for the greatest number but only a guaranty that he can continue to get what he considers essential from his land. What does he care if there are flamboyant dictators, senseless wars, or insurrections, so long as they do not affect his property? And, since he has the last word, any political change depends on him and on the system of which he is a part. What is the point in such a change if he can live in the capital city, or in Paris, or in Madrid? Why keep his

military and political lackeys from enjoying themselves and from
diverting the masses with parades, speeches, promises, and wars?
The more his manager can steal, over and above what the owner
needs, the more loyal he will be, the landholder tells himself.
And, the more the governor or military officer can amuse himself—and steal—the more he will try to defend the system that
supports him. Economic power rests firmly in the hands of the
big landholders precisely because they have been clever enough
to delegate political power, to throw it, as they would a bone to
a dog, to the politicians and soldiers willing to work as police-
men and major-domos.

"Liberal" Anticlericalism

Whenever some outstanding figure emerges—perhaps from the
very bosom of the oligarchy, with a troubled conscience and a
desire to change things—whenever the people in a flash of intuition want to collect the bill owed them for their deaths in war
or their peacetime misery, the men in power create a diversion.
Nowadays, as we shall see, they distract the people's attention
from their true interests by resorting to a so-called anti-imperialism; in the nineteenth century, they resorted to anticlericalism.

During the colonial period, the church enjoyed great power.
With independence, its power grew, for the clergy became one of
the groups in the oligarchies and had large landholdings in both
city and country. The clergy frequently intervened in politics to
impose their moral and religious points of view and to defend
their interests against other groups in the oligarchies. The liberals used ecclesiastical mortmain and unproductive properties
as a battlecry and, in the course of a long struggle, frequently
succeeded in getting mortmain abolished. At the same time, they
were distributing to individual Indians the lands once held com-
munally by them. On both counts, instead of aiding in the abolition of latifundism, they fostered the rise of new latifundists,
often foreigners, who paid ridiculously small sums for the lands
released from mortmain or purchased from the Indians, who had
never privately owned their land and let themselves be despoiled
without offering any resistance.[16] Of course, the liberals pursued

this course not in order to divert attention from the need for social change but as a matter of dogma, as we should say now, if we were discussing the Communists. But their policy did more to buttress than to weaken the oligarchic structure of Latin American society.

José María Luis Mora (1794–1850), a Mexican liberal who took the first tentative steps toward legal reform, realized that the ideas that had gained currency after independence militated against the formation of a Mexican nation: "The *esprit de corps* suffusing each social class . . . weakens or destroys the national spirit."[17] The absence of national spirit had consequences that the liberal Mexican leader Melchor Ocampo (?–1861) described in these words: "the profound disgust with which many look at public affairs, the selfishness with which others exploit them, the weakness with which idleness is tolerated, the lack of education, the property taken from its rightful owners and enfiefed to the clergy and the clergy's consequent wealth and insolence, the lack of integrity and foresight in supervising public expenditures, the prostitution of the so-called administration of justice."[18]

It was logical for the clergy to back the conservatives in order to defend themselves against the liberals and, when this proved unavailing, to encourage dictatorships or ally themselves with them if the dictatorships were disposed to defend their interests.

When Valentín Gómez Farías (1781–1858) tried to limit the wealth of the clergy in Mexico and to wrest control over education from them, the priests did not hesitate to promote a civil war; the army sided with the church, abolished the federation, and helped Antonio López de Santa Anna (1791–1876) to power. Lucas Alamán (1792–1853) estimated that more than half of the Mexican nation's real-estate wealth was under mortmain. The liberal reform of 1857 broke the entail on ecclesiastical property and on the native communities, too. The clergy, thereupon, plotted the installation of Maximilian, which provoked a long civil war.

During Central America's brief period of unity, the problem of church-state relations became acute. Francisco Morazán (1792–1842) abolished tithing and the traditional tribute of the harvest's first fruits, ended the entail on the property of religious communities, established freedom of worship, instituted a divorce law and a law granting the free bequest of property, converted the convents into model schools and prisons, and fostered public education. But later, Rafael Carrera, in Guatemala, returned to the clergy the prerogatives Morazán had taken from them, and the clergy wanted to canonize him. The victory of the liberal revolution in 1871, which brought Justo Rufino Barrios (1835–85) and Miguel García Granados (1809–78) to power, ensured the separation of church and state, confiscation of the clergy's property, and expulsion of the religious orders. Barrios was a shrewd and masterful middle-class mestizo. He began the construction of the Atlantic highway, provided for a statistical bureau and a real-estate registry, introduced the telegraph, telephones, and electric power, imported quinine from the East Indies, founded the National Bank with the proceeds of disentailed property, and encouraged coffee growing. But, before long, the church regained its influence. And, in our times, another dictator, Colonel Enrique Peralta, has seen to it that the Constituent Assembly, elected after his military coup, gave the church title to its real property, which undid what had been achieved in 1871.[19]

Serious conflicts between church and state also arose in Nicaragua and El Salvador. In Ecuador, Gabriel García Moreno dedicated the country to the Sacred Heart, arranged for the installation of foreign priests, and turned over the schools to them. Peru had a liberal clergy; hence, the lay liberals were rarely of a Jacobin cast. In Chile, during the period when Diego Portales (1783–1837) controlled the government, the religious orders won back their expropriated property and received the right to censor all publications, while religious ceremonies were restored at official functions.

Although the church did not possess economic power in the countries along the Rio de la Plata, its political influence there was considerable. Indeed, the struggle between church and state in Argentina became violent after the passage of a law establishing secular education in 1870. But the law was never fully accepted, and, in 1959, a law establishing "freedom" of education permitted the church to have its own schools and resulted in *de facto* abrogation of the older law.

Separation of church and state is a constitutional feature today in Brazil, Chile, Cuba, Ecuador, El Salvador, Guatemala, Honduras, Mexico, Nicaragua, Panama, and Uruguay. But, even in recent times, there have been conflicts, like the affair of the Mexican *cristeros* between 1926 and 1929. Not until very recently have Catholics supported social reform and the separation of church and state, and even then only in some countries and some segments of the clergy. In Peru, Chile, Ecuador, and a part of Brazil, some bishops have distributed church lands; in other countries the clergy are still interfering in politics on behalf of the oligarchy.

Since, throughout the nineteenth century, the church took the positions that "there always have been poor and rich" and that "Blessed are the poor since by their suffering they will gain the kingdom of Heaven," the power of its hierarchy stood in the way of incorporating the common people into society and thus forming a nation. The struggles of the liberals against *that* church were an indirect attempt to create nationhood, but their efforts were defeated by the encouragement of latifundism implicit in their own methods of abolishing mortmain.

Three Kinds of Evasion

If the liberals had had their way, they would have erased the entire colonial period and denied the influence of Spain. This attitude was an evasion of the urgent task of incorporating the people into society. In different places and at different times, this evasion assumed different guises. Some people looked back to the Aztecs and Incas; others, particularly in areas with a past not of Indian civilization but only of primitive tribes, turned toward Europe or the United States. These evasions served, unbeknownst to those who practiced them, the function fulfilled today by the nationalism of certain so-called left-wing groups: to salve the conscience and obviate sacrifice. Those who turned to the past, to Europe, or to the United States were part of the oligarchy; their material interest lay in preserving the existing social order, while their intellectual or moral interest lay in shaping its structure into a more humane, modern, and "civilized" (to use their word) political form. Absentee ownership had its counterpart in the absenteeism of the ideologue who lives mentally outside his country.

In 1844, José Victorino Lastarria (1817–88) delivered, at the University of Chile, a paper entitled "Investigations of the Social Influence of the Conquest and the Colonial System of the Spaniards in Chile." His critical words elicited a reply from Andrés Bello (1780–1865), who pointed to the positive features in the colony, regardless of all the errors for which it was responsible. In Mexico, José María Luis Mora wrote his *Political Review of the Various Administrations of the Mexican Republic Up to 1837*, in which he emphasized the colonial roots of most of the mistakes made by those administrations. In Cuba, José Antonio Saco (1797–1879), in his *History of Slavery*, pointed to the colonial basis of all the island's ills. In these and many other works of the same tenor, Latin American authors revealed "a past that should be denied, unlike the Europeans, who, in similar historical and sociological studies, have pointed to a past that should be affirmed."[20]

Others believe it axiomatic that Spanish *and* Indian influences were responsible for Latin America's inferiority. Juan María Gutiérrez (1808–78) asserted that Argentine poetry and popular music were spontaneous outpourings owing nothing to Spain. He considered it to Argentina's advantage that, in the colonial era, there was no literary or artistic culture in the Plata region emulating that of the viceroyalties of Peru and Mexico. He said such colorful things as that the dances in his country never shared the "sensual abandon and lack of reserve that are inherent in the songs and dances of the equatorial races, bound to slavery."[21] (Argentinians who lay claim to an ethnic superiority and "virtue" ascribe their good qualities to their climate. Since Argentina, like Europe, lies in the temperate zone, this must give it an advantage over countries in the tropical zone.)

Sarmiento felt that Catholicism should give way to an imported, non-Spanish Protestantism, and, in his linguistic theories, he advocated opening the door to "barbarisms" because, he said, modern thought would not fit the Spanish idiom. He and others put into practice their desire to imitate Europe. Rivadavia tried to change Argentina culturally by importing books, people, and capital from Europe (particularly England and France). Mitre, Sarmiento, and Alberdi asked help from abroad in order to transform their country's culture. Sarmiento went so far as to import a group of teachers from the United States. Article 66 of the Argentine constitution of 1853 ordered the national government to encourage the investment of private foreign capital.

This method of evading the basic problem, that of land, was presented as nationalistic because a proposal to transform the country was part of it. But it was at least better than some of the other types of evasion we shall study, since it was based on the premise that any change would have to be in the direction of greater freedom. Indeed, this group of Argentine nationalists affirmed as their basic principles popular sovereignty, freedom, equality, fraternity, the necessity of popular education, freedom of speech, and the separation of powers. "After long and painstaking research in the documents, Mitre concluded . . . [that] Argentine nationality antedated independence and that the nation was born democratic and liberal."[22]

Many of the Latin Americans who turned toward Europe—we should call them moderates today—greatly admired England and Anglo-Saxon political theorists. Others, more radical, wanted rapid progress toward freedom and the elimination of injustice and poverty but did not go so far as to demand the destruction of the oligarchic system. They turned toward the United States, for they believed it had known better than any European nation how to create the institutions, structures, and organizations that would safeguard freedom and aid progress.

The Argentine writer Esteban Echeverría (1805–51) argued, in his *Dogma socialista* that the ideal of independence could become a reality "by means of the organization of freedom, brotherhood, and equality, through the medium of democracy," on the model of the United States, for, "without England and the United States, freedom would vanish in this century."[23] And the man who really founded Chilean socialism, Francisco Bilbao (1823–65), who was as anticlerical, socialistic, and Utopian as Echeverría, did not mince his words either: "The North has positive values. It has freedom; it was born with it. The South, on the other hand, has the slavery that came with theocratic Spain." A hundred years ahead of his time, in his *Evangelio Americano* *(American Gospel)*, he proclaimed what only a few people dared to avow later: "We do not see in the land, or in the enjoyment of land, the definitive end for man; we offer the Negro, the Indian, the disinherited, the unhappy, the weak, the respect owed to the name and dignity of man. . . . Here is what the republicans of South America dare to place in the balance beside the price, wealth, and power of North America."

Bilbao and others who shared his ideas considered the Old World the seat of theocracy; they believed the future lay in America:*

There, monarchy, feudalism, theocracy, the ruling castes and families; here, democracy. In Europe, the pursuit of conquest; in America, the abolition of it. . . . In Europe, all the superstitions, all the phantasms, all the institutions of error, all the miseries and age-old platitudes of history accumulated among a people servile or made fanatical by glory and power; in America, the cleansing of history, the religion of justice that is deep and persuasive.

When Lincoln abolished slavery, Bilbao was moved to these words: "An alliance with the United States, cleansed of slavery, will give us control of civilization. . . . Civilization today is America and the republic."

These men understood better than the pro-Europeans that the American reality is unique, that it must be interpreted in a

---

* The United States held a certain fascination even for pro-European Argentinians, however, especially its open-door immigration policy and its way of absorbing immigrants. As Zea said, "The emigration of the surplus population of some old nations to the new ones operated like steam applied to industry: It multiplied the country's strength a hundredfold and accomplished a hundred years' worth of work in a day. That is how the United States grew and was populated; that is how we ourselves must expand; and the competition of Europeans is more needed by us than by the Americans, Sarmiento said. Alberdi . . . added, referring to Latin America, 'Insofar as the fatherland does not depend upon the foreigner, it is free; ·but the individual is not free so long as he depends upon the state exclusively and absolutely. The fatherland is free insofar as it absorbs and monopolizes the liberties of all its individuals; but the individuals are not free, because the government is the administrator of their liberties.' In the United States, on the other hand, 'the rights of man are equivalent . . . to the rights of the fatherland, and, if the state is free of foreign powers, the individual is no less free in relation to the state.' "

unique manner, and that its problems called for unique solutions. "What do the answers of European philosophy and politics matter to us," Echeverría asked, "if they do not lead to the end that we are seeking? . . . European science may be followed, but not its politics. Our world of observation and application is right here; we can touch it, we can feel it breathe, we can observe it and study its organism and its living conditions. Europe can be of little help to us in that."

This position was adopted all over Latin America by those who began to see the necessity of social change, who had begun to assimilate Utopian European socialism and were trying to adapt it to the needs of their own countries. Fourier and Proudhon strongly influenced some Latin Americans—Melchor Ocampo, for example, a theoretician of the Mexican Reform and possibly the only man who aspired to go beyond mere *political* change. Antonio Leocadio Guzmán (1801–84), of Venezuela; Santiago Arcos Arlegui (1822–74) and Martín Palma (1821–84), of Chile; Alfonso H. Lima Barreto (1881–1922) and Joaquín Nabuco (1849–1910), of Brazil; and Diego Vicente Tejera (1848–1903), of Cuba, are some of the names on that roster. They looked to the United States, not because they felt any great friendship toward it (particularly after its conflict with Mexico in 1847), but because it was a trail blazer. In a sense, it would not be wrong to call these men romantic populists. They were the first to realize that their countries could never become true nations until the submerged masses became part of society. But they reached this conclusion via populism, not nationalism—in other words, they believed that the people mattered more than the nation. (Echeverría was a possible exception.)

A "Decent Tyranny"

The people who turned to Europe wanted political change but succeeded in making only superficial alterations. Those who turned to the United States wanted social change, and, though they laid the foundations of the labor movement and anticipated the populist movement, which, decades later, fought to effect the same changes, they also failed. In the meantime, a desire for

economic progress, with only minor political changes and no social upheavals, was beginning to stir in the breasts of the landholding oligarchs. Some industries had been established, and a
proletariat was gradually forming. The nucleus of the new industrial bourgeoisie adapted themselves to the new forces and incorporated them into the oligarchies. The ideological enzyme that
permitted the oligarchies to digest the early forms of industrialization was positivism.

Latin American positivists wanted progress, but first they
wanted order, as others before them had wanted European or
North American influence. Order was an important political
desideratum in a system that reflected the landholder's indolence
and inefficiency. Many Mexicans believed they could put a stop
to the almost constant anarchy that was disturbing their nation
by applying the tenets of positivism. The Argentinians considered
it a suitable instrument for getting rid of those who clung to absolutism and tyranny. The Chileans saw positivism as an efficient
tool for realizing the ideals of liberalism. In Uruguay, positivism
furnished the moral doctrine capable of ending a long period of
corruption. Peru and Bolivia found in it a renewal of their
strength after their catastrophic war against Chile. The Cubans
found in positivism a justification for their longed-for independence from Spain. The Brazilians, on the other hand, used positivism to soften the effects of their belated abolition of slavery
and the Empire.[24]

Philosophically, the positivists followed Comte, but politically
and socially they fell closer to Spencer. England, then the chief
foreign investor in Latin America, fascinated both businessmen
and theorists of positivism. It was believed that the industrial
society extolled by Spencer had universal validity. The formula
for salvation seemed to be to renounce the past and imitate the
British. A Mexican positivist, Telésforo García (1844–1918),
wrote: "In the country where positivism has its roots in the national character, where the experimental method is applied to
every manifestation of life—in England, that is—freedom is most
secure and rights best guaranteed."

Latin American intellectuals and professionals in the last third
of the nineteenth century believed that they were destined to

guide and direct. They wanted to use science to solve all problems, including political ones. A group of young positivists, writing in the Mexican newspaper *La Libertad,* clamored for a new order. "Rights!" exclaimed one of them, Francisco Gabino Cosmes:

Society has rejected them already: it wants bread. In place of those constitutions filled with sublime ideas that have never been put into practice even for a single moment . . . society would prefer peace as a shelter to work quietly under, some assurance of its interests, and the knowledge that the authorities would hang kidnapers, thieves, and revolutionaries instead of chasing after an ideal. Fewer rights and fewer freedoms, in exchange for greater order and peace. . . . Furthermore, the day is not far off when the nation will say: "I want order and peace, even though they cost me my independence. . . . We have already been granted a wealth of rights that have brought nothing but misery and social ills. Now let us try a *decent tyranny* for a while and see what it will bring."

Gabino Barreda (1818–81), who helped to introduce positivism to Mexico and reformed its educational system, said many of the same things more subtly: "Let material order, preserved at all costs by the governors and respected by the governed, be our safeguard and our sure means by which to travel along the flowery path of progress and civilization."

All these points of view found expression in politics. In 1886, a number of positivists in Mexico were elected to the Chamber of Deputies. Some of them played an important role under Porfirio Díaz during the period of the so-called Scientists, in the 1880's. In 1892, the Liberal Union party issued a manifesto recommending a "scientific" analysis of social conditions in Mexico. "The nation would like its government to be in the position to demonstrate that it considers the present peace an accepted fact by reorganizing economically some branches of the administration." Once peace was established, once the needs of the rich were met and satisfied, then the rich should use their surplus wealth, "impelled by moral responsibility, as a public trust that society has put in their hands for the common good and for progress." The franchise was not the most important freedom, nor should it be granted to the people right away.

Although positivism attained its greatest political influence in

Mexico, in other countries it achieved a monopoly, if not of government, at least of culture. For decades, educated Latin Americans thought in positivist terms, or in terms they called positivist but which actually were an imitation of positivism, and used positivist jargon to justify the continued rule of the landholding oligarchies in alliance with the new, weak, vacillating bourgeoisie with "aristocratic" manners. In Brazil, positivism even determined the motto—"*Ordem e Progresso*"—that appears on the national flag, and Comte's religious fancies found fertile soil there and are preserved in a few positivist temples. In Chile, José Victorino Lastarria, a man of strong individuality, tried to instill a measure of national feeling into the country's culture by invoking positivism. "We *must* be original," he wrote. "We have within our society all the elements with which to be original, to convert our literature into the authentic expression of our nation."

Positivism became the justification of Guzmán Blanco's twenty-three-year dictatorial rule over Venezuela in the name of progress. In Mexico, Gabino Barreda secularized public education in the name of positivism; Valentin Letelier (1852–1919), in Chile, and Adolfo Ernst (1832–99), in Venezuela, did likewise—although, in fact, secularization left the people without schools, since most public funds for education went to the universities.

Refuge in the Past

With the first wave of modernization, late in the nineteenth century, a deep uneasiness began to permeate the upper strata of Latin American society. Doubtless, this was a provincial reaction (for Latin America was provincial at that time) on the part of people who feared the loss of their privileges or who were not sure they knew how to preserve and defend them in a modern society. Their close ties to the past now went under the guise of nationalism. What in Europe was the result of many centuries of historical development was expected to result in Latin America from a tradition less than four centuries old.

The oligarchs profited from the new trend that resulted from this development and that, with all the necessary demagoguery, was used whenever any other concept (emulation of Europe or the United States, the need for order) seemed to be gaining more than it should. This tendency was what we may call preterism. Like a sword-handler in a bullfight, it stood ready to draw the bull whenever he might charge (in Latin America, however, the "bulls" were very tame). It was the philosophy of seeking solutions for Latin America's problems of government not in the United States, in Europe, or in the idea of order but in the past —and not in precolonial times (for only Mexico, Peru, Bolivia, and Ecuador had a "usable" pre-Columbian history), but in the colonial period. The preterists called themselves nationalists, and historians were naïve enough to accept the label as valid.

This nationalism of evasion led to petty wars among the Latin American countries and took many picturesque forms, such as the theories built around "Argentinism," "Peruvianism," "Paraguay-anism," and so on, which ended up as little more than folk legends about the guitar, the dance, and the cuisine as distinctive expressions of so-called nationality. The most ironic and brutal example was provided by the dictatorship of General Juan Manuel de Rosas (1793–1877), in Argentina. Rosas owed his popularity in great measure to his long defense of Argentina against the French and British intervention he had deliberately helped to provoke.

Later, Europe again became the cynosure of Latin American eyes, but Latin American nationalism was reborn at another time of uncertainty, during the economic crisis of the late nineteenth century. This nationalism was cultural and economic, but it also contained elements of xenophobia and even racism, typified by Argentina's preoccupation with its international role and its expansionist and aggressive aims.[25] The same nationalism crept up again during the depression of 1929; later, through imitation and owing to certain unacknowledged ties between some military cliques and the Nazis, it turned into out-and-out fascism. This type of reaction has recurred in Latin America each time economic difficulties have given rise to the fear of losing traditional privileges.

Another expression of that type of nationalism emerged in the Chilean Andes, "where the oligarchy with Basque surnames controlled political power throughout the nineteenth century."[26]

Some groups found a model for their racial myths in the ravings of Nicolás Palacios (1854–1911) in his *Raza Chilena (The Chilean Race)*. Chile owed its merits and the order that reigned after the iron rule of Portales, according to Palacios, to the fact that the population was only slightly "Latin"; for, owing to some inexplicable process of selection, the Spaniards who came to the colony had more Germanic than Latin blood, being descendants of the ancient Goths.

The Oligarchies

Latin American countries, as we have seen, had stratified societies composed of a very compact oligarchy, some small intermediate classes, which among themselves made up a more or less structured society, and a formless submerged mass on the bottom —not a part of what politically minded Latin Americans considered the national society. To be sure, any present-day sociologist would consider them part of society, but that is of no significance; what a sociologist of today may think cannot affect the affairs of yesterday. The people of yesterday did not consider the submerged masses a part of society. On that, the great landholder, the shopkeeper, the lawyer, the general, the weaver, even the trade-union official, all agreed. So did the Indian in the mountains, the peon, the miner, the housemaid, and the miserable wretch in the city—all part of the submerged masses. The important thing for a nation is not what it is but what the people feel they are. In Peru, at most one-fifth of the people think of themselves as Peruvians; in prerevolutionary Mexico, perhaps 20 per cent felt like Mexicans; in Ecuador, probably less than one-tenth feel like Ecuadorians; and, in Guatemala, Nicaragua, El Salvador, Paraguay, and Bolivia, perhaps not even 5 per cent of the people have any sense of nationality.

Why should this have happened? In all instances, the answer is the same: because of the existence of a landholding oligarchy fearful of all change, who at best only tolerated political change. The war for independence did not do away with the landowners' holdings; on the contrary, it helped to enlarge them, and they continued to expand throughout the nineteenth century.

Between 1876 and 1893, 35 per cent of all the state-owned lands of Argentina—amounting to almost 12 million acres—changed hands, most of it cornered by favorites of the government or by foreign owners. Agriculture accounted for only 0.9 per cent of the country's surface; cattle raising and unproductive latifundia covered almost all of the land.[27] The state sold its own land cheaply, often from under the old-time settlers, who were forced to move on. In 1880, during a discussion of land sales in the Chamber of Deputies, Deputy José Hernández (1834–86) said, "We are going to depopulate the hills of Tordillo and populate the penitentiary."[28]

And this happened in Argentina, a country wide open to immigrants, where the arrival of new settlers inevitably helped to form a class of small farmer-landowners. But neither that new class nor any other group able to exert pressure—labor or the new industries—could prevent the cattle-raising oligarchs from halting progress. A revealing incident testifies to this. Between 1911 and 1914, a cabinet member, Ezequiel Ramos Mexía (1848–1935), and the American geologist Bailey Willis (1857–1949) drew up projects for industrializing northern Patagonia: a railroad, an industrial city with a technical college, irrigation, and the cultivation of wheat. But British interests, having no desire to see either progress in Argentina's wool-and-hide industry or the establishment of new railroads to compete with the British lines, opposed the plans. Thereupon, the oligarchy, or its more powerful or less intelligent members, killed the attempt to modernize Patagonia. The plans were burned by compliant bureaucrats, and Willis himself was in danger of being jailed. Ramos Mexía was forced to resign. The reasons for the oligarchy's fears were obvious: An industrialized south and lands given to the peasants would prove that its exploitation of land was not economical, and this would give rise to antioligarchic forces. Interestingly enough, ex-President Arturo Frondizi (1908–   ) has blamed the bureaucracy and the English, rather than the oligarchy, for this dark chapter in Argentina's history—evidence of the latter's continuing decisive role in the country's affairs.[29]

Ramos Mexía gave a clear explanation (figures don't lie) of what happened. In Paris, he was talking to Percival Farquhar, an

American who had built railroads in Brazil and other countries. Farquhar asked Ramos Mexía whether the big landowners might not someday yield to the temptation to expropriate foreign-owned railroads, and he replied that they earned 30 per cent on their capital investment yearly and would scorn the 4–7 per cent profit the railroads offer.[30]

If this could happen in the then most industrialized Latin American country, a country with almost no Indian population save the Patagonians, who were hunted like wild animals, what could one expect in countries with large native populations sunk in servitude since before the arrival of the Spaniards and in serfdom during the colonial period and after? Manuel González Prada (1848–1918), a Peruvian poet whose indignation drove him to embrace a passionate but nondoctrinaire kind of anarchism, clearly summed up his country's situation: "Our form of government boils down to a big lie, for a state in which 2 or 3 million individuals live outside the law does not deserve to be called a democratic republic."[31] He pointed out what everyone knows and accepts:

The axiom that the Indian has no rights, only obligations, is not written down, but it is true. In dealings with him, any personal complaint by him is considered insubordination; any collective protest is considered attempted rebellion. . . . Does the Indian suffer any less under the republic than under Spanish domination? Though *repartimientos* and encomiendas may no longer exist, forced labor and the military draft are still with us. The suffering we impose on him is enough to bring down upon us the curses of all mankind. We keep him in ignorance and servitude; we debase him in the barracks; we brutalize him with alcohol; we fling him into civil wars to his own destruction.

Official hypocrisy was not the most repugnant aspect of the situation:

The republic follows the traditions of the viceroyalty. Presidents plead for the redemption of the oppressed and call themselves the guardians of the indigenous race; congresses draft laws superior to the Declaration of the Rights of Man; government ministers issue decrees, send notes to the provincial governors, and appoint investigating committees—all with the noble aim of safeguarding the disinherited class. But messages, laws, decrees, notes, and committees amount to nothing more than hypocritical jeremiads, hollow words, palliatives, worn-out expedients.

The authorities in Lima who send stern orders to the departments know full well that they will not be obeyed; the governors who receive the admonitions of the capital also know that nothing will happen to them if they do not comply. What the Marquis de Mancera said in his *Memoirs* in 1648 bears repeating today; where he used the words *corregidors* and *caciques*, the text should read *governors* and *owners of great estates:* "These poor Indians have as their enemies the greed of their *corregidors,* their priests, and their *caciques,* all of them ready to get rich off their sweat."

This situation continues, thanks to a subtle political tactic:

An offensive and defensive alliance exists, an exchange of favors between the men in control of the capital and the provinces. If the landowner in the mountains serves the great *señor* of Lima as political agent, the great *señor* of Lima will defend the landowner in the mountains when he exploits the Indian. . . .

What has caused the expansion of the latifundium?

A large estate is the sum total of small plots snatched from their lawful owners; the master has the authority of a Norman feudal baron over his peasants. Not only does he influence the appointment of governors, mayors, and justices of the peace, but he also arranges marriages, designates heirs, doles out inheritances, and can force children to satisfy their parents' indebtedness by subjecting them to a servitude that usually lasts all their lives. He can order such terrible punishments as the stocks, whipping, the military pillory, or death; he can subject them to ridicule by shaving their heads or administering cold-water enemas. It would be miraculous if one who has no respect for lives or property were to respect the honor of women. Any Indian woman, married or unmarried, can be used to satisfy the lord's brutal desires. And yet, despite everything, the Indian does not address the master without first kneeling and kissing his hand. It cannot be claimed that the landowners behave in this fashion because of ignorance or lack of education: The sons of some landowners are sent to Europe, educated in France or England, and return to Peru with every appearance of being civilized people. But no sooner do they shut themselves away on their haciendas than they lose the European veneer and conduct themselves with greater inhumanity and violence than their fathers: The wild beast emerges again with the sombrero, the poncho, and the spurs.

Evidently, there is nothing new under the sun. The Black Shirts and the Brown Shirts could hardly have been acquainted with the customs of the Peruvian landowners, who on their own had invented methods of torture that today are considered products of the Fascist mentality.

Much the same things happened in Ecuador under the guise of a certain elegant and cynical legality. The constitution of 1852 required that a man be a landowner before he could vote or run for office. But it did not require that he be able to read and write.[32]

The Argentine José Hernández, by no means a revolutionary but familiar with the lives of the peasants, in his book *Instrucción del Estanciero (Instruction of the Landowner)*—a much less popular work than his "Martín Fierro" but no less revealing—said, "The *lépero* of Mexico, the *llanero* of Venezuela, the *montuvio* of Ecuador, the *cholo* of Peru, the *coya* of Bolivia, and the *gaucho* of Argentina have never yet tasted the benefits of independence, shared in the advantages of progress, or reaped any of the benefits of freedom and civilization."[33]

Politics was conducted in a vacuum, with the people taking no part. Hence, coups, countercoups, mutinies, plots, and intrigues could take place without jeopardizing the survival of the oligarchy; politicians and military men could play for power and seize it. It was all in the family. New proclamations were issued and new constitutions framed, but the people were not even aware of them; they seldom knew anything about such matters. This accounts for the picturesque style of Latin American politics. Newspaper readers in other countries, seeing reports of coups, shrug their shoulders and say, "Those Latin Americans, always so tempestuous. . . ."

Since conditions were more or less the same everywhere in Latin America, events everywhere were bound to take a similar course.

Ecuador had 35 revolutions in the course of a century. In Paraguay, only 6 presidents were able to serve out their terms since 1814: 3 generals, 3 civilians; the country has had 40 presidents in 78 years, and they have had to deal with 12 revolutions, 20 armed uprisings, and several wars with neighboring countries. In one anarchic 10-year period, Chile had 5 constitutions, and Freire, the chief of state, dissolved 3 assemblies he himself had convoked. In Nicaragua, in the short space of 14 years, 23 heads of state, called supreme directors, succeeded one another; from 1861 to 1893, the country lived in a state of virtual civil war. Mexico had 22 presidents within 39 years. In the Caribbean, there were 74 dictatorships. In Bolivia, 191 mutinies and *coups d'état* occurred in the 118 years from 1826 to 1944. Argentina could count 33 mutinies up to 1955.[34]

Every second-rate general or petty politician who climbed the ladder to the presidency wanted his own constitution. Either some pseudo-intellectual would whisper a panacea in his ear or he would concoct one in his own noddle. In either case, the ruler would be filled with the desire to leave, for the delectation of history, official evidence of his cure-all. This mania for solving problems on paper (a sure-fire substitute for actually solving them) resulted in a series of constitutions. There is no assurance that the long list of constitutions that follows is complete.

Argentina: 1813, 1819, 1826 (unitary), 1853 (federal, revised in 1860, 1866, 1898, 1949, and 1957)

Bolivia: 1823, 1826 (both Bolívar's), 1831 (the Bolivia-Peru Federation), 1843, 1861, 1880, 1938, 1955

Brazil: 1820 (constitutional monarchy), 1824 (the Empire, revised in 1832 and supplemented by the Additional Act of 1834), 1888, 1889 (republican), 1891 (revised in 1925, 1926, 1934, 1937, and 1946), 1965

Chile: 1818, 1822, 1823, 1833 (revised in 1871), 1925

Colombia: 1821, 1832 (revised in 1843), 1853, 1863 (the United States of Colombia, revised in 1864), 1866 (revised in 1910), 1930, 1936, 1937

Costa Rica: 1844, 1847, 1859, 1871 (revised in 1882), 1927, 1942–49, 1959

Cuba: 1869 (Guaimaro), 1895 (Jimaguayú), 1897 (Yaya), 1901, 1928, 1933, 1936, 1940 (revised in 1952), 1958

Dominican Republic: 1821, 1844, 1854 (dictatorship), 1858, 1865 (liberal), 1866 (constitution of 1854 adopted); in 1867, Cabral restored the 1865 charter; in 1868, Báez returned to the constitution of 1854, which was revised in 1877; then 1878, 1879, 1880, 1881, 1887, 1896, 1907, 1908, 1924, 1929, 1934 (revised in 1953), 1955, 1963, 1966

Ecuador: 1830 (revised six times before 1861), 1906, 1929 (revised in 1946), 1955, 1966

El Salvador: 1838, 1847, 1848, 1883, 1939 (revised in 1950), 1958

Guatemala: 1824, 1838, 1851, 1879, 1887, 1897, 1903, 1927, 1935, 1945, 1956, 1959, 1964

Haiti: 1790, 1801, 1805 (the Empire), 1806 (republic), 1846, 1849 (Second Empire), 1858 (restoration of 1846 constitution), 1867 (liberal), 1874 (conservative), 1876 (restoration of 1867 charter), 1879, 1932 (revised in 1946), 1955 (revised in 1963)

Honduras: 1824, 1848, 1924, 1936, 1960, 1965

Mexico: 1813 (Iguala Plan), 1814 (Apatzingán Plan), 1819, 1821, 1836

(Constitution of the Seven Laws), 1843, 1857 (revised in 1877), 1917 (revised in 1956)

    Nicaragua: 1838, 1911 (revised in 1913), 1939, 1948, 1950, 1957

    Panama: 1904 (revised in 1918), 1928, 1941, 1946, 1951

    Paraguay: 1870, 1940

    Peru: 1823, 1831, 1834, 1839, 1845 ("constitutionalism" of Castilla), 1856, 1860, 1919, 1933

    Uruguay: 1828, 1918, 1939, 1952 (revised in 1957 and 1966)

    Venezuela: 1822, 1830 (revised in 1857), 1858, 1914, 1928, 1931, 1936, 1947, 1953, 1956, 1959[35]

These constitutions were not simply scraps of paper. They influenced the everyday life of the people, their customs and their pocketbooks. Sarmiento lamented:

Comparison of the German and Scottish settlements with the villages of the interior evokes pity and shame: In the former, the small houses are painted; the front of the house, always neat, is decorated with flowers and charming shrubs; the furnishings are simple but adequate; the copper or tin pots are shiny; the beds are hung with pretty canopies; and the people are industrious and active. The cows are milked; butter and cheese are made; some families have succeeded in amassing vast fortunes and have moved to the city to enjoy life in comfort.

The native village is the reverse of this coin: Children, dirty and dressed in rags, live alongside a pack of dogs; men lie stretched on the ground in a state of complete inaction; slovenliness and poverty are on all sides; the furnishings consist of a small table and sleeping mats; wretched hovels serve as dwellings, and there is a general air of crudity and neglect.[36]

In some respects, things had retrogressed since colonial times: In the eighteenth century, maritime trade between Europe and South America was carried on in vessels built in South America; by the middle of the nineteenth century, however, to go from Rosario to Buenos Aires, one had to travel in ships built in Europe.

The Invitation to Imperialism

The oligarchs shipped capital abroad for fear that it would not be safe at home or because they lived in Europe. Consequently, their governments had to float loans to keep going, to build what was absolutely necessary, to conclude contracts that would open the way for the payment of graft to enrich the "heroes of their country." Such loans were made in Europe, particularly in England. The interest rates were merciless, doubtless because the lenders were greedy, but above all because the loans entailed a considerable risk, given Latin America's instability. The common interest rate charged by European bankers to Europeans was 5–8 per cent; to Latin Americans, 15–18 per cent.[37] Thus, because the oligarchs exported their profits to Europe, the home of the small *rentiers* who bought government bonds and thereby provided loans to Latin American governments or enterprises, the Europeans were virtually asked to become the owners of Latin American public utilities, mines, and industries. Imperialism came to Latin America because of the failings of the oligarchs. It was they who issued the invitation, opened the gates, and set the table for imperialism, without a thought for their own countries' interests. This began soon after independence. From 1822 to 1826, the Spanish American countries obtained ten loans from England, in the amount of £21 million. Of that amount, they actually received only £7 million; the other £14 million were held back to pay the interest.[38]

The situation continued to worsen; in 1896, the socialist Juan B. Justo (1865–1928) could say that Great Britain had succeeded, through her investments, in conquering Argentina, something she could not have achieved by force of arms. "We have seen the Argentines reduced to the status of a British colony by means of economic penetration," a development made possible, Justo believed, by the local oligarchy, "sellers of their country."[39]

Something had to be done to divert the sector of the public that was concerned about such things. For that purpose, military coups and nationalist demagoguery proved useful. In spite of this, the Latin American governments have never been able to work out coherent foreign policies, and their armies have never been of any use in defending their territorial integrity. When the conservatives in Mexico called in a foreign prince and set up an empire, the republican government had to call upon the people—the worker, the barefoot peasant, even the romantic poet —to fight and overcome the French Army and the troops of the conservatives, instead of calling upon the military men who so loved coups. This armed rabble (which depended on the support of the United States) proved more effective than the costly regular army. All this took place when, "owing to our weakness and divisions, not only the insolent France of Napoleon III but even the decrepit Spain of Isabel II could dream of new imperialistic ventures in our nineteenth-century America. . . . The Spanish American countries are at the mercy of any foreign fleet coming to collect the interest on its loans with cannons."[40]

When Cuba, the last corner of Spanish America that was still a colony, revolted in 1868 and again in 1898, no Latin American country's army or government came to the insurgents' aid. It was the United States that—for reasons of national self-interest, naturally—went to their rescue. But, when the United States rendered the bill for its aid, Latin America's governments, politicians, and nationalists, both professional and amateur, all protested, shouted, and criticized. It would have been much easier, more generous, and more honorable to have protested and criticized earlier, when it was obvious that the Latin American oligarchic governments were washing their hands of the Cuban struggle.

My insistence on the oligarchies' responsibility is not an *idée fixe*. Unless one recognizes the importance of this factor, it is impossible to understand the political and social evolution of Latin America or to solve the psychological riddle of the special kind of nationalism that boiled up in Latin America. The key to this understanding is the exclusion of the people from government, and this fact must be tirelessly stressed. The positivists recognized and tried to justify it. Lastarria said, "Democracy, which means liberty, is not legitimate, useful, or beneficent except when a people have come of age, and we are not yet adults. The strength that we ought to have employed to reach maturity—enlightenment, that is—was subjected for three centuries to satisfying the greed of a backward mother country and later spent on breaking chains and establishing an independent government."[41]

In Brazil, a country that was a long time abolishing slavery but finally did so without violence, the people also were not part of political life. Aureliano Cándido Tavares Basto (1839–1875) stated the matter clearly:

There is something that Brazil has forgotten completely: the lot of the people—not the great landholders, capitalists, newly created noblemen, university graduates, or other men of standing. Everyone keeps on talking about politics, extolling freedom, studying numerous aspects of contemporary history, attacking the ministries, and invoking the constitution. We write about Rome, Greece, France, and England, but nothing that bears any relation to the people. The country's scholars occupy themselves with studies of the autochthonous people's languages, the life of the Lepidoptera, and the geology of the backlands, but no one sets himself the task of studying the world we live in, no one worries about the creatures around us, and no one is interested in finding out what the lot of the people is.[42]

To sum up, the nineteenth century was marked by the paradox that the romantic populists, the only people with any concept of how to instill nationalism, tended, because of their belief in progress, to rise above nationalism. All others turned toward something other than the people, that is, other than the nation. In later days, the successors of those romantic populists were to take seriously the task of making the people part of society.

4

Attempts at a Positive Nationalism

The Liberals and the Radicals

Not until after World War I was any serious, conscious attempt made to foster, direct, and accelerate the development of nationality in Latin America. "Conscious," in this context, does not mean overt, for hardly anyone openly accepts the fact that the Latin American countries are not yet nations. Whoever would dare to say so publicly would find himself ostracized, the target of a flood of insults. Such a reaction might be evidence of the truth of the assertion, but it would not improve the political chances of the man who stated this truth.

But some people are trying to reach the masses. They hope to pull the people up from the substratum of society and to become the leaders of truly popular movements. As was the case with European socialism in the last century, they are members of the ruling classes, usually young, who break with their fellows and go over to the side of the masses. For some years, visitors to Latin America have received an impression similar to that received by visitors to Czarist Russia during the early days of the *narodniki*.

This trend toward espousing the interests of the people was not brought about by magic. It has roots in the past. The liberals, for instance, felt a need to concern themselves with the people. They supported agrarian reform, a more equitable system of taxation, the development of public works and services, the democratization of government, universal secular education, and the abolition of the political and economic power of the Catholic clergy.

But, as we have seen, liberal governments pursued an agrarian policy that had tragic consequences; it produced more generals, new great landholders, rich politicians, and, in some countries, new industrialists and bankers as well. These liberals, who had occupied a secondary economic position in nineteenth-century Latin America, never thought of supplanting the oligarchies; all they wanted was for the oligarchs to go a little easy in their methods of exploitation and institute more efficient economic practices. But, ultimately, they became part of the oligarchic system and lost their zeal for reform.

The provincial middle class and the peasantry, on the other hand, lent their electoral support—when elections were held at all —to the conservative parties. The church also supported the rightists. Any move by the reformers to destroy the caste system was countered by renewed efforts to preserve traditional forms on the part of the conservatives. "The peasantry, especially the small landholding Indians and those living on communal land, constitutes the major basis of the military dictatorship and the heaviest drag on revolution. Consequently, the rightists try to keep the old Indian communities in their original state."[1]

Nonetheless, the bourgeoisie and the working class continued to grow gradually. During the first three decades of the twentieth century, a number of bourgeois political parties developed and were joined by segments of the middle class: Radical parties in Argentina and Chile (who more or less imitated the French Radicals), the Colorado Party in Uruguay, the new liberals in some other countries. Whenever any of these parties came to power, they passed social legislation for which the labor movement had prepared the ground.

In its early days, the labor movement's aggressive character (an outcome of its being barred from the political path by electoral fraud or disfranchisement) frightened the middle class into supporting repressive legislation. Later, a new generation, seeing the problem of labor differently, became involved with the labor movement, and frequently furnished its leadership. The industrial workers supported the middle classes and their parties, which, in turn, wherever and whenever they came to power, passed reform laws demanded by labor. Although much labor legislation never got beyond the paper stage, some progress was made, and, on the whole, the workers gained a measure of social dignity and some rights they had not enjoyed before.

In many cases, however, the bourgeois parties eventually moved to the right, as they saw social progress going too far for them. The disintegration of these parties, which were concerned only with alleviating the most obvious economic injustices, not with changing the social structure, produced a political vacuum, which in some countries was filled by demagogic movements, sometimes of a Fascist type, like those of Juan Domingo Perón (1895–   ), of Argentina, and Getulio Vargas (1883–1954), of Brazil, and, in others, by populists wanting reform, not amelioration. The populists did not want to preserve the old structure; they wanted a new one that would represent an aggregation of the middle class, the proletariat, and the peasantry rather than the bourgeoisie alone.

The populists began with Marxism, or at least with a thorough study of it, but, in the end, they found that Marxism as a doctrine did not offer a usable theory for economic improvement. That was inevitable, for Marx held that socialism must arise out of capitalism, that it was capitalism that developed a country and converted it to an industrial economy. Precisely because the Latin American socialists never succeeded in creating a socialist theory of development, they could never put down roots, and they never managed to exercise an effective influence on Latin American politics. This deficiency obliged the populists to find and formulate their own theory of development.

The populists did not see the middle class as the classical Marxist *petite bourgeoisie,* vacillating but destined to turn proletarian in the end. On the contrary, they found that the middle class, which had arisen out of industrialization, was destined to be the main beneficiary of industrialization. The leaders of the middle class say that their interests coincided with those of society in general and, hence, that the middle class might bring the submerged classes to the surface and guide the development of Latin America without causing suffering or sacrifices not shared by all classes, and without bringing about unfair privileges or the suppression of any freedoms.

The Socialists and the Anarchosyndicalists

Two trends, both imported from Europe, paved the way for populism: socialism, especially of the Argentine type, since Argentina was the only country where socialism was well organized; and anarchosyndicalism, deriving particularly from the Peruvian González Prada's anarchism of protest and the syndicalists' experience in techniques of organizing, propagandizing, and fighting.

Many Latin American workers' parties were created by immigrants, and they still retain certain immigrant characteristics, although immigration to Latin America has almost ceased (except in a few countries, notably Venezuela).

Each immigrant hopes to find in America the opportunity for personal success that he can no longer find in Europe. His struggle, far more than a class struggle, is to find greater opportunities for individual triumph. He does not aspire to do away with the bourgeoisie; he aspires merely to acquire the same advantages as they, to be situated on the same economic and social plane. Hence, he may be closer to Spencer than to Marx. . . . He wants to come to terms with the bourgeoisie, not to destroy it.[2]

The labor movement was forming and growing during the period when positivism was spreading. Some positivists even believed that socialism and positivism should be reconciled: "Comte's doctrine will not be able to keep abreast of events unless socialism offers it the appropriate elements for its great work," wrote the Argentine positivist José Bianchi as far back as 1893.[3] The bourgeoisie found its justification in Spencer and Darwin, and the Latin American socialists sought in the same sources justification of the class struggle. This gave some socialists such as José Ingenieros (1877–1925) the theme for a strange racist theory; in 1915, giving himself a sociologist's airs, he said:

There exist definite factors of judgment by which to appreciate the advent of an Argentine white race, which will soon enable us to erase the stigma of inferiority with which Europeans have always branded South Americans. In the army, instead of Indians and Gaucho mercenaries, white citizens will be the custodians of the nation's dignity. . . . On Argentine territory, emancipated a century ago by the ideas and deeds of ten thousand Euro-Argentines, will live a race composed of 15–100 million white people, who, in their leisure hours, will read the chronicles of the extinct indigenous races, the stories of the Gaucho cross-breeding that retarded the formation of a white race.[4]

The explanation of the singular tolerance for this kind of writing no doubt lies in the fact that, although the labor movement (both trade-union and political) did concern itself with the dispossessed and oppressed people, it also gave these people both the hope of improving their condition and a certain sense of belonging to a privileged group. A glance at the extent of poverty, alienation, and resignation among the masses in Latin America makes one understand (however difficult this may be to justify ideologically) that the workers—less miserable, less alienated, above all less resigned—could feel nothing in common with the majority of the people, the submerged masses and, accordingly, felt little concern for them.

Juan Justo, on the other hand, blended Spencer's philosophy with that of Marx. He strove to naturalize Marxism, to adapt it to the aspirations of the Latin American proletariat, to prune it of everything that would not function in Latin America. He tried to formulate a theory to use as a weapon against the oligarchy, and he wanted the proletarian struggle to depend not upon abstractions or philosophies but upon science. "The idea of a sudden social change that would establish a perfect order of things in one stroke loses ground in the public mind in proportion as the people concern themselves more intelligently with everyday problems," he affirmed. What he wanted was "to hand over to all the people that function of leadership which is a monopoly of the privileged owner class today," not in order to establish a dictatorship but in order to obtain control of technology, then the possession of a few people. With the acquisition of this control, inequality would gradually disappear.[5]

If the Argentine socialists had won control of the government, they might possibly have done away with the oligarchy and granted "all the people" a voice in their government and, by taking such a step, might have started to create conditions under which the country might become a nation. But they never even came close to power.

Anarchosyndicalism in Latin America has a very individual style, and Manuel González Prada,* one of its theorists, exemplified it well. Concerning the socialist doctrine that places "education first," González Prada did not beat about the bush: "To him who says *school,* let us say *school and bread.*"[6] At one time, he believed that a new party might solve the problem of bread, and he founded the *Unión Nacional.* It never really materialized, however, but what he wrote concerning it was to have a decisive influence on the populist movement. In choosing the party name National Union, he wanted to make plain the need for all the people to take part in the struggle.

The National Union does not pretend to win converts or hybrid blocs; it breaks with political tradition and attempts to organize a force that will react against evil ideas and bad habits. We can attract sympathy and arouse an echo in the soul of the multitude in only one way—by being intransigent and irreconcilable. . . . The entire world of false legislation, laws, and constitutions alien to Peruvian actuality must be demolished. No more Utopias! A positive sense of reality is needed! The men of the past promulgated constitutions and laws, but they did not educate the citizens to understand and comply with them. . . . They ordered digestion without having the means to provide bread. . . . Of what use to us is free instruction, if we lack schools? What is the use of freedom of the press, if we do not know how to read? Of what use is free enterprise, if we do not possess capital, credit, or land to break with the plow? . . . The National Union can condense its program into two lines: to evolve toward the greatest freedom for the individual, we must set social reforms above political changes. . . . Down with politics! Make way for social reform![7]

* See pages 54–55.

The Populists

The populist movement drew upon anarchosyndicalism, the indignation of González Prada, and Justo's adaptation of Marxism to the needs of an oligarchic society. It was the populists who took the first tentative step toward seeing Latin American affairs through Latin American eyes. There was no moment of which we might say, "Populism began here," but there *is* a man who was able to draw together the various impulses in the atmosphere —the European experiences and the Latin American lessons— and to formulate a populist doctrine for the Latin American continent: Víctor Raúl Haya de la Torre (1895–   ). All the later populist movements—the Peruvian APRA (Alianza Popular Revolucionaria Americana); the Venezuelan Acción Democrática; the Paraguayan Febreristas; the Bolivian MNR (Movimiento Nacionalista Revolucionario); the PRD (Partido Revolucionario Dominicano), in the Dominican Republic; and, to some degree, the Mexican PRI (Partido Revolucionario Institucional) —all these found their inspiration in his interpretation of the Latin American situation. At one point, indeed, people believed that he would succeed in creating a continent-wide populist movement. This proved to be impossible, but, on the other hand, the idea encouraged a state of mind that embraced all Latin America and later even influenced President Kennedy's Latin American policy.[8]

All the populist movements were indigenous movements, formed after World War I, in which trade-unionists, anti-imperialists, and proponents of university reform were active and in which the Mexican Revolution and some surviving pre-Hispanic institutions were influential. The populists aspired to form mass parties and to establish a united front of peasants, the proletariat, and the middle class. Anti-Communist and democratic, they were independent of other international movements. They supported self-determination by the people as manifested through the vote; they were revolutionaries who conceived of revolution as an accelerated evolution destined to change the social structure of countries still dominated by the feudal system. They were anti-imperialists but rejected anti-Yankeeism. They were, finally, partisans of the political and economic integration of the Latin American countries for the defense of their sovereignty and the planned development of the continent.

Haya de la Torre's philosophy of history (especially his concept of historical space-time*) had a wide influence, but the program and organizational methods of APRA, which he founded in 1924, had an even greater one. However, each populist group coming to power has behaved in its own fashion. The first Latin American populist movement, then lacking theories or labels, was that of the men who accomplished the Mexican Revolution of 1910–17. They knew what one of the conservative leaders of the Revolution, Venustiano Carranza (1859–1920), pointed out:

The social struggle, the class struggle, must begin formidably and majestically. Whether we like it or not, whether its enemies oppose it or not, the new social theory will have to be imposed on our masses. And it is not only a question of apportioning land and national wealth, not just a matter of an effective suffrage or of opening more schools; it is something greater and more sacred; it is the establishment of justice, the search for equality; it is the removal of the powerful in order to establish an equilibrium of the national conscience.[9]

While the Mexican Revolution was going on, it was isolated from the rest of Latin America. But the Russian Revolution evoked great demonstrations of sympathy, particularly from the intellectuals, and inspired the formation of skeletal Communist parties. Yet, in time, the populists turned the Mexican experience to good account. (Indeed, Haya de la Torre formulated his first theories while exiled in Mexico.)

The populists were bound to react strongly against the widespread supposition, clothed in the "scientific" vestments of the

---

* This was an application of Einstein's theories to the sociohistorical field. Haya wrote: "With the juxtaposition of different stages of human evolution in the same space, time varies. Europe is living in a homogeneous time, in which all its countries are in the twentieth century. In Latin America, the twentieth century exists in Buenos Aires, . . . but, as we travel from the coast to the jungle, we pass from the twentieth into the sixteenth or seventeenth century, into the time of feudal and semibarbaric Andean agriculture, until we stumble on naked and hostile tribes in the tropical forests. . . . Each space-time area has its peculiar rhythm of development and, consequently, its own sociological characteristics." *Pensamiento politico,* p. 7.

sociologists, that Latin Americans—owing to the intermingling of races, the tropical climate, and a hundred other equally puerile reasons—were not fit for democracy. "The pessimistic philosophers were completely mistaken," said Rómulo Betancourt (1908–   ). "The people of Latin America are perfectly well able to organize economically, politically, and socially. We are a people who can be governed democratically and legally. We are resolved to find our own way, to make our own history; we do not want to continue in the contemplative attitude toward the past or to burn incense before the portraits of the Liberators."[10]

Still, the populists had to find a way to reach the people. If they wished to create united fronts, they had to awaken the country people, until then alienated from all political and social struggles, as well as the large portion of the proletariat that was still unorganized. The great historical merit of populism lies in its having succeeded in this task—at least in Mexico, Peru, Bolivia, and Venezuela. Acción Democrática, in Venezuela, in addition to promulgating its slogan "Plant Petroleum," which meant channeling the funds obtained from naphtha into the promotion of modern production methods, began a vigorous program of agrarian reform.

Bolivia's experience went further. The mines in Bolivia played the same role in the economy as that played by land in every other country. What was needed, therefore, was mining reform. Víctor Paz Estenssoro (1907–   ), a theorist of the MNR, said plainly:

We had to take the measures we took. They were determined by conditions in Bolivia. We had to nationalize the mines; we had to carry out agrarian reform. Nationalizing the mines entailed obvious risks, but they were the risks proper to our situation as a backward country, a country exploited for so long. We had neither capital nor technicians [of our own]; we might never have been able to nationalize the mines, precisely because, not being masters of our fate, we had neither disposable capital nor any technicians.

But, if the mines were the important element in the economy, the rural countryside was a basic human element. The miners numbered only 30,000, whereas there were 2 million or more farm workers. "Bolivia lacked a consciousness of nationality," and, to gain it, agrarian reform was essential, as much for economic as for social reasons, however great the risks involved.

A fundamental change in the system of landownership carries with it, as a consequence, a drop in production during the period immediately following the transition. In Bolivia, the upheaval was minimal because the peasant had already been indoctrinated and was conscious of his responsibilities. He made a great effort to keep to a minimum the drop in production. But agrarian reform was accompanied by an upheaval in the country, that is evident. . . . In Bolivia, we have wiped out serfdom; we have leaped from the Middle Ages to the contemporary period.[11]

The Anti-Imperialists

Populism offered, for the first time, a continent-wide outlook on Latin America's role in political history and in the world. Populists were, therefore, able to interpret imperialism in Latin American terms. Because of their oligarchies of absentee landlords who took their profits abroad with them, the Latin American countries had no ready capital with which to industrialize, and Latin American capitalism was, consequently, built at first with foreign capital. Thus, imperialism became the parent of capitalism. On several occasions, Haya proposed an economic chamber, to function alongside the traditional parliaments, in which foreign investors would be represented, so that they would feel assured of a safeguard for their interests and, conversely, would be obliged to feel some sense of responsibility to the country that had accepted their investments. The populists, however, believed that the best way to combat imperialism was to combat the oligarchies that had opened the doors to it and had created conditions that made foreign investment hazardous and capitalism possible only with foreign funds.

Latin American imperialism and anti-imperialism show unique characteristics. "In the years 1890–1900," said Haya, "this idea of intervention by the United States [as imperialistic] appeared in the United States; at the time, the Democratic Party called itself anti-imperialistic, and Bryan . . . called Theodore Roosevelt and the entire Republican Party 'imperialists.' The struggle between imperialism and anti-imperialism began in the United

States." British imperialism, which had become paramount in Latin America, at this point began to yield before the American drive. Haya wrote:

According to Lenin, imperialism is the final stage of capitalism. . . . We reply that, for our countries, it is the first stage, because the development of the European industrial economy produces the export of capital to underdeveloped countries and constitutes in them the beginnings of capitalism and industrialism. . . .

Imperialism inaugurates our industrialization. . . . On the other hand, it is dangerous, owing to what it may signify in terms of both an excessive control of our economy and political imperialism.

A political movement of resistance then appeared in Latin America, long in advance of Communism in its modern sense; it was an instinctive resistance to the trend fostered by those who were extreme in their stand favoring foreign investments and said, "We need foreign capital wherever it may come from, however it may come." The new movement . . . replies, "We need foreign capital under fixed control, with fixed coordination, so that it may stimulate progress to new stages of industrial accomplishment yet not menace the [nation's sovereignty] or even the nation's industrial economy—that is, without exploitation or injustice."

And he adds, recognizing what everyone knows but few dare to say, "Our . . . Latin American economy would be unable to move without the intervention of foreign capital. . . . [It] represents progress, the most advanced production technology, and so on, even though it may entail danger because of our disunity."[12]

As a logical consequence of their understanding of the problem of imperialism, the populists advocated both political and economic union for all Latin America. APRA sponsored the idea enthusiastically and energetically; other populist parties paid it lip service but took no action, although each time a dangerous situation arose, they united in their common cause. But then it was always too late. A Mexican proverb says, "They cover the well after the child has drowned," and the populist parties have done this over the years by failing to coordinate their own actions, the first step in the attempt to coordinate those of the various countries.

In the 1920's, APRA, striving to be a continent-wide movement, had branches in many countries, and the populist parties occasionally met to exchange points of view. The first Congress of Democratic and Popular Parties of America, in Santiago, in October, 1940, was attended by representatives from Mexico, Venezuela, Panama, Ecuador, Peru, Bolivia, Argentina, and Uruguay and by adherents from Colombia, Paraguay, and Brazil. But, when some of the populist parties came to power after 1944, they failed to take advantage of this to coordinate their policies with those of other populist governments. Not until military coups drove them out did they try to do something along that line, as they did at the first Inter-American Conference for Democracy and Freedom, in Havana, in 1950, attended by populist delegates and members of some trade-union groups.[13] Ten years later, when dictatorships had fallen in almost all the Latin American countries, a second conference was held (many of the delegates who had been exiles when the first conference met being now ministers and senators), and, whereas the first conference gave special attention to political problems, the second was devoted almost entirely to social questions.[14]

Finally, however, in August, 1960, there was a meeting in Lima of representatives of the Bolivian MNR, the Costa Rican National Liberation Party, the Paraguayan Febreristas, the Peruvian Apristas, and the Venezuelan Acción Democrática, to coordinate a plan for action throughout Latin America. And in March, 1961, nineteen Latin American parties returned a favorable answer to President Kennedy's proposal for an Alliance for Progress.

The 1960 Declaration of Lima is important because it defines the populist position on a number of problems, including that of Cuba, that had caused schisms and heated debates among some of the signatory parties. The Declaration states, "Historical experience in Latin America demonstrates that parties of the people, that is, national and revolutionary movements, formed as a front of the exploited classes, with a genuinely Latin American doctrine and program and with roots in the civic majorities, are the most efficacious instruments with which to consummate economic independence and establish social justice in our countries." The problems of each Latin American country "constitute parts or variants of a continental problem; its solution requires the closest coordination of our countries on the economic, political, and cultural levels, with a view toward a federation of peoples." But "the existence in the Western Hemisphere of two clearly defined zones, one industrialized and capitalistic, like the United States, and the other economically underdeveloped, like Latin America, and the virtually uncontrolled system of exploitation by the first of the second, which has predominated until now, creates a problem of international injustice and disequilibrium." This is "the source of a legitimate discontent among our people that may induce them to opt for totalitarian formulas of political organization like those prevailing in other continents, in order to accelerate, by any means whatsoever, their economic development." At the same time, the signers of the Declaration of Lima refused to play the anti-Yankee game, and they asserted their "unalterable rejection of Communist totalitarian penetration of Latin America, against which our parties have always fought, as much because of an insurmountable difference in social and political philosophy as because of the deviationist and prejudicial activity and frequent complicity with dictatorships and reactionary forces that have been typical of Communism in Latin America."[15]

Three Stages of Populism

For a time, just after World War I, there was in some countries a real collaboration between trade unions and the groups of students and intellectuals then struggling for university reform. The "popular universities" in Peru and elsewhere were the fruit of that collaboration. These future leaders of the populist parties had personal experience of "going to the people," and this gave their parties a bent toward organizing the submerged masses from the start, taught the propagandists to speak to the people in language they could understand and that would arouse their interest, and made them familiar with the problems, psychology, and aspirations of the masses. As a rule, unions in Latin America were nonpolitical, but soon their leaders began to emerge from the populist movements or became affiliated with them, since, for the first time, people who had not come from the labor rank and file were taking an active interest in workers' problems and trying, without paternalism, to help them to solve them. That was the road toward the creation of nationality—toward making the submerged masses a part of society. For a time, the trend seemed about to become established, to turn into something permanent in Latin American life that would yield far-reaching results.[16]

But the populists were always a part of opposition movements and were invariably persecuted. Haya de la Torre founded APRA in 1924 as a continent-wide movement and as a Peruvian party in 1931; in 1962, the Apristas won in the elections, and then, as twice before, the armed forces staged a successful coup against them. Acción Democrática won in the elections in Venezuela in 1948, and, a few months later, the armed forces there seized power. The MNR in Bolivia lost the elections of 1951 and seized power by violence; then, in 1964, the military took over. The Paraguayan Febreristas governed for a few months, only to be replaced by an endless series of dictators. In Guatemala, the Communists corrupted the various populist parties. Only in Mexico was populism able to remain in power for several generations. (It may succeed in doing so in Venezuela too, as a result of the success of the Betancourt government of 1959–64.)

However, whenever populism has held power, the movement has seemed to become paralyzed. The threat of a military coup (that is, the extreme form of oligarchic reaction) puts the populists on the horns of a dilemma: Either they foment political action by the masses and, as soon as success seems imminent, are confronted with a military coup; or they try to appease the armed forces—meaning, in the last analysis, the oligarchy—and abandon their efforts to awaken the people; this automatically puts them at the mercy of the military's whims and means surrender to the garrison gang.*

Populism had two periods of apogee besides its initial heroic period. The first came in 1944–45, in the flush of the Allied vic-

---

* Venezuela is a special case that cannot yet be judged. There are indications that something is brewing that may turn out to be not unlike what happened in Mexico, where, although a populist government had begun to integrate the people into society, this was followed by indifference to the people on the part of the privileged groups that emerged or expanded thanks to this integration.

tory in World War II, when populists won control in several countries. Perón's fall initiated a second wave of democratization, which Kennedy's victory in 1960 reinforced. But, when populism had both impetus for change *and* revolutionary zeal—in 1944–45 —it received no support from the United States; by the time Kennedy offered this support, it had lost the latter. In 1944–45, the populists tried to enroll all the people, to govern with the people and for the people; in 1960, the middle class and the organized proletariat, both indispensable to populism, wanted government for their benefit, but they no longer aspired to revolution, because their living conditions had improved so greatly (at the expense of the submerged masses) that they fancied they could enjoy the benefits of a revolution without having to risk their necks by making one. The populist parties, or their old guard at any rate, were nostalgic for the revolutionary period but had to speak and act in accordance with the thinking of the new membership.

The Mexican Example

Mexico is, perhaps, the country that shows most plainly the effects of the historic lack of synchronization between Latin American populism on the one hand and on the other a clear understanding in Washington of the real interests of the United States and the mutuality of interests between the peoples of Latin America and North America at any given stage.

The Mexican Revolution of 1910–17 was, essentially, a nationalistic revolution on the part of the middle class for the purpose of establishing conditions that might lead to the creation of a national capitalistic system and a rural middle class. The people played an active part in the Revolution.[17] One of the results of the Revolution was a recognizable "new Mexico," insistent

. . . on the role of the Indian and the process of cross-breeding, that is, the blending of European and Indian elements of the population. Although philosophers may discuss this question of racial intermingling as an intellectual matter, even as a spiritual mystique, its effect on actual social relations was the partial removal of class barriers to upward movement, which was marked by a change from the earlier belief that the upper classes were "white" and the lower "Indian" or "colored" and by the official enthronement of an ideology according to which social distinctions based on particular differences were replaced permanently by distinctions based on vocation or success. This change permitted the development of a great many small and medium-sized businesses and encouraged bigger ones to enlarge. Similarly, it fostered a great and rapid increase in industrial production. And, even though the increase in agricultural production lagged far behind that of industry at the start, it, too, has recorded a remarkable advance in the past few years. The reorganization of the social structure, which was the final result of the Revolution of 1910, has laid the groundwork for what one author called "Mexico's industrial revolution."[18]

According to Luis Cabrera (1876–1954), author of the agrarian law that set a standard for the objectives of the Revolution, the Revolution was a "violent and deep-seated social movement, the object of which was to restore the economic and political balance that must exist among the different human components of the nation."[19] This balance was to be achieved not by an illogical rhetoric of "peaceful revolution" or "democratic means by which to establish democracy" but by change-making action that did not wait for the sanction of technicians, studies by experts, or the backing of international bodies. On March 19, 1915, in the midst of the Revolution, *The Mexican Herald* showed how to do things when there is a real conviction that the social structure must be changed and when the people are ready to oppose their strength to the strength of armies. The newspaper printed a decree by the Governor of Morelos:

In order to begin to make effective the reforms that the Revolution will bring about, and in order to alleviate a little the critical conditions through which the people are passing, I make this proclamation:

Proceed at once to organize in the municipality in your charge a land guard, after first convoking a board of residents so that they, in agreement, may appoint [as its head] the person who combines the best qualities of honesty with the knowledge needed to carry out his work, and [once in office] this official will provisionally dispense allotments of land for cultivation to those who solicit them. . . . Each individual who receives an allotment will be notified that this division is temporary, pending an order from the secretary of agriculture that the Agrarian Commission make a definitive division of lands.

Reform, Freedom, Justice, and Law.

General Lorenzo Vázquez, Provisional Governor
Cuernavaca, March 8, 1915

For several decades, the government of Mexico tried to maintain an equilibrium between the new forces—the professional middle class, the new industrialists, the farmer-capitalists, and so on—and the people. The people had media of expression and means for defending themselves, both of which they owed entirely to the Revolution: the national legislature, the peasants' leagues, and the trade unions. In Congress, there was no hesitation about attacking the government: no personality cult surrounded the president; unions staged violent strikes; and peasant leagues ordered the occupation of lands whenever the bureaucrats were remiss in applying the agrarian-reform laws. But the moment a military uprising jeopardized the regime, the unions, the agrarian leagues, and every other popular organization rushed to fight in defense of the administration (except the Communists, always ready to seize their chance in such unstable situations to apply mechanically Moscow's slogan "All power to the Soviets").

Thus, by constant struggle, the country gradually consolidated its still basically agrarian economy and went ahead with the building of a middle class and the stabilization of its political system. Everything changed radically during the administration of Lázaro Cárdenas (1895–   ), from 1934 to 1940. Cárdenas did what any president would have done in a similar situation. He nationalized petroleum, not in obedience to principle, but in reaction to a wound to his nation's dignity produced by the incredible stupidity of foreign companies. Cárdenas may go down in history, when his image tumbles from its pedestal, for less positive accomplishments; it was he who—when obliged to win adherents to counter the influence of ex-President Plutarco Elías Calles (1877–1945), to whom he owed his election—destroyed the media of public expression and overruled parliament and made it a congress of servile politicians. He corrupted the trade unions and peasant movements by attaching them to the government and granting privileges to their leaders and to the workers too. He vitiated the agrarian reform that aimed to create a rural middle class, and made the *ejidos* (communal lands), which were regarded as transitional schools for small landowners, into permanent institutions, an act that proved injurious to the economy and prolonged the poverty of the peasants. To do this, Cárdenas created a bureaucratic apparatus (over the *ejidos,* in the trade unions, and in politics) that is still a burden on Mexico, owing to the enormous weight of self-interest it has acquired. Luckily for the country, however, the Revolution left behind a residue of conviction that the government should take upon itself the duty of defending the people against the greed of the new middle class. Cárdenas' successors have tried, without undue upheavals, to mitigate the harm he did, particularly in agrarian affairs. Thanks to its tutelary system, Mexico is the only country in Latin America in which the people's standard of living has appreciably improved, albeit with exasperating slowness. Nevertheless, the Mexican middle class, once revolutionary, has turned its back on the people. How much more natural was it for this to occur in the other Latin American countries, where populism won power for the middle class and then either was abandoned by it or had to turn its back on the people to stand with the middle class.

In the matter of developing nationality, all this translates into a great advance for Mexico over the rest of Latin America in achieving a national consciousness in the period before Cárdenas while the people were struggling, speaking out, and voting, and, after Cárdenas, into a step backward as the people again became wards of the government. Among the offspring of post-Cárdenas society, nationalism has again acquired the sterile vociferousness it always uses as a substitute for true awareness of nationality. Thus, during the Olympic Games held in Tokyo in 1964, Carlos Montoya, a Mexican athletic coach, remarked, "What these Olympic Games reflect is the extraordinary advance of sport on other continents, rather than the stagnation of Latin American sport."[20]

For all that, Mexico even now has a more clearly defined nationality than any other Latin American country. And the Mexican governments, I repeat, have tried to protect the people. But they have done it all from above, in the face of indifference of the newly prosperous and even the new poor, who are less poor than the old poor. Insofar as the middle class, even in a country that fought a revolution, has turned its back on the people, its thinking, including the arguments dredged up by its economists, has begun to take on the gloss of oligarchy. Or might it be said that the middle class became an oligarchy—not a landowning or absentee oligarchy but an urban and industrial one?

These are not idle words. Statistics indicate that, in 1952, real per-capita income had jumped from an index of 100 in 1939 to 160; however, in 1939, profits accounted for 26.0 per cent of the total national income and salaries and wages for 30.5 per cent, whereas by 1952 profits had risen to 41.4 per cent and salaries and wages had dropped to 23.8 per cent.[21] From 1950 to 1964, that part of the national income received by the wealthiest 10 per cent of the population rose from 49 per cent to 60 per cent. Conversely, the portion that went to the poorest 60 per cent of the people dropped from 26 per cent to 20 per cent—and this in the Latin American country where the government is most concerned over those who are not rich.[22]

At the same time, some ironic paradoxes have arisen. Mexico is one of the countries where the laws covering foreign investments are enforced most rigidly and where, in all business enterprises, 51 per cent of the capital must be in the hands of Mexicans. Mexico's so-called left inveighs constantly against foreign investment; yet, at the same time, Mexico has the largest proportion of foreign investment in all Latin America, and foreign capital feels most secure there. In 1964 and 1965, because the Swiss banks, having an excess of "refugee" capital, raised the cost of holding it, some of the capital in flight from Latin America found its way to Mexico, which, thus, had on hand more capital than could be invested at home. The Mexican newspapers did not report this, but it was possible to guess it from some news items; for example:

Three Mexican factories designed for the manufacture of nylon, acetate, and Dacron textiles have been opened in San Juan, P.R. The three Mexican companies are the first of their kind in Puerto Rico. It is hoped that they will be operating at full capacity by January, 1965, and that their annual sales volume may total $5 million. It is anticipated that 40 per cent of their production will remain in the local market and that the remaining 60 per cent will go to the United States.[23]

Better markets might be found to the south, however, as another item indicates:

Promexa, the company devoted to the manufacture of Volkswagen automobiles in Mexico, is looking for a million more square meters of land to fulfill its immediate plans for expansion. It is estimated that the company will be able to produce 25,000–30,000 cars a year, especially if it is taken into account that Promexa will undertake to supply the Central American market with vehicles assembled in Mexico for export. By mid-1965, Promexa should be able to use 70.3 per cent of the parts manufactured within the country, in accordance with the agreement signed with the government. The production of spare parts here will soon permit their export to the United States also.[24]

Here is another significant news note:

Venezuelan entrepreneurs and investors are studying the possibility of associating themselves with Mexican industrialists in order to establish plants for fabricating steel into various articles that are now being imported and that are greatly in demand. The economist Humberto Piñero Alvarado, who heads the promotion department of the Corporación Venezolana de Fomento, has reported on the visit he has just made to several steel-fabricating plants operating in Mexico. In his judgment, there are broad possibilities for an association between Mexican and Venezuelan capitalists for the purpose of developing the fabricational branch of the iron-and-steel industry.[25]

Perhaps, in the near future, we may have a sort of financial and diplomatic vaudeville show in which Mexico will demand from other Latin American countries guaranties of the investments made by Mexican firms (even those made with Latin American capital). Of course, the same kind of guaranties were labeled "imperialistic" by Mexican "leftists"—and by Mexican industrialists too, when they were suggested at a meeting of the International Monetary Fund in 1964.[26]

The Failure of the Middle Class

Populism, we see, has provided proof, the length and breadth of Latin America, that being right is not enough, that nobody is a friend of the masses unless he sees some advantage in it for himself. What the masses will achieve, they will have to achieve for themselves. If they do not succeed in integrating themselves into society, the countries of Latin America will never succeed in becoming true nations. The populist theses may continue to be valid, but new ways must be found to apply them.

A commentator in the United States wrote, in 1965:

The fact that the welfare state is financed in large measure by middle-income groups—who in turn receive the most benefit from it—explains the widely based, powerful political opposition to all efforts toward direct aid to the poor. Middle-income groups have no interest in the redistribution to others of their hard-won gains, and insist on the principle of equal treatment for everyone.[27]

This, which is true in the United States, a country that has succeeded in becoming a nation and that saw its middle class arise *when it was already a nation,* is all the more true in Latin American countries, which could have become nations with the help of their middle class but in which the middle class, upon becoming rich, substituted nationalistic rhetoric for a struggle for nationality, that is, for the people.*

* The reader may consider my treatment of the populist movements very gentle, whereas, since the populists were the only group that understood the necessity of going to the people, they should merit more severe treatment. But, if one takes into account the fact that the populist leaders were the only ones (outside of the socialists, anarchists, and anarchosyndicalists of another epoch) who made sacrifices, fought at the risk of their lives, and demonstrated the sincerity of their convictions, and if one remembers the enormous obstacles they encountered and the indifference of those who ought to have understood and supported them—the people of the United States and even the diplomats in Washington—it will be seen that this apparent gentleness is only justice.

5

The Nationalism of the Emperor's
Clothes

The Law and the Staff of Law

At this point, the reader may be thinking, "This author is obsessed by *idées fixes*. He sees oligarchies everywhere; to him, everyone is either an ally or a servant of an oligarchy. The oligarchies are to blame for everything."

Exactly: Like many another before me, I am trying to cure
myself of my obsession, not by closing my eyes, not by searching
scapegoats, but by talking about its cause. For oligarchies *do*
exist in Latin America. The truth is that, at this very time, when
even some American diplomats acknowledge the existence of the
oligarchies, when experts refer to the oligarchies in cleverly
veiled words, the oligarchies themselves have found a means of
making people forget their existence. That means is nationalism.
The oligarchies, the basic cause of the Latin American countries'
failure to arrive at nationhood, are now putting themselves forward as ultranationalist. They behave like one of those fat, stri-
dent sopranos with pendulous bosoms and triple chins who come
on stage wrapped in the national flag and launch into the na-

tional anthem to ward off jeers that would otherwise greet their offkey renditions.

It is high time for someone with an obsession like mine to be naïve enough to forget his personal ambitions and shout that the emperor is going through the streets without any clothes, perhaps because he has sent his last suit to the Swiss banks.

The oligarchies have created certain political and social actualities that must always be kept in mind by those who desire to change the situation for the better. Only rarely do the members of an oligarchy concern themselves with the masses or desire to serve them. The founders of APRA belonged to that honorable band of turncoats, but, in the several decades since, it would be hard to find any new cases. But where now is the socialist, populist, or merely "leftist" Latin American leader who has emerged from an oligarchy? Those we know of came from the middle class; a few, from the working class; almost none came from farm labor; many, from the professional or intellectual ranks; but, from an oligarchy, none. This is a fact of prime importance. In Latin America, the oligarchs are *all* partisans of their oligarchy. As a social class, they are probably the most class-conscious group in the hemisphere.

No authentic political life can exist if the masses play no part in politics, and the best-organized parties have only a few thousand members and a few hundred militants. To be sure, there are "small political retinues marked with all the signs of senility —sullen introversion, fondness for intrigue, the tendency to become bureaucratic, and reactionism—but never any capacity for expansion or projection."[1]

Latin American governments are formed out of those political retinues which are given oxygen by the clubs—the Union Club, the National Club—the seat of oligarchy, where gentlemen bore one another with their talk when they are not playing roulette at Monte Carlo or drinking at the Waldorf-Astoria. Honest Latin American writers have described these governments well:

For decades, the government has been able to be judge and gendarme. What a judge! What a gendarme! There is no larcenous act or outrage that the judge has left unattempted. The army is a praetorian guard that holds him up or topples him, depending on circumstances.

When he topples, a few of the big shots are exiled or killed, but most of them go on to fill the ranks of the new administration, which is thus kept in readiness for the next coup. This simple mechanism explains the frequency of the changes in the presidency.[2]

Is it any wonder that, with such political customs, only slightly modernized by television, electoral campaigns, etc., the oligarchs despise the people? An anecdote will illustrate their scorn. The Argentine General Lucio V. Mansilla (1831–1913) traveled among the Ranquel Indians, about whom he wrote a famous book. He was a friend of the political leader Bartolomé Mitre, and once, on a visit, he found his friend writing.

"What are you doing?" he inquired.

"I'm translating Dante," was the reply.

"Bravo!" said the General. "We've got to screw those gringos!"*

The General was "nationalist" enough to hate the Italians and other foreigners who were then settling in Argentina in great numbers; as for the Indians, he wrote in his book, "My studies of the Indian's intelligence have demonstrated that they have a better understanding of the staff of the law than of the law. Symbols impress the imagination of the masses more deeply than allegories do. Consequently, in every part of the world where there is a constitution and a congress, the man most feared is the president."[3]

Today, the staff of the law is not enough. The president has permitted himself to be deposed too many times at no risk to himself; sometimes, he has even organized the military coup that ousted him. Too often, he has appeared as an accomplice of the very people he pretended to oppose, and he has actually become the butt of their ribald and obscene jokes. The people no longer respect him, no matter how many special ambassadors, famous personages, or guests invited from the ends of the earth he has around him as he takes office. (The practice of putting on a show of legitimacy by gathering together celebrities—inherited, doubtless, from the elaborate and pompous coronations of the past—lives on in Latin America.) The people do not respect him, but they will flatter him if they want something from him; they will detest him when they can get nothing from him. They despise

* In Argentina, *gringo* refers to any *foreigner*.

him, for they know that he will quit the executive mansion after mouthing a couple of bombastic phrases or staging a parody of a hunger strike, but he will never draw his pistol when he hears the jingle of spurs. The people have learned to see the government and the president as enemies from whom occasionally they may be able to wring some little advantages but in whom they can never believe. The staff of the law is no longer respected, because it has too often come down on the shoulders of the people only, never on those of the rich, the uniformed, the *distingués*.

A few examples will serve to show why the oligarchic Latin American states have reached the critical stage in which they feel obliged to demonstrate that they are as nationalistic as the most vociferous "anti-imperialists."

The Bolivian "Turn of the Screw"

Many years ago, Bolivia had little Anglo-Saxon capital. The owners of the tin mines were Bolivian. (There was also some Chilean capital.) On the average, the miners, victims of tuberculosis or pneumoconiosis, seldom lived beyond the age of twenty-seven. In 1923, miners in the Uncía workings, owned by Simón Patiño (1862–1947), demanded an increase in pay. The president of Bolivia, Juan Bautista Saavedra (1870–1939), promptly ordered a massacre of the workers. Yet Saavedra was an able politician who decreed the first laws compensating workers for accidents on the job and for job-connected illnesses.

For several decades, the country's political life revolved around the question of how to evade compliance with these social laws, which, unenforced, brought little improvement in the living conditions of the miners but, nevertheless, set them apart from the peasants. (The latter, subjected to such demeaning practices as the *pongaje*,* merely existed under subhuman conditions.) Finally, the political activities of the oligarchy came to life. The country entered into a war with Paraguay over the oil-bearing border regions of the Chaco. The Bolivian Army, although

---

* A personal service the peasants were obliged to perform. Owners of rural property would give them small parcels of land to cultivate for themselves; the peasants were expected to subsist on the yield from these plots. In exchange, they had to work a certain number of days without pay on the owners' land.

trained and commanded by German military experts, was decisively defeated.

The majority of Bolivia's population is Indian; hence, the army was composed almost entirely of Indians. "But what were the Indians in Bolivian society? They were serfs. What did the Indians own that was worth defending in a war? What was their country to them? Their country was a stepmother; it had never given them anything; it had never bothered about them. It demanded duties of them; it demanded the maximum that a human being can give—his life."[4]

The rout in battle exasperated some of the young military men, who behaved in a fashion we now might call Nasser-like. Colonel Germán Busch (1904–39) seized power but finally killed himself when he saw the futility of his efforts. Then, Colonel Gualberto Villarroel (1910–46) was installed in the National Palace, and he sought to achieve reform under the slogan "I am not an enemy of the rich, but I am a greater friend of the poor." He forced the mining companies to build 5,000 dwellings for their workers and convoked a peasant congress to give the Indian delegates a chance to explain their needs. He decreed the abolition of the *pongaje,* and, in Villarroel's time, the owners were required by decree to pay a wage for peasants' labor.

In 1946, the political machinery of the oligarchy, the "screw," turned again and ousted Villarroel; a mob hanged him from a lamppost in the center of La Paz. A succession of oligarchic governments followed, supported by the Communist-controlled PIR (Revolutionary Party of the Left), and, when the MNR won the elections, the then president, Mamerto Urriolagoitia, fell before a coup led by General Hugo Ballivián and engineered by the President himself. In 1952, the MNR moved out into the open; the miners fought, the army was disbanded, and the MNR came into power, nationalized the mines, started a program of agrarian reform, and governed the country for twelve years. The administration made mistakes and was guilty of excesses; there was corruption and dissension; but, in spite of everything, the agrarian reform converted the Indian into a peasant and, by nationalizing the mines, made the miners full citizens. The country was on its way to becoming a nation.

Then, in November, 1964, a military coup under the leadership of General René Barrientos overthrew the government of Paz Estenssoro at the very moment when, for the first time in history, Bolivia had managed for two successive years to achieve a 6 percent economic-growth rate, and also for two years had not had to import foodstuffs, thanks in great part to the agrarian reform and the removal of 250,000 peasants from the highlands to the fertile lands in the east. Central Bank reserves had risen by that time to $20 million, an amount that had not been achieved since 1952. Thus, for the first time, the country had something worth seizing.

Allied with the military, urging it on and advising it, was an odd mixture of elements. The miners, led by Juan Lechín, opposed any decrease in the number of workers in the nationalized mines or any reduction of their privileges, even for the purpose of balancing the country's economy or making possible a continuance of agrarian reform. They had been the shock troops of 1952, but now they were privileged veterans of the 1952 revolution and determined to keep their advantages. Members of the middle class, who had profited from the revolution and held almost all the leading positions in the country, had no desire to take any risk in defense of a revolutionary government, for they knew that in no political situation would it be possible to do without them. The Falangists (the party of the extreme right, which had assimilated all the groups vanquished in the revolution) were longing to get even and to halt agrarian reform. The Communists too entered the fray. One of the first proposals of the military was to take the vote away from the illiterate, which meant disfranchising most of the peasantry who were loyal to the MNR.

In 1952, Barrientos had been a lieutenant in the army and a member of the MNR. He had risen rapidly and, by 1964, was vice-president under Paz Estenssoro, a position he had been given in order to hamstring Lechín, who wanted the presidency. His coup was delivered to "save the revolution." But, soon afterward, the forces of the right were in control, and after some days of fighting, the miners had to accept conditions more stringent than those proposed by the MNR before the coup. The men with presidential ambitions who forgot their country's best interests as they pursued their own ends were completely thwarted. The screw was turning again, not in the service of the mining oligarchy but in the service of a new oligarchy of professional men, businessmen, and army officers—the middle class that had emerged from the revolution. The peasants were the losers. Bolivia's progress toward nationhood was sidetracked for who knows how long. The 1966 election of Barrientos to the presidency did nothing to change the situation.

Chilean "Democracy"

If Bolivia was beginning to fight its way out of centuries-old chaos and terrible poverty, its neighbor Chile, the victor in an earlier war against Bolivia and Peru, could boast of a political life that ran more or less smoothly. Chile had had a military government only once in the twentieth century. Chileans were wont to say that the "civilization of the vine" was dominant in their country—in other words, that they were very European because their country was the one spot where the Spaniards permitted the cultivation of grapevines and because the indigenous portion of the population was small and the descendants of Irish, German, and Basque immigrants were numerous. All well and good, but, in this Chile that fancied itself so different, copper miners and workers in the nitrate fields had already organized into unions at the end of the nineteenth century. Although deeply divided, the labor movement, in which socialists and anarchosyndicalists took part, exercised strong pressure. Before the laborites succeeded in organizing the farm workers, the oligarchy gave in.

In 1920, the labor vote gave victory to a liberal presidential candidate, Arturo Alessandri (1868–1950). The conservatives, with a majority in Congress, wanted to prevent his inauguration. Monsignor Crescente Errázuriz (1839–1931), Archbishop of Santiago, persuaded them not to interfere, and Congress ratified Alessandri's election. Alessandri proclaimed a series of labor laws, double-edged in that they authorized unions, permitted strikes, and established pensions and safeguards against exploitation but required that all unions be under government control. Industry-wide collective bargaining was not permitted, and pensions were arranged by crafts, thus helping to create rivalries among the various union groups. There was no attempt at agrarian reform.

In 1938, the Communists succeeded in forming a popular front, which elected the Radical candidate Pedro Aguirre Cerda (1879–1941)—whom the people called *Don Tinto* (Mr. Red Wine) because he owned extensive vineyards—by only 4,000 votes. The conservatives voted for him in Congress, although everyone expected them to oppose him. Naturally, no effort was made to achieve agrarian reform. In 1946, another popular-front candidate, the Radical Gabriel González Videla (1898–   ), won office. Two of his cabinet members were Communists—one was minister of land and settlement. More legislation favorable to labor and the middle class was passed, but no one even mentioned agrarian reform.

The bourgeoisie, which might have pushed the country toward progress, was a timid social group, not opposed to the oligarchy but submissive to it. Economic development was the result more of chance than of will, and, while it might have served to diversify foreign trade, nothing was done along those lines, so Chile today still depends on the export of minerals, which is on the downgrade. The Depression in the 1930's caused an abrupt drop in Chile's import capabilities; exchange controls were introduced, which gave domestic manufactures *de facto* protection; this stimulated an industrial growth of 300 per cent in the past thirty years, compared with only 70 per cent for agriculture and 144 per cent for services. (Mining fell 12 per cent.) These changes did little, however, to alter Chile's dependence on the export of minerals for about three-quarters of its total dollar income. One of the most serious obstacles to industrialization was the tightness of the domestic market, which confined industry to an uneconomic scale of production. Agrarian reform might have expanded the market, but no one made a serious effort to attempt it. Stock companies have not achieved the needed growth and so have been unable to attain their objectives. Investment trusts are virtually non-existent, as are savings-and-loan companies for home building. The nation's industry is overprotected, functions under monopolistic conditions, is inefficient, and turns out low-quality products.[5] For all the oligarchy's cleverness in holding on to its power, it is quite unable to use this power to protect the country's economic stability.

Inflation, a perennial from the demagogic and pro-Peronist administration of Carlos Ibáñez (1877–1960) to that of the conservative Jorge Alessandri (1906–   ), and made bearable only by foreign loans, had forced half of the $600 million Chile receives annually from its export sales to be set aside to pay the interest and amortization on its debt. This debt had climbed to $2.5 billion—the highest debt in all Latin America. In addition, Chile had to spend $120 million a year to import needed foodstuffs.

Jorge Alessandri's government of conservatives, liberals, and radicals passed an agrarian-reform law that was nothing more than a joke; its only purpose was to permit Chile to continue borrowing abroad after the Alliance for Progress demanded changes in the agrarian structure as a condition for granting loans. The government's reforms consisted in letting the oligarchy keep its productive lands and give its uncultivated land to a few peasants. In the cities, a million people live in hovels; 3 million rental tenants earn wages amounting to 30–80¢ a day. Of every 1,000 children born, 127 die before they are a year old, one of the highest infant-mortality rates in the world.[6] When the Christian Democrat Eduardo Frei was elected president in 1964 on a promise to inaugurate a "revolution in freedom," two-thirds of the arable land in the country was in the hands of 2,800 landowners. The oligarchic members of Congress succeeded in delaying approval of a real but moderate agrarian-reform law until 1966. And this in a country that considers itself a model of democracy, with an oligarchy that prides itself on being white, "European," refined, and cultured. Money from Chile paid for the ballet of the Marquis de Cuevas, but the troupe never performed in Chile.

Oligarchy and Bourgeoisie in Peru and Argentina

No ballet financed by Peruvian money ever appeared in Europe, but Peruvian landowners were assiduous clients of the French casinos. The coastal oligarchs developed, modernized, and mechanized their plantations, invested in banking (their private preserve today), and even agreed, in 1965, after having brought about the election of Fernando Belaúnde Terry (1912–) (with the help of the army and the Communists and Castroists), to the sacrifices imposed by a moderate land-reform law on condition that the sacrifices were made by the ruder and more implacable mountain oligarchs. The bourgeoisie is still timid, but it may prove more capable of evolution than the oligarchy.

Any bourgeoisie that can be characterized as aggressive, venturesome, and chock full of initiative does not exist. People prefer the safe and immediate: savings, investment in real estate, and mortgage bonds. On the other hand, agriculture based on sugar and cotton, the two great export products, is rising to its zenith on the coast of Peru. Investment in mining and banks is starting, too. And [so is] insurance. . . . The middle class, almost nonexistent shortly before then [1940], began to make itself felt. . . . Now, a sector of the bourgeoisie is undertaking important enterprises, being audacious, aware of the risks it runs; its members are ready to seek solutions never tried before.[7]

But that same bourgeoisie bears the stigma of its association with the oligarchy; hence, there is no reason to wonder that social cynicism reaches the lofty height exemplified in this news item of 1965:

Only authentic beggars will be able to solicit alms on the public streets, according to a mandate of the Municipality of Lima. Others will be arrested and tried. . . . The municipal government is taking a census of beggars for the purpose of identifying them, and it will issue them a card if they have no available resources or are not in a condition to work. They may be recognized by the cards they will wear on their chests.[8]

There is a bourgeoisie of the same sort in Argentina. Its influence has been diluted by the absurd political situation, resulting from the stubbornness of an oligarchy that preferred to break with civil tradition, enthrone the military, and end up with Perón rather than yield its privileges. An example of how the oligarchy has colored the thinking of the bourgeoisie is the assertion, so often repeated by Argentinians, that "there is no agrarian problem" in their country. Of course there is,[9] but almost everyone seems to have agreed to conceal the fact. Former President Arturo Frondizi once wrote:

The crisis we are going through is the fruit of our predecessors' lack of foresight. In the golden days of our export trade [at the beginning of the century], we did not know how to program the investment of the profits yielded by export. We used them to finance the importation of consumer goods, many of them luxury items, or we simply spent them to support a high standard of living for a minority, instead of channeling them into the construction of a basic national industry that, in a half-century of prosperity, would have armed us to resist the later deterioration of the balance of trade. In a more recent period, steps were taken to distribute income socially, a demand doubtless urgent and just, but, again, there was a failure to understand the need to channel a part of that income into productive investments, which would have made possible the laying of a permanent and immutable foundation for social justice.[10]

If the former President recognized the oligarchy's lack of capacity for administration, he took care not to suggest that agrarian reform was essential if a better distribution of income were to be attained. Consider this survey of seventy-eight families living in the Chaco region, not far from the provincial capital:

Total number of persons in the surveyed group 507
Total number of children 351
Average number of children per family 4.5
Total value of foodstuffs found in the 78 family dwellings $25.80
Value per family $0.33
Value available to each child $0.07
Value available to each person $0.05
Land owned by the 78 families (in acres) 1,097*
Average extent of land owned per family (in acres) 14.06
Total income of the 78 families in the 3 months prior to survey $240.00
Average monthly income for the group $80.34
Average daily income for the group $2.64
Average daily per-capita income . . . . $0.005[11]

Of course, the Argentine oligarchy is not to blame for this— not so far as the press and politicians of the country are concerned. Meat constitutes almost half of the country's exports; most of it is sold to Great Britain, which thus has been in a position to set prices, which have been falling ($415 per ton in 1962; $378, in 1963 . . .). One might expect the outbreak of a fierce campaign against Great Britain. But no. The English—

* The parcels ranged from 2.5 to 37 acres.

thanks to the octopus-like way their influence has spread in the
Plata region since the last century—have managed to deflect to the
United States the anger of the Argentinians. So the oligarchy began a press campaign against the United States; *La Nación* (Buenos
Aires) has accused it of starting a "trade war." "The groups most
representative of . . . livestock capital have been the ones demanding a strong policy to put the brakes on the 'economic
war,' just as it was the multimillionaire agrarian interests who
sponsored trade with the Communist countries."[12]

Central American Cockfighting; South American Coffee

Some of the Central American oligarchs—who are perhaps,
among the most ferocious, unlettered, brutal, and corrupt of their
breed—have been Maecenases, of cockfighting at least: "Fighting
cocks of the former president of Nicaragua, Luis Somoza, will
meet the cocks of Mexico and El Salvador in bouts with short
knife spurs, for the benefit of the National Neurological Institute
of Guatemala."[13] In this same Guatemala, which has a fiscal
system so rudimentary that the minimal taxes on coffee plantations are not sufficient to support the Neurological Institute, other
phenomena have been equally significant. Take this revelation
from the Office of Catholic Information for Latin America:

> The expulsion of the [Spanish] priest Father Luis Gurriarán was re-
> lated to his pioneer work in the cooperative movement among the
> poverty-stricken Indian population of El Quiché Province and to his
> personal differences with the provincial governor, Colonel Rubén
> González Rivera. . . . It has been learned that business interests put
> pressure on the governor to expel the priest because they considered
> plans drawn for the establishment of a cooperative store in Quiche a
> threat to their own financial interests. . . .
>   The Bishop of Sololá has announced that a new priest will be named
> to the parish of Quiché. But the people living there, who had abound-
> ing admiration and affection for Father Gurriarán, are not satisfied.
> They have asked for a reconsideration of the priest's expulsion and for
> Colonel González Rivera's resignation. This constant agitation has led
> to the arrest of eight of Father Gurriarán's close collaborators in the
> cooperative movement. . . . The arrests were the reason for an Indian
> delegation's trip to the capital, where it presented vigorous protests to
> several government officials and members of the National Constituent
> Assembly.[14]

To be sure, Guatemala is a backward country that has nearly always been ruled by dictators. Things like this do not happen in more educated countries with a long tradition of representative democracy—Columbia, for example—but other things do.

In the early 1960's, Colombia had been expected to be a showcase for the Alliance for Progress; experts and diplomats had become impressed by the fact that liberals and conservatives had agreed to take turns in controlling the government after years of muted civil war. But it became clear that this relative political stability did not mean economic progress—much less, economic democratization. The Colombian oligarchy makes its money from coffee (Colombian coffee is among the best in the world), but it was more and more evident that in a few years coffee exports would not keep the country's precarious economy afloat. Instead of diversifying production, though, Colombian administrations fought to keep up the price of coffee by means of international agreements and closed their eyes to the inevitable future. A 1962 development plan, within the framework of the Alliance for Progress, offered a scheme for increasing coffee production as the basis for economic progress, even though there is no possibility of the demand increasing commensurately or of prices being maintained. An agrarian-reform law passed in 1963 is a farce, calling for little more than the distribution of uncultivated lands, and it has been applied with an eyedropper. Under these circumstances, it is logical to expect a withholding of foreign investment, and, in fact, in the three years between 1961 and 1964, new foreign investment amounted to only $13 million.

The United States, in those years, granted aid totaling almost a quarter of the combined value of Colombian exports. In 1964, Colombia received $160 million in American aid. The importance of this sum may be seen when one compares it to the $525 million Colombia obtains annually from its exports. Colombia has received another, indirect annual subsidy of $80 million to maintain coffee prices. But instead of being applied to promote industry, diversify production, and implement measures for social progress, these sums have been sent abroad as capital belonging to the oligarchy, although no figures exist to prove this.[15] In the first half of 1965, American aid fell to about $30 million because it was evident that the aid was only helping a minority, of which the Colombian secretary of the treasury, Diego Calle Restrepo, said mildly, "Some people have been taking their capital out of the country."

Optimists declare that Colombia's economy is stagnant. Pessimists say that it is moving forward for the oligarchy and backward for the people. But in any case, the value of the Colombian peso is declining. What has the government done to protect it? Nothing less than this:

The Colombian Government today [1965] began to take steps to control the tendency of the free dollar to rise on the open market, as shown by its listing on the exchange at the unprecedented figure of 15.10 Colombian pesos. The Secretary of the Treasury, Diego Calle Restrepo, announced that the government had decreased the payment the Colombian coffee planters must make to the Bank of the Republic on the basis of an estimate of their volume of export to international markets. The coffee exporters are the leading purchasers of dollars on the open market. At the close of operations, the dollar was quoted at the rate of 14.90 pesos.[16]

Some explanation is needed to make clear the marvel of this trick. When planters export coffee, they must enter on their books a certain percentage of the value of their dollar sales abroad; this is known as the *reintegro en dólares,* that is, reimbursement in dollars. The coffee planters buy their dollars on the local market. Very well; it occurred to a cabinet minister (that is, to a member of one of the twenty or thirty families who have supplied most of Colombia's presidents, cabinet officers, and generals over the past century and a half) that the best way to cut down the demand for dollars, and thereby lower the price of the dollar on the Colombian market, would be to arrange matters so that the coffee planters would pay back in dollars a smaller amount than the actual required value. In other words, the planters would end up with more dollars and the country with fewer. What a dazzling stroke of intelligence! Particularly since Secretary Calle Restrepo had been complaining about the export of capital.

Let us not think that the powers that be are racking their brains to find new and original arguments. For decades, it has been said that industry would be ruined if the working day were shortened, yet this proved not to be so. Similarly, it has often been repeated that increased wages would lead to greater poverty, but that did not happen either. Now an equally tired old war-horse is being trotted out. At a meeting of ministers of labor held in Colombia in connection with the Alliance for Progress in 1963, the Colombian minister of labor, a great landowner of Antioquía named Jaramillo Restrepo (another Restrepo!) asked, "How can we propose higher wages while the price of coffee is so low?" He had to be shown the figures that reveal that when the price of coffee was high, wages were *still* low. But these statistics were not entered in the minutes.

Coffee is important not only to Colombia. It is equally so to Brazil, and for the same reason—the inertia of the oligarchy, the stubborn refusal to diversify production lest it demand more capital, gray matter, and action. Nevertheless, while Colombia's economy is stagnating, Brazil's is "moving ahead." By this I mean that there are more factories, more industrial production, more skyscrapers in Rio and São Paulo, more paved streets in the main sections of the large cities, and more millions in the bank accounts of Brazilians living abroad. But the people's standard of living is falling, there as elsewhere in Latin America—not so much in statistical terms as in terms of what is wanted and what can be bought.

A great deal has been written about Brazil. I suspect that it is one of those countries that most easily deceive the visitor. (Stefan Zweig wrote a book in which he marveled at Brazil's racial tolerance. Now while it is true that no one is in danger of being lynched because he is a Negro or a mulatto, there is not a single dark-skinned man in the diplomatic corps or in a high administrative position; conversely, no white people sweep the streets or live in *favelas*.) An American sociologist has written of Brazil, "South American nations like Argentina, Uruguay, and perhaps Chile may imitate Europe; Brazil has to find her own formulas by which to combine modern civilization with a tropical environment. This is not an easy task, but the country lends itself to ingenuity."[17] Brazilian ingenuity, however, is most frequently manifested in demagoguery masking the oligarchy's interests.

Actually, an urban middle class, sprung from the industrialization of certain limited areas, has grown more rapidly in Brazil than in other Latin American countries. That restless and demanding middle class might have been able to go to the people and mobilize them had it not been for the demagogues who turned them from this path and led them along another, falsely labeled "left" (of that, more later). It is of enormous significance that the Latin American chief executive who moved farthest along the road to fascism, Getulio Vargas, was, during his first period as dictator, the same man who later, when he had been elected president after World War II, would set the guidelines of Brazilian demagoguery that Janio Quadros (1917–) and João Goulart (1918–) were to follow with considerably less intelligence and with notably less courage and strength of character.

Many people say that another sign of Brazil's tolerance is that its army does not intervene in politics. Of course, that is not true. The Brazilian armed forces are as militaristic as those in any other Latin American country, but their way of injecting themselves into politics is not via coups (except in 1964) but by settling men in office, demanding copious purchases of playthings of war from them, retiring with the fantastic rank of marshal, and showing a clear police spirit. Gilberto Freyre (1900–), who is far from being a revolutionary but is one of the few who try to see things as they are, describes the situation as follows:

> There was a time when the police of the state of São Paulo were almost as powerful as the Brazilian Army. They had their own French military instructors and other appurtenances of a national army. The same, or almost the same thing, has happened in Rio Grande do Sul and in Minas Gerais. One time I left Minas Gerais with the impression that I had been in a Brazilian Prussia. A vast amount of public funds has been spent on maintaining a police force almost as powerful as the national army, instead of on public works or for the permanent well-being of the people.[18]

The most characteristic program of the Brazilian oligarchy is its coffee policy. It has operated to keep down world coffee production (and sometimes cacao production too) by manipulating the prices set by the international cartels (for the international agreement on coffee is just that). Some of us can recall the fueling of Brazilian locomotives with coffee beans during the depression of 1929–31. The oligarchs use their country's diplomats and nationalist leaders—a Vargas or a Goulart threatening the phantom of Communist control of Brazil—to force foreign consumers to pay a higher price for coffee than they otherwise might. President Kennedy promised that he would try to put through Congress a measure approving American adherence to the international coffee agreement that fixed a price of 32–33¢ per pound in American money. But the Brazilian oligarchs, after frightening the Americans with a bogeyman—they alleged that Goulart was "going over to the Communists" (Goulart, a great landowner and coffee planter; remember!)—and then tossing him out with a great hue and cry from the armed forces, demanded that Brazilian coffee sell for 45¢ and that this price be upheld by subsidies and more or less covert aid from the United States.

They had a still better trick up their sleeves. A World Bank technical mission to the part of New Guinea that was not under the control of "anti-imperialist" Indonesia had issued a statement that the land there was incomparably good for producing coffee and cacao at low cost. At present, the island yields seven sacks of coffee per acre, and there are millions of acres suitable for planting coffee. The figure of seven sacks falls only a bare 16 per cent below the highest coffee productivity in the world (Costa Rica's). What has Brazil done in the face of this threat? Just what it has been doing for many years—it is threatening to break the international agreement and establish an accord of its own with other coffee-producing countries, then to try to force the price up. And this when Brazil has an enormous supply of coffee that cannot find a market. In the end, the losers are the people of the United States and Western Europe, who drink coffee that costs more than it should. The people of Brazil have never benefited by a penny from the high prices.[19]

Diversionary Tactics

The oligarchies, then, have no national consciousness. Their politicians employ the rhetoric of nationalism whenever it is convenient to distract the people from their true interests, but they do nothing to integrate the nation. On the contrary, they leave

80355
SOUTHERN COLORADO STATE COLLEGE LIBRARY

an enormous vacuum in industrial activity and public service. Local capital, whether exported or in flight, will not fill the vacuum, but foreign capital will. Foreigners have undertaken the work of industrializing Latin America. For decades, British and American capital competed in this. (It is common knowledge, though of course there is no documentation to prove it, that, in the Plata region, where British capital predominates, certain newspapers, calling themselves anti-imperialistic but really anti–United States, were financed by British firms in order to hoodwink the public.) The table below shows the various stages of this struggle, which has gone on under the rejoicing eyes of the Latin American oligarchs, the impotent gaze of the middle class, and the indifferent glances of the masses.

Foreign Investment in Latin America
(in millions of dollars)

	1913	1929	1940	1950	1959
Great Britain	4,984	5,891	4,954	4,050	4,010
United States	1,242	5,587	6,110	6,800	8,400

Source: Mario Hernández Sánchez-Barba, *Las tensiones históricas hispanoamericanas en el siglo XX*, p. 77.

Latin American governments were not interested in trying to mitigate the effects of excess foreign capital by balancing it with local capital. They preferred to use their ingenuity to find means of muting the echo of the Mexican Revolution in their countries.

Why had the Mexican Revolution, which reflected the yearnings of all the leftist Latin American groups, no influence in the rest of Latin America? Why have no parties elsewhere proposed a revolution on this model? Why did it remain an isolated phenomenon? Partial explanations for this may lie in the nature of the Mexican Revolution and the psychology of the Mexican people. But I think the most fundamental explanation is that the Mexican Revolution found its cause in conditions very like those in many other Latin American countries; it was nearby; it was imitable—and therefore it represented a threat to the oligarchies. To distract the masses' attention from it, the oligarchies tolerated and even looked with a measure of good will on movements applauding the far-off Russian Revolution, which was much less likely to be imitated. The Mexican Revolution was bloody, violent, and hard-fought. Latin Americans who desired a change did not dare to acknowledge the need in their own countries of such a bitter struggle; instead, they discreetly ignored it.

This timorous attitude is conspicuous among the intellectuals. Latin American writers and professors come from the middle class or the oligarchies. Many cultured oligarchs turn very democratic and, above all, very anti-imperialistic—in writing, and this kind of writing exerts a steady influence, which, in part, accounts for the ineffectuality of populism's attempts to do away with the oligarchies and their byproducts: militarism and foreign capital.

This attitude is synthesized in some verses Rubén Darío (1867–1916) addressed to Theodore Roosevelt:

> You are the United States
> You are the future invader
> Of the naïve America that carries indigenous blood,
> That still prays to Jesus Christ and still speaks in Spanish.

Here are all the commonplaces that José Enrique Rodó (1872–1917) popularized in prose and that still color the image of the United States. Rodó said of the United States, "Its prosperity is as great as its utter inability to fulfill its mediocre concept of human destiny. . . . [The people of the United States] live for the immediate reality of the present, and, therefore, they subordinate all their activity to the selfish ends of a personal and collective well-being."[20] At the time he thus reproached the United States, peasants in his own Uruguay were living miserable lives, and police and armed "nationalist" gangs in neighboring Argentina were shooting down labor leaders who were fighting for a "personal and collective well-being." Strikers in the Chilean nitrate fields were being slaughtered by the hundreds; Indians in Bolivia were living as serfs, as were those in Peru and Ecuador. To show oneself refined, concerned with "spiritual values," and disdainful of "personal and collective well-being" was a way of being anti-imperialistic that perfectly suited the oligarchs. But in fact, the Latin American masses needed (and still need), first of all, most of all, the "personal and collective well-being" that struck Rodó as a sign of selfishness. Apparently, Rodó believed it was humanity's destiny to knuckle under to the oligarchs while a few dozen intellectuals hurled thunderbolts against the "unrefined," "unspiritual" countries that were so selfish as to grant some importance to personal and even collective well-being. None of those anti-imperialistic intellectuals acknowledged that, if "imperialism" influenced Latin America, it was because the oligarchies had never given a thought to investing their own capital for the progress of their countries, and had opened the doors to foreigners.

Reactionary Anti-Yankeeism

The nationalism of these writers is tinged with reaction, with a desire to return to the past. This could satisfy only the interests of the oligarchs, but their readers, dazzled by the harsh words flung at the United States and its "materialism" and by the praise of their own "spirituality," might never be aware of the writers' oligarchic bias. It was as if the exploiters and mockers were less reprehensible than the foreigners simply because they were fellow citizens. To illustrate this point of view, let us take the nationalist Ricardo Rojas (1882–1957), an Argentine writer with a wide and lasting influence, the inventor of a mysterious political ectoplasm called "Argentinism."

Rojas maintained that, even though Argentina won political independence in 1810, she had been turning more and more into a colonial country in her cultural and economic life. The cause was what he called "cosmopolitanism." The enslavement of the Argentine people by foreign capital and foreign ideas was a product of cosmopolitanism, which, he said, led to "the downfall of the old moral nucleus, indifference to political matters, a growing forgetfulness of traditions, corruption of the language, and a lack of national unity." Since this cosmopolitanism originated in Argentina's schools, the "nationalist restoration" must begin in the schools. The national government must control education and create a community of ideas, with the object of restoring the national spirit and rescuing the schools from the "foreign clergy, foreign gold, and foreign books." Spain was a source of cosmopolitanism, but the principal root of it was in the United States (not Britain, whose interests were closely linked to those of the Argentine oligarchy).

Although Rojas believed that democracy was the "fruit of Argentinism," his disciples parted company with him at that point. The poet Leopoldo Lugones (1874–1938), for example, began as a socialist and ended as a Fascist. Manuel Gálvez (1882–   ) adopted some Fascist tenets and even went so far as to demand that Argentina declare war on Brazil, in the hope that Brazil would win and defeat would produce a national catharsis. When the Depression led to the military overthrow of President Hipólito Yrigoyen (1850–1933), Gálvez published a book entitled *Este pueblo necesita* (*This Country Needs*), in which he asked his countrymen to do away with the constitution "copied from the United States" and establish an authoritarian government similar to those of Mussolini and Hitler.[21]

Moving northward, we find the Mexican José Vasconcelos (1882–1959), who, after he became a Catholic and a reactionary, struck out at the United States:

What can anyone expect today, when the United States has become the leading power in the world and we are helpless satellites, morally weakened by the treason of liberalism? [In such a situation,] only a return to the religious community that constituted the strength of Spanish America of old, a return to its Catholicism, supported by U.S. Catholicism, can offer any hope to our luckless people.[22]

Vasconcelos, in his *Historia de México,* depicts his country's nineteenth-century political struggles as reflections of the divisions among American Masonic lodges. Another Catholic thinker, the Nicaraguan Ycaza Tigerino, thought that all Latin American liberalism was inspired by the United States:

The implantation of this liberal anarchistic democracy was not the exclusive work of minorities of hallucinating doctrinaires who fought against the Liberators and their realistic plans of government. These doctrinaires served, in many cases, simply as tools of North American imperialist policy, of an imperialism [as old as the United States], born at the time of that political abortion we call Spanish-American independence, which left twenty peoples—weak in their social structure because their racial integration was not yet complete—at the mercy of the people [of the United States], who, by eliminating all the complications of cross-breeding, were born with the solidarity and unity of an old civilized race and with a ruling caste experienced in the exploitation of other races, a caste of slave-trading Puritans convinced that they were predestined to be rulers and with a utilitarian feeling for money and wealth. Liberal democracy was encouraged by North American imperialism as a debilitating anarchistic element within our nations, to further its ends of territorial annexation and social and economic exploitation.[23]

History was a continuing plot to destroy Catholic and Hispanic tradition: "Propaganda in our countries for ideas and doctrines destructive of our spiritual and political foundations, of our traditional Hispanic essence, has been the basic method of Yankee imperialism in pursuit of its primary aim of economic exploitation." Even an interest in the indigenous peoples is suspect:

The Pan-Americanistic cult of the indigene, which strives to civilize the Indian, to raise his standard of living, seeks above all else to enable him culturally and economically to be a possible consumer of North American industrial products. On the day when thousands of Bolivian, Peruvian, and Mexican Indians become accustomed to drinking Coca-Cola, chewing gum, and using Colgate toothpaste, on the day when they can buy Ford cars and General Electric radios and equip their dwellings with bathtubs, electric refrigerators, nylon curtains, vacuum cleaners, and canned goods, the aspirations of this commercial interest in the Indians will have been fulfilled.[24]

So, in order to maintain tradition in its essential purity and protect society from "Yankee materialism," the Indians must be prevented from having bathtubs, refrigerators, and curtains in their houses, not to mention the even more horrendous imbibing of Coca-Cola instead of healthful and inoffensive beverages like pulque or rum. Since this is precisely what the oligarchs would like, this anti-imperialism, when all is said and done, translates into pro-oligarchism.

The much circulated statement that Latin America is to serve as a bridge between East and West, that the South American mestizo will become a sort of universal man, a member of a "cosmic race" (Vasconcelos' dixit), leads to the same result. So does the business of considering the Latin American as living a kind of protohistory, as Martínez Estrada said of the man of the pampas. (Writers as dissimilar as Count Keyserling and Waldo Frank agree here, possibly because they obtained the informational basis of their interpretation from this type of Latin American intellectual.[25]) A consequence of these ideas is a willingness to leave to the future—a far-off future—any solution to the problems of the present.

Of course, the intellectuals who see things in this way do not serve the oligarchies deliberately; they are merely trying to escape the responsibility to protest against the present or help to change it. Nevertheless, by looking out for their own moral convenience, they are indirectly serving the oligarchies. In fact, their nationalism is a simple diversionary tactic—first, as regards the uneconomic and inhuman in the social structure and, also, with regard to their own mediocrity. "There is a tendency," Mariano Picón Salas pointed out, "to excuse our misdeeds because we are still young, to interpret what seems dark and amorphous as a sign of being [Latin] American. In certain types of Creole utterance, the worn theme of autochthonism is only a crude fetish for the negligent or mentally confused."[26]

The Oligarchy's Anti-Yankeeism

When nothing runs right, when tariffs protecting rachitic local industries make the cost of living high, when the people have to pay when the prices of their country's exports drop on the world market yet get no part of a price increase, how do Latin Americans console themselves? Nationalism of the narrowest and most myopic, aggressive, and bizarre kind is the aspirin for such headaches. At times, racism, particularly in the southern South American countries, goes hand in hand with this nationalism, especially in the form of anti-Semitism, while, in the Andean countries and Central America, it is manifested as contemptuous paternalism toward the Indian masses. Depending on the particular time, that brand of nationalism strikes a note of antilabor patrioteering or of puerile chauvinism. "A *sui generis* antiforeign autochthony is cultivated so intensively that the sight of some pedigreed breeding rams brought from England to improve the flocks evokes the exclamation 'Down with the mangy foreign sheep!' "[27] No doubt, the superiority of "national" sheep was what inspired a book marking Argentina's centenary of independence, entitled, modestly, *Argentina poder mundial* (*Argentina, World Power*).[28] Because of a boundary dispute with Ecuador, the Peruvians have suppressed by postal censorship any printed matter bearing a map of the country not in accordance with the government's stand on the boundary lines. Of course, the grotesquerie mounts when a dictator is involved. Trujillo ordered the "Dominicanization of culture" and made this slogan a tool of his personality cult.[29]

We must not think that the oligarchy waited until the present time to put nationalism to its own use. Back in 1885, an Argentine oligarch, Carlos Pellegrini (1846–1906), stated, "We must strive resolutely for our financial independence," and considered it shameful that his country should have to turn to Europe each time it needed to scrape together funds. Pellegrini believed that financial independence could be won only by establishing a single bank, and he himself organized that bank after the crisis of 1890.[30] At the beginning of this century, when the oil-bearing deposits at Comodoro Rivadavia were discovered, the conservative government decreed that they be exploited exclusively by Argentine companies, but, as the oligarchs did not invest in such enterprises, exploitation was slow and inefficient. It was also a conservative government that established the system of Yacimientos Petrolíferos Fiscales, in 1936, to produce and distribute Argentine oil.[31]

In the course of time, the methods of utilizing the sentiments of nationalism became more refined. To be sure, the old, brutal, spectacular, dirty movements continued—in Argentina, the *Tacuara** movement, the Nationalist Restorationist Guard, led by a priest, the Nationalist New-Day Youth, even the Nazi Brotherhood; in Chile, the National Socialist Party—all of them anti-Semitic and made up of old-style Catholics and (a revealing fact) Castro sympathizers.[32] But those movements are never very effective; they simply provide the shock troops to do the dirty work. Much more subtle is the official government activity, which distracts public attention with protests against Washington or

---

* The name *Tacuara* comes from the word for bamboo rod used on the pampas to beat cattle. It designated a Fascist organization of Catholic, nationalist, anti-American, and pro-Nazi orientation.

with "nationalization"; both have become quite fashionable. The most demagogic as well as the most moderate governments practice them; generally, they nationalize enterprises that are failing, as Perón did with the railroads, or those of little influence, as Brizola did with the telephone companies. Every time a cabinet member in an oligarchic government mentions nationalization, it is a sure thing that something is amiss. An oligarchy is ready to nationalize everything, absolutely everything—except land. And now that the church is beginning to distribute land in some countries, the oligarchies would nationalize the church too, if they could. If nationalization did not exist, the oligarchs would have to invent it, just as they invent boundary disputes.

No one who talks about Latin America says these things. The Latin Americans are silent because those who are able to speak eloquently feel bound to an oligarchy in one way or another—now by complicity, now by their impotence to destroy it. North Americans hold their tongues for fear they will be tagged imperialists. And the few Europeans who write on Latin America, since most of them know little about it, generally do not understand what is happening; they get out of the difficulty by employing the clichés circulated by both the oligarchs and the Communists.

The press offers constant proof of the oligarchies' use of nationalism. For example, the Peruvian government of Belaúnde Terry, oligarchic by nature, which won election with the help of the Communists and Castroists, announced with much éclat in 1965 that "it will not lend any kind of aid to the United States in Vietnam."[33] At the same time, it accused the United States of being responsible for the crisis in Peru's sugar industry. What happened, however, was that, a year earlier, Peru had offered its sugar on the world market, where higher prices prevailed, and had chosen to sell only smaller quantities to the United States, which has a quota system; in 1965, when prices on the world market fell below the American price, the Peruvian Government wanted the United States to buy its sugar, but the American quotas had already been fixed in accordance with the sales made the preceding year. It should be said that the sugar workers and the people in general had not profited from the high prices of

1964, and that the oligarchic government, pursuing its nationalistic campaign (in a matter concerned only with markets), tried to make the people pay for the decline in the sugar producers' profits.[34]

In Brazil, where the military conservatives took the reins when they saw that Goulart's demagoguery, sponsored by the oligarchy, was going too far, they adopted the ruse of nationalizing industry as a proof of their boldness. They proposed to nationalize eleven American public-utility companies—and, at the same time, to grant concessions to other American companies.[35] Eventually, the business grew monotonous.

But, at times, it takes on almost magical qualities, as in cases where the interests of all the local oligarchs coincide, for example, where the prices of raw materials were involved. Reading the speeches delivered by oligarchic cabinet members on such matters, one feels oneself to be in a world of Orwellian doublethink. The ministers are very anti-imperialistic; when necessary, they take the "third force" position between East and West; they are very radical in condemning the differences in the wealth of nations, while they tolerate and even maintain much crueler and more easily remedied differences of wealth within their own countries. All they ask is that the European or American man in the street be made to pay more for Latin American products so that the Latin American oligarchs can continue to take their capital to Switzerland or use it to support their armies' high spirits.

Not once, not a single time, has anyone in power offered to establish a system that would share with the people the profits from these high prices. No one seems to recall that, when the Korean War brought a fabulous rise in the prices of raw materials, there was in *no* Latin American country any improvement in the standard of living either of the people as a whole (which would have been only fair) or even of the workers and peasants directly related to the materials' production. Bolivian miners continued to earn the same wages; so did Chilean miners and Central American cotton pickers and the sugar workers in Cuba and Peru. In Latin America, the people are not informed of a rise in prices. However, the oligarchic governments, with the zealous help of Communists, Castroists, and false leftists, set out to put it into everybody's head that the United States and other industrial countries are to blame when, in peacetime, prices fall in the world market. Of course, this does not stop these same elements from thundering against "war-mongering imperialist policy."

The Wrangle over Foreign Policy

In that spectral world created in Latin America by the joint propaganda of the oligarchies and the bogus left, nationalistic fever reached its highest pitch in September, 1964—at a meeting of the International Bank for Reconstruction and Development, in Tokyo. Something truly memorable happened then. The nineteen Latin American countries opposed the establishment of an Arbitration and Conciliation Center (optional, not obligatory) to mediate disputes between governments and foreign investors from member countries of the Bank.[36] The Latin American oligarchic governments cried to high heaven and rent the garments they wore as vestals of national sovereignty. The very governments that, when their country's feudal structure was threatened, took power through *coups d'état* that made a mockery of constitutionalism, the very governments that have never permitted their people to enjoy real self-rule, the very governments that have "intervened" among their own people by occupying the land with armies and police—these very governments, in Tokyo, brought out and polished up all the magical, fashionable formulas: constitutionality, self-determination, national independence, nonintervention.

These governments knew that that they needed foreign investors, and they tried to attract them. Not infrequently, their cabinet members sit on the boards of companies created with foreign capital. They declare themselves, loudly and often, the partisans of free enterprise and private initiative. Why did they object to an optional board of arbitration that might provide a safeguard to foreign investors? They took the ultranationalistic position for two reasons: (1) because it was in their interest to leave the door open to the possibility of easy nationalization of foreign industrial enterprises, either when this would seem necessary to pacify certain very nationalistic and "revolutionary" groups allied with the oligarchy or when nationalization would serve to distract attention from the basic need to nationalize the latifundia; and (2) because they had nothing to lose by adopting a "nationalist" policy in international affairs (a policy that, in any case, will not prevail), since they could use that policy to buy the neutrality and even complicity of the bourgeoisie and intellectuals who have made a *de facto* alliance with the oligarchy but who seek to ease their consciences by echoing the Communists' slogans.

The latter motive is of strategic importance in Latin America today. Whenever a government—whether it calls itself conservative, liberal, or revolutionary—wants domestic peace at a time of social crisis or tension, it will play the old tricks of issuing "nationalist" statements on foreign policy, of opposing some suggestion by the United States, and thus of ensuring that the "revolutionary" elements accept its conservative domestic policy. Carlos Julio Arosemena (1919–) did this in Ecuador, and Quadros and Goulart did it in Brazil. None of these governments (and many more could be mentioned) did anything to change agrarian policy in their countries, although they made many promises, but, on the other hand, they maintained a demagogic foreign policy (medals for "Ché" Guevara, speeches against the United States, tentative diplomatic overtures to Communist countries, etc.). In this way, they succeeded in making the groups that called themselves leftists (but were so only verbally) forget to press for changes in the land-tenancy structure, which were the basic need, and be content with considering that they had won a victory in foreign affairs. That the peasants cannot eat the votes cast in the United Nations General Assembly or sow their fields with neutralist declarations is of no concern to the false leftists, who are more interested in their own "revolutionary" consciences than in the welfare of their countrymen.

Hence, when journalists or diplomats come out waving their arms, tearing their hair, and shouting about the threat of Communism under Goulart or Arosemena, the effect is grotesque. Communism is not the real danger, for the Communists and the bogus leftists are satisfied with statements by their governments that may annoy the United States; the real threat is that the people's lot will become all the more wretched as their governments, behind the screen of foreign policy, continue to favor the oligarchies.

Naturally, this habit of taking the word for the deed—a habit shared by Latin American pseudoleftists, American commentators, diplomats, and European instant experts—works out in the end in favor of the oligarchies, since it falsifies the data upon which an interpretation of the Latin American actuality might be based. Consequently, much of the writing on Latin America gives the impression of referring not to the real Latin America, where the things I am describing do happen, but to an invented one. As a result, many sincerely nationalist and revolutionary politicians, and a good many diplomats, apply a policy that would be appropriate for the invented Latin America but that is either useless or harmful to the real Latin America.

I have heard in the United States the observation that not a single Latin American president attended President Kennedy's funeral. In three cases—Mexico, Venezuela, and Bolivia—the domestic situation forbade the president to leave the country, but the other heads of state could well have made the gesture. They did not, but their absence was the most revealing homage they could have paid to President Kennedy's Latin America policy. They were not present at Arlington Cemetery because Kennedy's death had delivered them from an enemy of the anachronistic social system they had made it their mission to defend. And, by not going to Arlington, they also catered to the sentiments of the anti-American "leftist" elements. Similarly, they paid President Kennedy further homage a year later:

President Guillermo León Valencia, of Colombia, canceled his proposal to bring together the heads of the Latin American governments in Washington on November 22, the first anniversary of the assassination of John F. Kennedy. Apparently the decision was made because most of the executives had excused themselves from taking part in the ceremony, on the grounds that administrative matters made it impossible for them to leave their respective countries on that specific date.[37]

What Nationalism Protects

The use made of nationalism and of the anti-Americanism that is its usual expression in present-day Latin America has brought important consequences to the Latin American people. The oligarchies use nationalism and anti-Americanism for their own protection, and, at the very least, such self-protection also requires the maintenance or even aggravation of the social conditions I have described. This is no mere phrasemaking. What follows is fact:

Statistics on Latin America's land-tenancy structure are out of date and frequently not worthy of credence. Nevertheless, it is safe to say that, in Latin America, only 5 per cent of the arable land surface is under cultivation, as opposed to the world figure of 7 per cent and the United States figure of 18 per cent. In Peru, 76 per cent of the cultivated land is owned by 1.6 per cent of the people; in Colombia, 1 per cent of the people own a quarter of the cultivable land; in Argentina, where current myth denies the need for agrarian reform, 5.1 per cent of the people own 74.5 per cent of the land; in Bolivia, before the revolution of 1952, 91.1 per cent of the land was the property of 6.3 per cent of the inhabitants; in Chile, 2.2 per cent of the landholders own 73.2 per cent of the land; in Brazil, 50.9 per cent of the land belongs to 1.6 per cent of the people (yet Brazil has had no fewer than 200 agrarian-reform plans, 58 of them within the past twelve years, a good way of making sure none of them would be approved).[38] Although in Chile and Colombia, for example, there have been plans for land reform, they have made such a cruel mockery of the aspirations of the landless peasants that Eduardo Frei's first step upon assuming office in Chile was to present an agrarian-reform plan "totally opposite to the earlier one passed during the administration of Jorge Alessandri."[39] Frei's plan was approved by Congress in 1966.

Some useful statistics, compiled with great difficulty,[40] sum up the material consequences of the oligarchs' stubborn hold, often disguised or excused by the type of nationalism they sponsor:

Farm Distribution in Latin America, 1950

Size of Property (in acres)	No. of Owners as Percentage of Total Owners of Farm Properties	Percentage of Arable Land
0–60	72.6	3.7
60–250	18.0	8.4
250–2,500	7.9	23.0
More than 2,500	1.5	64.9
Total	100.0	100.0

Nothing good can be expected from a structure like this. However numerous the efforts toward industrialization may be, the results can benefit only a minuscule proportion of the people, and, furthermore, they strengthen the oligarchies, for those who profit feel an unacknowledged solidarity with the oligarchs and, like the *demi-vierge* of the last century, will hide their blushes behind the fans of nationalism. But facts speak louder than words. The Latin American agrarian structure is uneconomic, as the table below reveals:

Comparison of Farm Acreage and Production Between
1948–52 and 1957–59
(1948–52 = 100)

	Cultivated Land Surface	Average Yield	Annual Rate of Change Surface	Yield
Latin America	124	107	2.7	0.8
Europe	103	124	0.4	2.7
U.S. and Canada	93	125	−0.7	2.8
World Total	114	121	1.7	2.4

Discontented and often hungry peasants, anachronistic work methods, deficient technical supervision, absenteeism—all result in diminution of Latin America's productivity. That is happening on a continent where the population in almost every country is growing more rapidly than agricultural production. A simple comparison of the following data should shame the Latin American latifundists, if they are still capable of blushing.

Rate of Increase in Yield of Six Selected Products*
(in bushels per acre)

Product	Latin America		U.S. and Canada		World	
	1948–52	*1963–64*	*1948–52*	*1963–64*	*1948–52*	*1963–64*
Wheat	10.5	14.1	11.6	17.2	10.1	12.1
Rice	17.0	18.5	25.6	44.2	16.0	20.5
Corn	10.5	11.1	24.9	42.3	15.8	21.6
Barley	10.6	12.1	14.5	19.0	11.4	14.4
Potatoes	52.6	61.2	156.1	218.5	106.9	112.5
Cotton	2.1	3.0	3.2	5.8	2.4	3.4

* Acreage planted with these six products represents 75 per cent of the total cultivated land surface in Latin America.

Source: Montague Yudelman, *The Inter-American Development Bank and Agricultural Development in Latin America,* p. 46.

How is this possible? Simply as a result of the workings of nationalism and the habit of accepting the *status quo?* No. Frei described well the political process that permits the continued existence of this situation:

The scattered peasant masses lack organization, power, and, at times, an understanding of their true interests. As a result, only the great landholders appear before the people as representatives of agriculture, and, when they solicit better conditions for agriculture, the urban masses—and sometimes the rural masses themselves—think this will favor not agriculture itself and those who work in it but a group of privileged people.[41]

The dominance of uneconomic latifundism is reflected in the thinking of those who ought to be the most powerful force for change. In the words of a Colombian sociologist, this brings, among other consequences,

Lack of patriotism in the moneyed classes, and a consequent flight of Latin American capital into Swiss and United States banks

Lack of flexibility in cooperating, especially in commercial enterprises of the stock-company type, to share risks among a greater number of persons

A propensity on the part of all social classes to practice "conspicuous consumption," instead of saving and investing

Tying up of middle-class and upper-class savings in the acquisition of real estate, fundamentally an unproductive activity

Economic insecurity because of dependence on a single export product, in turn reinforcing the desire to invest in real estate

Tax structures that penalize initiative in productive fields and, again, reinforce the desire to invest in land and livestock

Class stratification that has taught the middle class to scorn manual labor, to emulate the upper class in conspicuous consumption, and to pursue security by seeking employment in public or private bureaucracies that do not require initiative, activity, risk, or the use of the hands[42]

Apathy and Melancholy

Naturally, the adverse effects of oligarchism are not confined to the economy. They are reflected also in culture and politics. Roberto Fabregat Cúneo, who believes that the Brazilian *bandeirantes* were the last pioneering adventurers on the South American continent, perceives this clearly:

In the vast interior, on the great river tributaries, even on the shores of the ocean, conformity, routine, and apathy have prevailed against the expeditionary and transcendental spirit. The migratory impulse, the zeal for interchange, the desire to confront the unknown have become exceptional. . . . Gravity, melancholy, and misery are the salient popular moods. . . . One might say that, on our entire continent, there is not a single expression of exuberant joy, of overflowing vitality, of satisfaction with oneself. . . . Also, and this is worth underlining, the call to the future, the impulse to dare, and the desire to conquer far-off places are lacking. And this in a natural setting that is almost always an invitation to travel, to adventure, and to conquest.[43]

There are great differences between the European and the Latin American, but, since these differences also exist between the Creole and the European, they cannot be accounted for by what is commonly called, with unconscious racial bias, "Indian blood." "European festivals are almost always a fulfillment, a reaching out to communicative elements, and a collective euphoria achieved by the use of ritual; South American celebrations are more like an escape. [Consider] the different roles popularly assigned to the gifts of Bacchus: The European would say that he drinks to be gay; the Creole, to forget."[44] Even the proverbs of Latin America reflect despair and fatalism derived from an over-all philosophy of pessimism. The Latin American is bitter even in his humorous outbursts.

They say that the typical Latin American never looks ahead,

that he will not save for the future. But why should he, if experience has proved to him that saving is futile and that no future exists for him? The future is only for the oligarchy and its servants and allies.

It is significant that Fabregat Cúneo's work, in which he documents such statements, fell into a void despite, or because of, the truths he so forcefully drove home. How can anyone comment significantly on a descriptive synthesis like the following? "Therefore, South America is, at present, a prodigious admixture of progress and barbarity, of political progressiveness and feudal retrogression, of open democracy and senseless despotism, of superior culture and collective ignorance on the level of the crassest illiteracy. That is why it is a continent of European cities and Asiatic deserts."[45]

The Farce of Politics

The consequence of all these facts is that "the people's feelings have remained quite inchoate, never having achieved the unity that is the condition for attaining the uniformity of culture that is expressed in the idea of nationhood, and also for the normal exercise of freedom."[46] This is true even in the functioning of the simple electoral machinery, even where clean elections take place and in the exceptional countries in which their results are respected. Actually, the general level of Latin American electoral participation is at about 20 per cent of the citizenry; that is, one out of every five inhabitants is registered to vote; the level falls still lower if those who are registered but fail to vote are subtracted. In the 1964 Mexican elections, 21.5 per cent of the population participated. In Brazil in 1967, 17.3 per cent participated. In the United States, average participation in presidential elections is about 55 per cent. In Great Britain, almost 70 per cent of the registered voters vote. Venezuela heads the list of Latin American countries; in the 1963 elections, 39 per cent voted.

There is no universal suffrage in Latin America. The basis for limiting the vote is not the census of taxpayers, as it was in the nineteenth century, but the education census. Today, illiteracy is the dodge by which the people are kept from voting, as poverty was yesterday. Power and representation are apportioned among the 20–25 per cent of the people on the highest economic and cultural level.[47]

But, if there are few voters, there are plenty of candidates. Existing and functioning political parties, although most of them are active only around election time, number no fewer than 193 —nearly 200 parties for about 200 million inhabitants, or a party for every million people. This total is broken down as follows[48]:

Country	Number of Parties
Argentina*	29
Bolivia	6
Brazil	13
Chile	10
Colombia	8
Costa Rica	3
Cuba	1
Dominican Republic	7
Ecuador	11
El Salvador	11
Guatemala	8
Haiti	1
Honduras	4
Mexico	7
Nicaragua	12
Panama	14
Paraguay	5
Peru	19
Puerto Rico	5
Uruguay	8
Venezuela	11
Total	193

* Before the military coup of June, 1966, which banned all parties and seized their property.

Such an array of parties is obviously no sign of democracy. It indicates the opposite: cults of personality, *caudillos,* personal wrangling and envy, a lack of convictions, ideological confusion, Byzantine ideologies, the absence of programs, and a shortage of political personalities strong in character and ideas. Clearly, the people are deprived of a voice just as they are generally deprived of the vote.

Things being as they are, who—outside of the technicians, who forget that the economy reflects the political situation—could wonder at a study showing that, from 1960 to 1963, a period in which undernourished or ill-nourished Latin Americans numbered 100 million, there were no appreciable increases in Latin American crops or livestock:

The volume of production is growing slowly with respect to the preceding year, an increase that was nullified by population growth so that, during the period in question, no improvement was recorded in farm and livestock production per inhabitant as compared to 1958; on the contrary, there was a slight decrease. If the comparison is carried back to the prewar period, the situation becomes even more dramatic, for we note a diminution in the production per inhabitant of nearly 8 per cent. . . .

This grave situation not only has resulted in a lower increase in the income from crops and livestock and a shrinkage in exportable surpluses but has also prevented any appreciable improvement in the low standard of nutrition among the great masses of Latin America. The slight rise in average yield, traceable to the modest technological advance shown in the region, has been one of the salient characteristics of Latin America in the last decade, and the increases achieved in some countries are based, in general, on an increase in the land surface under cultivation.[49]

This is happening in an area of the economy that is under the direct control of the latifundists. But the problem is not limited to agriculture, for, "as for the manufacturing industries, the growth rate slackened in the period of 1960–63. Latin America's industrial production has weakened to such a degree that the rate of increase in the volumes recorded between 1960 and 1963 was the lowest for the entire postwar period."[50]

In the face of such figures, the cabinet members follow their old routines. They hold meetings, solicit reports from experts, have round-table discussions with technical experts, seminars with specialists, press conferences, and television interviews. They meet to recognize the fact that the Latin American land-tenancy system is "unjust and antiquated"—an enlightening and epoch-making evaluation on which the secretaries of agriculture all agree, whether they come from the few countries that have achieved agrarian reform or are part of dictatorships intent on fighting off at sword's point any pressure for change. In an inevitable response to this evidence, the secretaries hasten to demand a rise in the prices of Latin American products for export.[51]

6

Negative Nationalism

Political Concubinage

The oligarchs have had a steadfast ally in their efforts to use
nationalism as a means to pressure Washington for their own
benefit. This ally seeks profit for itself; it aims to make difficulties for the United States, and these include difficulties between
Washington and all sectors of Latin American society. I refer to
the Communist movement.[1]

Communists have been manipulating Latin American nationalism for several decades; one approach they have used has been
what I call the "political concubinage" they have offered the
dictators, which more pedantic commentators have described as
"critical support."

Trotskyists invented the latter phrase in the days when Perón
ruled Argentina, when they supported some of his positions and
criticized others. But the expression "critical support" characterizes, more exactly than it does that attitude, the stand the Communists took even before the time of the Popular Front and,
above all, during the Cold War.[2]

The shifts and turns in Communist policies everywhere have always surprised naïve observers, who cannot fathom how members of the Party manage to accept such abrupt changes of line or why these changes have not weakened the Party itself or hampered its subsequent development. Perhaps this phenomenon can be seen more plainly in Latin America than elsewhere. The Communist parties in Latin America are much smaller than those in the Old World and are more bureaucratized, which contributes, in large measure, to the acceptance of each change in tactics. The fact that the bureaucracy and its basic ideology endure despite all the tactical shifts explains why militant Communists and fellow-travelers have grown accustomed to regarding the Party as a sort of super-Machiavellian organism with the ability to turn its alliances to its own indubitable advantage, and it also explains how, since their faith in the Party's systematic dogma and its ultimate objective does not lessen, they pragmatically, though often blindly, accept each tactic as it comes along. On the other hand, we can see clearly how, because of these tactics, the Latin American Communists, who use various theoretical justifications, have always been adversaries of the democratic and revolutionary movements, and allies—sometimes overt but most often covert— of reactionary dictatorial forces.

Let us look at the historical manifestations of this alliance between the Communists and the reactionaries.

From "Social Fascism" to the Popular Front

Almost all the Communist parties of Latin America emerged as splinter groups from socialist or anarchist parties. Communists also split the labor movement, with the intention of creating their own unions, which they called "unitary" organizations and which, in 1929, formed the Confederación Sindical Latinoamericana (CSLA). But the Communist movement made no great progress. Other parties, particularly those of the populists, attracted the masses, while the Communists had to content themselves with whatever advantage they could gain from the bedazzlement produced among intellectuals and students by the Russian Revolution. Naturally Communists used the catch phrase "social fascism" to brand other parties of the left, including the populists and anarchosyndicalists. In the 1920's and 1930's, APRA was their main target. Haya de la Torre attended the congress in Brussels that created the Anti-Imperialist League in February, 1927, but he came out against both the resolution on Latin America passed by the congress and the formation of such leagues, because, he said, the struggle against imperialism should be carried on not by a party representing a single class but by parties integrating several classes and viewing imperialism as an ambivalent economic phenomenon. He did not believe that Latin Americans should attack imperialism with the tactics the Communists used in industrialized countries. The Aprista delegation was the only one to state formally reservations regarding the final conclusions of the congress, and Haya did not attend the later Anti-Imperialist League congress at Frankfurt, in 1930.[3]

The Soviet Union was rather skeptical about the possibility of a Communist-led revolution in Latin America. S. A. Losovsky, who directed Communist policy in Latin America from Moscow, wrote, in a pamphlet on the Latin American union movement:

Fascism is impossible in backward countries that cannot support the complex economic, political, and social machinery necessary to a Fascist regime. . . . At present, we have a young movement in Latin America, a movement that lumps together hundreds of thousands of workers but is very confused, from the ideological point of view, and very weak, from the organizational point of view. Revolution is not accomplished by manifestos; strikes cannot be called every twenty-four hours; and it is not enough to have a weekly publication or a hundred militants for the struggle against the bourgeoisie. What is needed is to have available an organization sufficiently strong to combat and overthrow the capitalist state. There is too much talk in Latin America about social revolution. All Latin American letters end with *Viva la Révolución Social!* That is all very well; I am not against it. But there are a certain number of comrades who have too primitive a notion of social revolution. They believe that, if the socialist revolution did not arrive yesterday, it will come tomorrow.[4]

During the same period, APRA was subjected to harsh governmental persecution, as were most of the other populist and socialist parties against which the Communists were fighting. No explicit alliance existed between the dictators and the Communists, but they directed their fire at common targets. Naturally, the Communist attacks ceased during the lifetime of the Popular Front, but the populist and socialist movements had had their fingers burned, and only in Chile—and to a lesser degree, under another name, in Brazil—was a transitory alliance formed with the Communists. In order not to alarm their allies of the moment and the Western powers, the Communists tried to restrain the leftist movements. They carried this new tactic to the extreme of virtually opposing the nationalization of Mexican petroleum—an episode almost ignored but worth remembering.

In March, 1937, the National Union of Petroleum Workers in Mexico called a strike. The walkout was on the point of success when the Confederación de Trabajadores de México (CTM), led by Vicente Lombardo Toledano (1894–   ),* intervened to persuade the union to call off the strike. The Communist Party of Mexico proposed, at the time, to increase the production of a small government-owned oil company to offset the effect of the strike and any intervention by the companies affected by the strike "in case of the prolongation of the movement." But it never mentioned nationalization, which it feared would be a revolutionary measure that might shatter the Soviet Union's alliances by affecting the private interests of countries that maintained friendly relations with Moscow. For this reason, the Communists could not publicly espouse any such move. But they did support the Mexican Government's *fait accompli* when the oil companies were nationalized a year later.[5]

World War II and After

During the two years when the Soviet Union and Hitler's Germany were joined in a nonaggression pact, the Latin American Communists followed the Moscow line by denouncing the war as an imperialistic one. At the Thirteenth Congress of the Communist Party in Uruguay, Secretary-General Eugenio Gómez demanded a "united front of all progressive and peace-loving forces to struggle against the imperialist war, for the defense of the Soviet Union, the homeland of socialism." Blas Roca (1909–   ), the Communist Party's secretary-general in Cuba, defended

* The pro-Communist lawyer who had founded the CTM in 1936.

the idea of keeping Cuba out of the war on the grounds of expediency. Indeed, the Communists came up with a formula for "socialist neutrality" for all Latin American countries.[6]

The Communists' position, as is well known, changed as soon as Hitler attacked Russia. This shift was manifested in a stubborn effort to help maintain the *status quo* in Latin America. Many Latin American democrats thought that, because of the war, the moment was ripe for the overthrow of the dictatorships, but the Communists opposed these aspirations.

In 1942, Lombardo Toledano, who had founded the Confederación de Trabajadores de América Latina (CTAL) in 1938, toured Latin America, enjoying the prestige and influence bestowed on him by his position as secretary-general of that organization, which had absorbed most of the labor unions on the continent. On his return from his travels, he issued a public report in which he called Carlos Arroyo del Río (1893–   ), president of Ecuador, his "friend" (three months later, that same president unleashed some very harsh and repressive measures against labor and socialist leaders in Ecuador) and also eulogized other dictators: General Enrique Peñaranda Castillo (1892–   ), of Bolivia, whose administration was marked by the terrible slaughter of the miners of Cataví, and General Anastasio Somoza (1896–1956), of Nicaragua. Of the latter, he said, "General Somoza is an intelligent and faithful man who has done good for his people in his fashion and who is what we might call a paternal dictator to his people."

The Communists' general policy in that period can be defined in terms of the objectives set forth by Lombardo Toledano in his report: "(1) not to struggle for an increase in pay, (2) not to provoke any strike, (3) to declare a *status quo* on questions concerning Central and South America."[7] He expressed this position again at the CTAL congress in Cali, Colombia, in 1944: "We are very far removed from those romantic and sterile attitudes that led us to utter fervent cries against imperialism. . . . During the war against the Nazi-Fascist Axis, the working class must not use the strike as a normal weapon."[8]

In Venezuela, the Communists supported General Isaías Medina Angarita (1897–1953) from 1941 until his overthrow in 1945 (and fought to the last ditch in his defense). Cuba's case is even more revealing. In 1933, when a general strike was called against the dictator, Gerardo Machado (1871–1939), he summoned César Vilar, the leader of the Cuban Communist Party, and offered legal status for the Party and government jobs for its members if Vilar could abort the strike. At once, the Party's Central Committee published a manifesto asking the workers to call off the strike. On May 4, *La Correspondencia Internacional* stated, in justification of this, that the Central Committee had judged that "the armed struggle against Machado would lead directly to imperialist intervention." When Machado fell, the Communists opposed the revolutionary government of Ramón Grau San Martín (1887–   ), overthrown in January, 1934, by Sergeant Fulgencio Batista (1901–   ). The latter soon sought the support of the Communists. In 1937, he permitted the organization of a disguised Communist party, the Unión Revolucionaria, led by Juan Marinello (1898–   ); in 1938, he gave permission for the publication of the Communist newspaper *Hoy,* and, immediately, the tenth plenary meeting of the Central Committee of the Communist Party ruled that "a more positive attitude must be adopted toward Colonel Batista" because he was no longer "the point of convergence for reaction but the defender of democracy." As a consequence of a meeting with Blas Roca and Communist Party Secretary-General Joaquín Ordoqui, Batista permitted the legal organization of the Party. In January, 1939, the Confederación de Trabajadores de Cuba (CTC) was organized, under Communist control, with Lázaro Peña (1908–   ) as its secretary-general. In the 1940 elections, the Communists formed a part of the Social Democratic coalition that supported Batista's candidacy, and they won ten seats in the Chamber of Deputies and more than a hundred posts as municipal councillors. In March, 1943, Batista invited the Communists to take part in his administration—he was the first Latin American chief executive to have Communists in his cabinet. Juan Marinello was appointed a minister. And, in the elections of 1944, the Communists were still a part of the coalition supporting him. But the democrats won, and Grau San Martín was returned to power.[9]

At the end of the war, the Communists began a phase of ministerial collaboration. There were Communist ministers in the governments of France, Norway, Belgium, Italy, and Holland, as well as the countries of Eastern Europe. In Chile, in five months of 1946 and 1947, during the term of President González Videla, who had been elected by a popular front, Carlos Contreras Labarca became minister of communications, Miguel Concha became minister of agriculture, and Víctor Contreras became minister of land; they all served until the president removed them because the other cabinet members refused to continue working with them.[10]

But, in the countries that had freed themselves of dictators—Brazil, Peru, Venezuela, Guatemala, and Cuba—the Communists did not succeed in entering the government. Their wartime collaboration with dictators was too recent. (Let me point out, in passing, that, upon the dissolution of the Communist International, several of the Latin American parties affiliated with it changed their names. In Haiti and Costa Rica, they became the Popular Vanguard; in Cuba and Colombia, they took the name Popular Socialist Party.) Preparing for this stage, Lombardo Toledano had said, in 1944, "This is not socialism's hour . . . for we want nothing but fulfillment, disinvolvement, development, and progress based on the ideas of yesterday, enriched by new modalities and forms for applying them."[11] Consistent with this position was the labor-management pact between the CTM and the Mexican Chamber of Manufacturing Industries, of which Lombardo had this to say: "We propose to respect the vested interests because we are respectful of private property—mark these words—and because we are Partisans of private property at the historical stage through which Mexico is now passing."[12]

But, as soon as the Cold War began, the Communists changed their tactics. Until that moment, support of dictators or virtual alliance with them had been a result of pragmatic adaptation to circumstances, but from them on, it became a systematically employed tactic, used not so much in obedience to orders as because it suited the mentality and interests of the Communists themselves and also satisfied Moscow's demands on them.

Two conditions were needed to make the new tactic effective: local and international circumstances should favor its applica-

tion; and a means should be found to wipe out the memory of
the tactic when a dictator should fall, die, or retire. The first
condition existed almost continuously in the decade 1948–58,
during which a succession of dictatorships took control in Argentina, Venezuela, Peru, and Colombia, while in Nicaragua,
Paraguay, the Dominican Republic, and Haiti, others survived
from previous years. The second condition was fostered by the
Communist parties' splitting into two separate groups, each with
a different mission, both of which maintained relations with
Moscow. This phenomenon, or tactic, existed only in Latin
America. Probably, it began spontaneously and later was used
and repeated deliberately and for specific purposes. In all the
countries, the positions taken by both groups of parties with regard to international affairs were identical, and the only difference between the two groups lay in their choice to support or
oppose the local dictator.[13]

What was gained by this policy? The Communists won tolerance for the organization of their groups, the training of new
militants, and the spreading of a network of influence through
public institutions including universities and schools; this enabled them to propagandize with their Soviet slogans and generally keep in readiness to exert strong pressure if a more or less
democratic regime should be re-established. Often, they took
over the leadership of trade unions whose democratic leaders had
been persecuted or imprisoned by a dictator.

The dictator, for his part, received the benefit of the Communists' experience in organizing the masses, an art of which the
military know nothing at all. He also gained Communist help in
eliminating the antidictatorial elements in the unions. Furthermore, the dictator could pose as an anti-Communist who had out-
lawed the Party, while he really tolerated its activity and furi-
ously persecuted the democrats. This happened in Venezuela
under Pérez Jiménez, in Peru under Odría, in Nicaragua under
Somoza, in the Dominican Republic under Trujillo on two occasions, in Brazil during Vargas' second administration, and in
Cuba under Batista.[14]

What tactics do the Communists follow where democracy has
been restored? In such situations, the use of the inexperienced is

the psychological basis of Communist tactics. In Latin America, this approach not only was used in Chile during the time of the Popular Front;[15] it later had greater success in Guatemala. The experience acquired in Guatemala during the years 1945–54[16] was then applied in Cuba and, doubtless, will be applied again.

The objectives of the tactics based on this approach are (1) to gain control of the masses in order to force non-Communist leaders to ask for the support of the Party, (2) to obtain government subsidies to finance the Communist movement, (3) to create fellow-traveler movements with many ramifications and force the leaders of other parties to sign their manifestos and protests so that these can be presented as non-Communist, (4) to impose on governments the prescribed attitudes toward international affairs, and (5) to set a trap by instigating moves that will provoke the United States to intervene and, thus, provide an invaluable pretext for use in anti-American propaganda.

There are three prerequisites for carrying out such tactics: inadequate political training of non-Communist leaders, the presence of reactionary forces that will play the game for their own immediate ends, and an American foreign policy that will make miscalculations and be constantly obsessed with the "Communist peril." These requirements were met in Guatemala and in Cuba and may be met in other Latin American countries.

But conditions are not always so favorable to the Communists as they were in Guatemala and Cuba. That is precisely why they have chosen to make use of the unwary. For example, in many elections, they have supported the candidates who were least experienced in politics—often military men such as Rear Admiral Wolfgang Larrazábal (1911–   ), in the Venezuelan elections of 1958, and Marshal Henrique Teixeira Lott, in the Brazilian elections of 1960—and, in so doing, have been at the side of the most conservative forces in the country. Elsewhere, they have supported new, and hence inexperienced, parties—the Christian Social Party of Peru, for example, in the elections of 1956. In still other places, they profited from the confusion and disappointment of defeat to ally themselves with the forces conquered by the democratic elements, maneuvering with them while trying to seize control of them, as they did with the Peronists in Argentina. They also have supported Castroists who had split off from democratic movements, as happened with the Movimiento de Izquierda Revolucionaria (MIR) in Venezuela. The tactic was always basically the same: to take advantage of the political inexperience of a party or candidate in order to use, mortgage, and hide behind it or him whenever that seemed advisable.

The Betrayal of the Peasants

The tacit alliances between the Communists and the oligarchs and dictators would have been impossible to establish had the Communists ever taken any serious interest in the land question. But Party dogma, which obliged them to imitate Soviet agrarian policies even though the circumstances of Russian land problems were different, acted, so to speak, to protect the Communists against the temptation to concern themselves effectively with the peasants.

The tactical use of the agrarian problem by Latin American Communists passed through three stages of dogma:

1. Only action by the proletariat can solve the land problem. This held from the Communist Party's earliest days until the Popular Front period.

2. The land problem is secondary and can be alleviated by technical and financial means; there must be no talk of land reform. This occurred during the period of the Popular Front.

3. Land reform is the motive power that will mobilize the masses. This was the situation during the period of Castroism.

Lenin had laid it down at the Second Congress of the Communist International in 1920 that, "The urban and industrial proletariat directed by the Communist Party is the only body capable of freeing the working masses in the rural regions from the yoke of capital. . . . The working masses in the country have no chance of salvation other than to seal an alliance with the proletariat, to lend self-abnegating support to their revolutionary struggle to throw off the yoke of the landowners and the bourgeoisie." (Lenin, it will be remembered, distinguished six agricultural types: the farm workers; the farm semiproletariat; the small, the medium, and the rich peasant farmers; and the owners of large estates.)

This theory that the proletariat must lead the struggle of the peasants created a major problem for the Communists on a continent where the vast majority of the people live in the country and most of the exploited are peasants. Speaking at a Communist trade-union conference in Montevideo in May, 1929, M. Contreras, secretary of the organizing committee, avoided the problem by using the term "farm proletariat" instead of "peasants." This made no sense for most Latin American countries, since the owners of the semifeudal latifundia still pay no wages.

A report on the land question was presented at the same conference by Leopoldo Salas, of Uruguay. He was a bit less hard and fast, pointing out that there are farm workers, poor and rich peasants, and great landowners, which recalls Lenin's distinctions, but he stated that, against the wishes of the peasantry or with the peasantry neutral, "the Latin American industrial proletariat is absolutely incapable of winning a victory for its cause." The peasants, on the other hand, would be unable to better their living conditions and certainly could not win their "emancipation from the feudal yoke" unless they fought alongside the urban proletariat.

The Indian problem, always related to the land problem, was also noted at the conference, in a paper prepared by the Peruvian José Carlos Mariátegui (1895–1930),[17] but the conference did not approve Mariátegui's theses; it tabled the question for future study, with the understanding that, meanwhile, "the utmost effort must be directed toward winning over the great indigenous proletarian and peasant masses, while planning an immediate redress of grievances in each country according to its particular situation." Mariátegui's was the only document presented to the conference that referred to agrarian reform (although, of course, it did not use this expression, which had been anathematized by Moscow).[18]

A month later, in June, 1929, a congress of the Communist parties of Latin America met in Buenos Aires, and a principal subject of debate was the nature of revolution in Latin America.

The delegates agreed to define it as "agrarian and anti-imperialist." As the semifeudal landholding oligarchs had allied themselves with imperialism, it was decided the struggle against the latter must be coordinated with the fight against the system of latifundia. The congress worked out a number of slogans on the agrarian problem: "Land for those who labor, and expropriation without recompense of primitive latifundia for distribution among the peasants." "Dedication to cooperatives for agricultural workers on industrialized latifundia." The congress ordered intensified organization of unions for farm workers and worker and peasant blocs. It recommended arming the workers and peasants. It asked for the suppression of laws "onerous to the Indian or the Negro," and it recommended that the agrarian struggle be coordinated with the struggle for the emancipation of the indigenous masses.[19]

It is interesting to consider some examples of how these slogans had already been applied. The Latin American Communists did attempt to form worker and peasant blocs, and they succeeded in Argentina, Brazil, and Uruguay, even if only on paper and through letterhead organizations directed by Communists. The only country in which they were able to achieve really substantial success was Mexico. There, they had managed to get a Workers and Peasants Bloc set up with some skeletal "unitary" unions led by the Communist Party. (One of these unions was a curious Railroad Workers' Party; another was the powerful National Peasant League, headed by Ursulo Galván, a leader of great prestige.) The president of the Bloc had been the famous painter Diego Rivera (1886–1957), then a member of the Communist Party; all but three of the Bloc's nine directors had been Communists. But the Bloc had been isolated from Mexican reality. On the very day that President-elect Alvaro Obregón (1880–1928) had been assassinated, the Bloc had issued a manifesto demanding, *inter alia*, the replacement of the legislature by assemblies of workers and peasants. In March, 1928, a military coup had been attempted. The National Peasant League and the Railroad Workers' Party had lined up with the government against the military, but the Communists had taken advantage of the situation to demand the handing over of lands and factories and to attack the government. The Party had expelled Galván, and the League, in turn, had expelled its Communist directors. The Workers and Peasants Bloc had then been dissolved, but the Communists continued to use its name in propaganda attacking the "Social-Fascist government, a traitor to Mexico."[20]

In 1922, a Socialist Revolutionary Party (SRP) had been founded in Colombia, and it grew rapidly. It relied on the support of prestigious intellectuals and had a certain influence on the infant trade unions. In 1926, the Communists, led by Mahecha, decided to take it over because their own group was not prospering. Two years later, a French delegate from the Montevideo Bureau of the Third International ("Austine," whose real name is unknown) arrived in Bogotá at a time when agitation among the peasants in the Magdalena River Valley was strong. Workers on the plantations had won three strikes and were preparing another against the United Fruit Company in the banana-growing region of Santa Marta. The only purpose of the new strike was to win a redress of grievances; it had no political motive. But, on the decision of "Austine," the SRP decided to make the strike the opening move in an uprising. Mahecha was sent to Santa Marta to "orient" the imminent strike of 40,000 agricultural workers; he collected money, stored provisions, and did an excellent job of organization. On November 12, 1928, the strike was called. The strikers disarmed the soldiers in some villages, and there were fights between peasants and soldiers. In all, 1,004 were killed, more than 300 were wounded, and 500 were arrested, of whom nearly all were sentenced to long prison terms. The strikers failed to find support in the rest of the country, and, as soon as the Communists in Bogotá saw how the struggle was going, they confined themselves to sending Mahecha a communique, which reached him after the fight was over, in which they advised him, "Don't confuse the strike with the insurrection [sic]."[21]

Until 1928, the Communist Party of Argentina, largely composed of intellectuals, showed no concern over the agrarian question. The leaders of the few peasant groups that played a part in politics were socialists or radicals. There was an Argentine Agrarian Federation, founded in 1912, which the Communists accused of being allied with latifundism. Not until after the Perón regime ended would the Party change its attitude toward this organization and begin to infiltrate it. It was at the Eighth Party Congress, in 1928, that talk of the land problem began. The theses approved at the Congress admitted that "the Party, as such, has been unconcerned until now with the peasant question. . . . It is the duty of the Party to link its work in the rural regions with the anti-imperialist struggle. Furthermore, the Party must launch and support the slogan of a worker-and-peasant government."[22]

As long as the Latin American Communist movement was under the direction of the Comintern and bound by its rigid slogans, it had no influence among the peasants. The popular-front strategy made possible a new approach to them, at least in some countries, but again, the Party wasted its opportunity, although for different reasons. Whereas formerly the Communists had been isolated from the peasantry by their dogmatism, now, with the Popular Front, they were isolated by their too great flexibility.

Throughout the period of the Popular Front, the Communists never raised the issue of land reform in Latin America. At most, they recommended measures for technical improvements in agriculture. In Chile, as I mentioned earlier, the Communists held cabinet posts immediately after World War II, in the government of González Videla. One of these Communist cabinet members, the minister of land, made good use of his stay in office to help the Communists to organize and infiltrate the rural regions, but he did not put forth any plan for agrarian reform and took no steps that would change the conditions prevailing in the countryside. In Cuba, General Batista's government had a Communist member; he also did not raise the land question, but this question was later to be the subject of one of the strongest planks in Fidel Castro's platform.

The agrarian program of the Cuban Communist Party was ultramoderate, probably because the Communists did not want to create difficulties for Batista. In 1944, the fifth point of the "socialist program" approved by the Second Congress of the Popular Socialist (Communist) Party was to give the peasants "full possession of the land they work," so as to "accomplish the intensification and diversification of agricultural production [which are] the indispensable bases of national economic emancipation." (At that time, the Cuban Communists opposed the theory of complementary economies, but they accepted it under another name in 1962, when they were, evidently, no longer interested in "national economic emancipation," since, by then, the Cuban economy depended on the Soviet-bloc countries instead of the United States.) The Party proposed the passage of a law regulating land rentals, the creation of an agricultural loan bank, the establishment of a rural housing program, extension of rural education, and a number of measures such as irrigation, formation of cooperatives, road building, technical aid to farmers, and granting of state-owned lands. (The Communists fought those same measures in other Latin American countries in 1960 and the following years, when they were part of the plans related to the Alliance for Progress. Not once did the phrase "agrarian reform" appear; neither could it be found in the other resolutions passed by the party.[23])

In Argentina, where the government was neutral during the war and there was no popular front, the Communists might have been able to apply a more vigorous program but did not, doubtless hampered by their mimicry of Moscow and adherence to its shibboleths. One of the few men who attempted to analyze the Argentine agrarian situation in Marxist terms concluded that Argentine agriculture was vested with capitalist forms, and he proposed merely the establishment of systems for working the land "on a technical and cultural level higher than that already reached," without moving backward to limited exploitation by individual effort.[24]

Mexico is a good touchstone by which to judge the attitude of the Communists with regard to land reform, because the Mexican Revolution preceded the Russian Revolution. In 1927, the Communist Confederación Sindical Unitaria (United Trade Union Federation) maintained that private ownership of land should be abolished and argued that worker and peasant control of the government and of the *ejido* organizations was necessary. During Cárdenas' administration the Communist Association of Socialist Agronomic Engineers[25] tried to devaluate the Mexican Revolution: "The Revolution of 1910 was nourished on the spirit of the French Revolution, [which came] in a period when small land ownership in France already was known to have failed. The Revolution in Mexico was a sentimental and extemporaneous copy of the French Revolution."

Although Cárdenas hoped to transform the *ejidos* into a system for communal labor, the Communist engineers wanted to go further: "The *ejido* is not the appropriate unit for solving the land problem. Only large-scale collective cultivation of the land, put into the hands of peasants by means of collective exploitation, will solve that problem."

Later, with the coming of the Cold War, they changed their position. Lombardo Toledano believed that, even though the system of latifundia had been broken, agrarian reform could not be said to be over. What he advocated was not the socialist revolution but an "antifeudal, popular, and anti-imperialist revolution."

The case of Guatemala is more complex. In Mexico, the Communists were in the opposition; in Guatemala, however, they infiltrated the administration of Jacobo Arbenz (1914–   ) and virtually took control of it.[26] In 1951, the Party (there called the Partido Guatemalteco del Trabajo) agreed, in its Fifth Plenary Session, to work for a land reform "that would end feudalism and move toward capitalism." During the debate on the projected land-reform law, the Communist deputies in the Guatemalan legislature said they would vote for the plan but added that their final objective was to abolish private property, although this would become possible only when power passed into the hands of the alliance of workers and peasants, that is, "when a regime of popular democracy or socialism is established." Meanwhile, they proposed changes: nationalization of a portion of the land and the granting of it not for full ownership but for usufruct. At the same time, the Party was training a corps of organizers to assume the task of tying the land issue in with the peace issue by affirming that the imperialists were intent on unleashing a local war to prevent land reform. The Sixth Plenary Session indicated that the Party must take advantage of "the class contradictions that agrarian reform will make more acute

. . . for the purpose of furthering the struggle against imperialism." Clearly, the Communists intended to use agrarian reform as a tool, not as an end in itself.

Communist Party members held all the important posts in the Agriculture Department (except that of the department head, the mere existence of whom provided them with a screen) and at least 35 per cent of all the positions in the department. Consequently, the people who received land grants were under the impression that they were indebted to the Communists; those already owning land believed that they could thank the Communists for allowing them to keep it; those who wanted land hoped to get it from the Party men.

Years later, the Party admitted that its agrarian-reform policy had been justly criticized. But it assessed the blame for such "errors" on "adventurer-leaders" in the government. J. Rodríguez expressed this in the usual phraseology:

Errors were committed in the application of agrarian reform by both the right and the left, but the latter were the more important. These consisted, for example, in annexing the lands of some peasants [those who did not submit to the Party], which meant ultimately that they were treated the same as the landholders. In other cases, they pressured the peasants in order that they themselves, on their own initiative and without waiting for the dispositions of the National Land Department, might distribute the land or take measures not considered in the Agrarian Reform Law. These errors were made principally by the leader of the [Communist] National Peasant Federation, who had an adventurous political orientation.[27]

Rodríguez added something that, though it referred to Guatemala in 1954, was to be equally applicable to Cuba in 1962: "As experience with counterrevolution in our country has taught us, the errors of the left can, for a time, put some peasants in the reactionary camp."

The Bolivian revolution of 1952, which erupted while the groundwork for land reform was being laid in Guatemala, was a different matter. In it, the Communists were never a part of the revolutionary movement there. But once they had organized, divided, and subdivided, the Communists had won control of the PIR (Revolutionary Party of the Left) and nominated José Antonio Arce as their candidate to run against Colonel Gualberto

Villarroel in 1944. Later, after Villarroel was assassinated, the PIR had cabinet members in the reactionary administration of Enrique Hertzog. But, although the Bolivian Indians (who constitute the majority of the population and all of the peasantry) have retained to this day a strong pre-Columbian tradition of communal living and working, the PIR was never able to take advantage of this to infiltrate the rural regions.

In 1952, the revolutionary government established a Department of Indian and Peasant Affairs whose first task was to organize unions of peasants. Though the Trotskyists dominated some of these organizations, the Communists never succeeded in winning control of a single one. In January, 1953, when a Commission for Agrarian Reform was empowered to draft legislation transforming the Bolivian rural structure, Communist Party Secretary-General Sergio Almarás introduced a plan of his own because, he said, there could be no true land reform unless the industrial proletariat directed it, and he asked for the formation of a Patriotic Front for National Anti-imperialist and Antifeudal Liberation. Almarás suggested an alliance between the revolutionary government and the wealthy peasants and the granting of the latifundists' lands to the poor peasants. At the same time, he warned against the danger of right deviationism (taking the latifundists for wealthy peasants) and left deviationism (taking the wealthy peasants for latifundists). No doubt, this sounds very familiar to the reader, and that is how it seemed to non-Communist Bolivian leaders. It did not take them long to discover that the plan was a faithful copy of Mao Tse-tung's agrarian law of 1950. Eventually, the government adopted a plan for nationalizing the land (by expropriation of the latifundia and compensation by means of an issue of twenty-five-year bonds), and, on August 2, 1953, agrarian reform became law and was put into practice. Since then, the Communists have not succeeded in increasing their minimal influence among the Bolivian peasants, even though they exercised some in the labor unions and among the intellectuals.[28]

In Brazil, during the same period, the Communist movement tended to try to neutralize its possible adversaries. This led to rather peculiar reasoning on the subject of the peasantry, as Luis

Carlos Prestes (1898–   ) made clear: "The [Party] program deals appropriately with all the progressive claims of the peasants, including wealthy ones, whose properties must not be confused with those of the latifundists."[29] Party Secretary Diógenes Arruda insisted on this strategy of appeasement (adopted at a moment when the Party was eager to find allies among the bourgeois parties) because, he said, "By safeguarding the property of the wealthy peasants, the program . . . reflects an objective economic reality. In this way, we shall attract the wealthy peasants to the side of the proletariat and broaden still further the possibilities of attracting the middle-income peasants to the proletarian side."[30] Five years later, in Cuba, the world was to see how Communists treated both rich and middle-income peasants.

Communist tactics on the agrarian question, since the establishment of Castroism, have been characterized by four elements:

1. The Communists talk of land reform (abandoning the old thesis that the agrarian problem can be solved only by revolution) and relate it to the anti-imperialist struggle. Since this correlation is considered almost certain to unite several social classes, they do not insist on the Leninist thesis of the hegemony of the industrial proletariat.

2. They criticize (not always without reason) land-reform plans and introduce others that tend to limit the extent of private land ownership without providing for compensation. Often, such counterproposals are introduced not by the Party itself but by a coalition of front organizations or peasant unions.

3. The Party has left the task of agitation to the Castroist movements and reserved for itself the harder but more profitable task of organizing the peasants. In some countries, a ban on the organizing of peasants facilitates the Party's work, for it eliminates the competition of democratic movements, which, by their nature, are incapable of undercover work.

4. Where circumstances are propitious and there is spontaneous agrarian agitation, the Communists try sometimes with success to channel the unrest toward occupation of the land, to force the police or army to intervene. This maneuver has enabled the Communists to play the role of defenders of the peasants and to shake the people's confidence in land-reform plans.

The purposes of this fourfold tactic are to frustrate every effort to change the land structure and, thus, to demonstrate that only the Cuban method can be effective. Experience has taught the Communists that only circumstances like those that prevailed in Cuba—collapse of the state, inexperienced non-Communist leaders without solid political organizations—would enable them to seize control.

In this respect, the case of Venezuela is worthy of special study. A democratic government began land reform there in 1960. At that time, the Communists, who were not merely in opposition but in incipient insurrection, were supported by reactionary forces and Castroist elements. Essentially, the motive behind this obstructionism was not only to cause agrarian reform to fail but also to bring on the collapse of the entire populist regime, which had proved by its success that there were other, less costly ways to social change. But the Venezuelan peasants who had received land or were confident they would receive it were the first to act, often spontaneously, in defense of the government.

In short, today, as yesterday, the land question serves the Communists as a tool with which to carry out their policy. Sometimes, they use it to neutralize their adversaries; other times, to torpedo democratic efforts to bring about reform; and still other times, to win support for the Cuban revolution. In Guatemala and then Cuba, the Party took absolutely no interest in the fate of the peasants beyond using their aspirations to achieve its ends. The cases of Guatemala and, especially, Cuba further demonstrate that wherever the Communists are in a position to solve a land problem, they practice not what they preach but what the U.S.S.R. and the "peoples' democracies" have practiced without success. In an exchange of opinions on "the agrarian question and the movement for national liberation," published in 1961 by the *World Marxist Review,* an organ of the "Communist and labor parties,"[31] the formula was repeatedly echoed: "The peasant in Argentina must struggle against not only the landowners but also the imperialistic monopolies" (J. M. García, Argentina). "The struggle against semifeudal latifundism in Guatemala is intimately bound up with the struggle against United States imperialism and the struggle for national independence" (J. Rodríguez, Guatemala). "Uruguay cannot rise from the depression without destroying the latifundia, without simultaneously struggling against imperialism, ownership of large tracts of land, and precapitalistic vices" (R. Arismendi, Uruguay). "The struggle for agrarian reform is closely bound, in our judgment, to the struggle for national independence and against imperialist domination" (J. del Prado, Peru). "The question of agrarian reform is one of the fundamental aspects of the struggle for national liberation" (P. Saad, Ecuador).

The Communists know that the peasants' desire is not for nationalization but for direct possession of the land they live on. Accordingly, they demand land reform (which they opposed in the years before the Popular Front) and conceal their ultimate objective—state ownership and control. For example, the Argentine Party program reads as follows: "The big farm operations will be handled by the state or handed over to cooperatives. . . . The state will establish tractor stations." (This proposal came after the abolition of tractor stations in the U.S.S.R., but, no doubt, the Communists in Argentina foresaw that such installations might help to establish state control over the peasants.) In the Uruguayan Party program, there is the same sort of thing: "Those technologically developed estates that are the property of the latifundists will not be divided but will pass into the power of the state." Here, the possibility of creating cooperatives to work the land is not even admitted; it was only suggested that "a parcel of land to be held as personal property will be turned over to the peons and peasants who work on these estates."

In Colombia, between 1947 and 1957, the agrarian situation took a turn that surprised the Communists—a guerrilla war of the peasants against the forces of the conservative government, with innumerable skirmishes, in which about 200,000 people lost their lives. The Communist Party, which had not foreseen the struggle and was not prepared to share the fate of the peasants, called the bloodbath "self-defense by the masses," in the hope of evading any need to take part in the fighting. Of course, the Party made contact with some of the guerrillas and, in 1952, organized a National Conference of Guerrilla Fighters, but it recognized the failure of this policy: "The course of events may have indicated that the platform of the said conference was too lofty for the actual level of political consciousness among most of the Colombian guerrilla fighters," said the Communist leader Gilberto Vieira. With the fall of the dictatorship, the guerrilla bands dissolved, but, after the emergence of Castro, whose partisans were very active in Colombia, guerrilla bands began to form in areas where there had previously been none. This time, the Party let the Castroists assume the risk of the struggle and contented itself with proposing an alliance between the guerrilla fighters and the working class and *petite bourgeoisie* of the cities to fight the "anti-imperialist and antifeudal revolution."[32]

After the inception of the Alliance for Progress, governments with little desire to bring about real land reform but a great desire to receive credits from the Alliance developed a tendency to give the name of land reform to measures that might better have been called land colonization: the opening up of virgin lands, transfer of villages, new irrigation systems, mechanization of agriculture, etc. The populist parties opposed this perversion of agrarian reform, and the Communists denounced it, too (but also accused the populists of complicity with the falsifiers).[33] The problem of the Latin American Communists has been to make such propaganda compatible with the agrarian policy pursued in Cuba, where Castro's style is to establish state ownership over the land as a means by which to place the peasants under state control. Indeed, cooperatives and small landholdings were converted into state farms during the second stage of Castro's land reform. This step had been advocated earlier by Blas Roca, who, in his report to the Eighth National Congress of the Popular Socialist Party of Cuba, held in Havana, in August, 1960, had said that one of the most important tasks in the field of land reform was "to further the development of cooperatives of every type."[34] When we understand that the so-called agricultural cooperatives in Cuba are actually state farms, we can realize the true import of this advocacy of state ownership.

It would be well, however, to be not overly confident of this contradiction between Latin American theory—not theory, really, so much as strategy—and Cuban practice. The Latin American masses and many political and intellectual leaders have been unable to perceive its subtleties. This contradiction is not what has hindered, up to now, the Communists' efforts in the rural regions Their main stumbling block is the fact that their influence is primarily among the middle class, which is little inclined to concern itself over the peasants.

A Look at the Indians

The problem of land is very closely related to that of the Indian masses. Mariátegui, as we have seen, pointed this out. For some time, the Communists were concerned over the Indian question whenever and wherever it seemed that the Indians offered good human material to build on. At the Montevideo Conference of 1929, the Peruvian delegate, Saco, pointed out that the Communist International was fighting the nascent "Negro Zionism"—a movement advocating the return of Negroes to Africa for the purpose of establishing there a revolutionary state of their own—and he asserted that, "similarly, the constitution of the Indian race into an autonomous state would not be conducive, at the present moment, to a dictatorship of the Indian proletariat, and certainly would not contribute toward the formation of a classless Indian state, despite what has been said to the contrary, but, rather, it would lead to the establishment of an Indian bourgeois state." He opposed the application here of the principle of self-determination, lest this entail a massacre of whites, workers included. "Peters," a representative of the Young Communists' International, protested because he saw this statement as an implied criticism of the nationalities policy that the Soviet Communist Party was said to be pursuing. No delegate even mentioned Mariátegui's essays on the Indian problem (only one referred to him and that was to call him a Trotskyist), and the position taken by some Communist intellectuals—for instance, in Mexico—who sought to resuscitate Indian culture as a form of national expression, found no sympathizers.

Shortly afterward, the Mexican Communists raised the question again, and two of their leaders, Alberto Lumbreras and Vicente Guerra, wrote a paper on the subject during a visit to Moscow in 1932. The Indian tribes, they wrote, still as wantonly exploited and oppressed as they had been in the Spanish colony, were long-lived, historically developed, with their own languages, lands, economic life, and psychology, all manifest in a cultural identity. Since 1930, only the Communist Party and Mexico's revolutionary trade unions had raised as a national question the problem of how to deal with these tribes, but their statement of the problem was confusing. The phrasing of the Party program of 1932—"For the indigenes, neither emancipation nor betterment exists under the capitalist regime"—was theoretically false and politically harmful, said Guerra and Lumbreras, for the international Communist movement never has denied the possibility that an oppressed nation can win its freedom within the capitalistic system. The 1932 statement continued: "The cultural development of the indigenous peoples and tribes must be national in form, but socialistic in content." The formula was theoretically sound but, as applied in the case of Mexico, incorrect, Lumbreras and Guerra said, since in Mexico it is a question not of a socialist proletarian revolution but of an antifeudal and anti-imperialist and agrarian one; this would not preclude the possibility that an Indian bourgeoisie might head some of its own free Indian republics or that it might reject the Soviet system.[35]

This argument is interesting—although Communist proposals of this kind, such as the American Communists' notion of setting up a Negro republic in the South of the United States, never had any practical result—for it shows that the Communists were aware that it would be useful to "create" nations and that this could only be accomplished from below. Yet, when they had a chance to exercise some real influence in this direction, within a much broader framework than that of the Indian groups, they did not, because, at that juncture of history, it would not have been in line with the diplomatic interests of the Soviet Union.

The Manipulation of Nationalism

By collaborating with oligarchic dictatorships, the Communists did not increase the likelihood of the masses being incorporated into society or of the Latin American countries beginning to make themselves into nations. But the Communists were able to pretend that they were strong nationalists, particularly during the period of the Popular Front, which gave them a respectability they had never before enjoyed and the opportunity to come out of isolation. Logically, their first objective was to win over the intellectuals, for their only hope of influencing the middle class was to work through them. The Communists had to devise a platform that would permit them not only to attract the intellectuals emotionally but also to pull them into political complicity. An effective means was to enter into contact with liberal professors, leftist journalists, and revolutionary students—but also with politicians who were a little to the right of center and with conservative businessmen. The tactic they chose was a new, radical, yet negative form of nationalism. Its postulates were abstract and illogical slogans extolling "national glories" and "pre-Columbian civilizations."

In the mid-1930's, many Latin American intellectuals were in a peculiarly vulnerable state of mind. Like many of their confreres in Europe, they were oppressed by a deep sense of failure. Neither their teachings, their writings, nor their protests had prevented the survival or restoration of dictatorships, which then ruled in Argentina, Uruguay, Paraguay, Brazil, Bolivia, Peru, Ecuador, Venezuela, Nicaragua, El Salvador, Honduras, Guatemala, the Dominican Republic, Haiti, and Cuba. In all other parts of Latin America, the situation was unstable. Bitter memories of certain interventions by the United States lingered on.

For several years, the charms of the Communists' new "nationalism" wrought a change in the ideological orientation of the cultural world. There were, naturally, exceptions, especially among the outstanding figures, but most Latin American intellectuals and artists gradually adopted this type of nationalism, which has continued to exercise a strong influence ever since. To gauge its intensity, we must know its characteristics:

1. It is isolationist and autarchical. Among the favorite themes of many writers of the past thirty years are the beliefs that native tradition is the sole source of progress and that the national culture has no need for European or any other influence.

2. It is separatist. Its adherents speak not of Latin American

culture but of Uruguayan, Salvadorian, or Mexican culture. This has brought things to an absurd point: Countries with the same traditions, similar economic and political organizations, a common language, and similar aspirations refuse to consider themselves culturally interdependent.

3. It turns back to ancient times. The negative nationalist has searched the past for literary subjects and other avatars to support his current attitudes. Lombardo Toledano's case is typical. In 1952, when he stood as a candidate for the presidency of Mexico, he began his campaign by taking a "loyalty oath" in front of the alleged tomb of Cuauhtémoc (1495–1525), an Aztec emperor who was assassinated by the conquistadors. The dispute among archeologists concerning the authenticity of the remains, which had been discovered a short time earlier, immediately took on a political character and ended with the epithèts "reactionary" and "pro-imperialist" being ascribed to anyone who, for scientific reasons, did not accept this authenticity.

4. It is symbolistic. Generalized, symbolic themes have replaced concrete ones. This fondness for symbols is less evident among writers with no Communist affiliations, but few have managed completely to escape the influence. Almost always, the symbols are abstract—the nation, the enemy of the nation (first Nazism and now "American imperialism"), peace, warmongers, etc.

The deep infiltration of arts and letters by this negative nationalistic ideology was not achieved by Communist propaganda alone. Beyond a doubt, the call was persuasive and the audience receptive, but the Communists' success would have been less resounding if they had not availed themselves of the more compelling tactic of administrative persuasion or, to put the matter more bluntly, blackmail. During the time of the Popular Front, many Party members and fellow-travelers infiltrated a number of institutions in the fields of culture and information—newspapers, publishing houses, private and public cultural organizations—vantage points from which they could reward their friends and punish their enemies. In short, they set up an informal censorship, refusing jobs or media to those who would not bow before the cultural precepts they sponsored. Eventually, some of the artists who had been reluctant to obey the call of the Communists had to surrender to this harsh method of persuasion and were absorbed into the conformity then in vogue.

The policy of negative nationalism, which started off with a plan to seduce and placate the intellectuals and the liberals, soon went even further. Not only was the integrity of the left wing subverted, but it was also lulled to sleep, with the object of leaving the Communists free to court the political right. We have seen how this permitted them to dedicate themselves to their alliance with the dictators. Thus, a nationalistic campaign that began as a simple attempt to attract the intellectuals through propaganda became a systematic method for infiltrating every aspect of Latin American life. The result was that, for the first time, Communism became a strong factor in the political environment of Latin America.

The years after World War II, with their political frustrations and their economic and social rewards for everyone but the voiceless masses, offered fertile soil for negative nationalism. The Communists no longer have a monopoly of this; now that it has become more refined intellectually, more "liberalized," and more modernized, it is open to anyone.

7

Nationalism as an Opium of the Conscience

Effects for Causes

If the oligarchies make use of nationalism to distract the people from their real problems and to put pressure on Washington to pay higher prices for raw materials exported for their exclusive benefit and to get more aid; if the Communists use nationalism to serve the interests of Soviet diplomacy and make it little more than anti-Yankeeism, the situation is reversed when it is a question of nationalism among the nonoligarchic social groups that prosper in one way or another at the expense of the masses. These groups, composed of the bourgeoisie—especially its younger and more recently arrived members—professionals, intellectuals, bureaucrats, and students, use nationalism to compensate for their guilt feelings (when they have them) and frustrations. Nationalism is the ploy that permits them to bear, with a clear conscience, the exploitation of the submerged masses. They sign manifestoes favoring Castro, or peace, but they let their own people be harassed. They are not Communists and more often than not have no sympathy for Communist methods, but they end by being manipulated by the Communists, since they reduce their nationalism to simple anti-Yankeeism.

Of course, this type of nationalism cannot create nationhood, since its object is the continued submersion of the masses. It may be said that such a nationalism is a sort of opium of the conscience, in the same sense in which Marx called religion the "opium of the people." It does nothing to improve the situation out of which it arose.

I must confess that, in the mid-1950's, I believed and wrote that the social groups I have listed were emancipating themselves from the negative nationalism of the Communists and that they would be in the vanguard of the forces creating conditions for genuine nationhood. True, there was an awakening of social conscience and a withdrawal from negative nationalism. But, at the same time, there was a rapid improvement in the living conditions of those groups and an increase in their influence. There ensued a conflict between conscience and self-interest. To resolve the conflict, the drug of nationalism was used and scarcely anyone was aware of its significance. I had failed to take into account the extraordinary human capacity for self-deception and invention of compensations.

In the nineteenth century, anticlericalism served to soothe the liberal Latin American's conscience: While the liberals were combating the influence of the clergy, they told themselves, they were doing their duty; consequently, they were able to prosper at the expense of the Indians and the early industrial workers. The anticlericalism of today is anti-imperialism. Of course, I am not condemning the anti-imperialism that had (and still has) a historical function. I am trying to show that certain social groups have, for reasons of prestige, designated as anti-imperialism attitudes that are directed toward the same social ends as those envisioned by holders of the complex of attitudes called anticlericalism a hundred years ago.

Yesterday's liberalism influenced social groups that were rather like, but numerically much weaker than, those that "compensatory nationalism" has brought together: the middle class, the intellectuals, the professionals, even the young men in the armed forces who are more cultivated than those of higher rank. The early liberals mistook effect for cause and failed to see that the intervention of the clergy in politics was possible only because it suited the oligarchs, who therefore tolerated or promoted it. To-day, anti-imperialists also fail to see that imperialism is solely an effect and not a cause and that it has existed only because it suited the oligarchs and was therefore tolerated and, sometimes, in the past, promoted by them. In each case, owing to timidity, intellectual complicity, or political cowardice, the opposition has preferred to do battle with the effects rather than the causes. In each case, the result could only be the same: to leave the masses submerged and the nation a mere hypothesis for the future.

Politically, the nationalism in question finds expression on quite varied grounds. On one side are certain leftists—neither populists, socialists, nor Communists—who, consciously or un-consciously, play the Communists' game and exhaust themselves in bizarre parochial quarrels. On the other side are sectors of the Christian Democratic movements, particularly in the unions, who set out to win adherents by lip-service to radicalism. Other groups, although they have not yet found a clear political voice, include the young industrialists and military men.

The Scholars' Clichés

The background of this compensatory type of nationalism lies in the first half of this century. The historical record will show how men of strong intellectual character, true savants, able to think for themselves in other matters, curiously let themselves be seduced by the most absurd clichés whenever the matter of re-lations with the United States arose—for that provides the sub-stance of their nationalism.

Manuel Ugarte, a socialist and one of the first to propose a union of Latin American countries, voiced utter nonsense in speaking of the "two Americas": "The warm America of Spanish origin, of Italian influence, and French culture, which has frat-ernized with the aboriginal races, can boast of a unity and a physiognomy that separate it basically from cold North America, where the spirit of England, Holland, and the Scandinavian countries has flourished, with all its promiscuities and other philosophic tendencies."[1] Ugarte came close to racism and to depreciation of what is truly Latin American. To him, resistance to the United States was the result of Spanish and French influence—which only proves that his nationalism was not true nationalism but mere anti-Yankeeism:

It is undeniable that, until now, the Yankees have reaped some disappointments in the south. But that cannot possibly be attributed either to the former's incapacity for conquest or to the latter's vigor in defense. Here, we have two independent forces at work: our Spanish origin, which makes us hostile to any approach to the enemy race; and the tastes, ambitions, and antipathies—the ideals—that France has suggested to us ever since our first steps on the road to independence. Left to ourselves, we might perhaps have weakened."[2]

Such a Bergsonian philosopher as the Mexican Antonio Caso, who fought a successful battle against positivism and produced some very original works, could write, "There are people in the world who do things, but without any moral greatness; that is why the United States has dominated and still dominates. But it is necessary to think about the fact that the exalted spirit and high ideals the Latin American people carry in their hearts must sooner or later soar above all imperialisms."[3] Leopoldo Zea described this kind of reasoning well:

Each of the Americas, it is also said, possesses qualities the other lacks. The Anglo-Saxon America possesses great technical capability; the Latin, or Hispanic, America has a strong cultural capacity—that is to say, a spiritual one. . . . This interpretation, common not only to Spanish-American thinkers but also to some North Americans, falls into error by assigning to each section of America a quality that is the negation of the other. One has material capability but denies the spiritual . . . ; the other has spiritual capability but denies the material. . . . In Anglo-Saxon America, there has been no lack of men capable of spiritual direction, and they are not lacking [today]; neither is there any lack of Hispano-American men capable of realizing a strongly material world.[4]

Nevertheless, the intellectuals of Latin America today, or the majority of them at any rate, derive great satisfaction from their devotion to anti-Yankee commonplaces. The intellectuals are influential, but their attitude meets indifference on the part of the masses, toward whom they in their turn are so indifferent.

But, in the final analysis, the intellectuals' abnegation of the right to doubt and analyze, their behaving like a flock of sheep in caps and gowns, may conceivably cost them their prestige. They are preparing a very hard tomorrow for their successors. More's the pity, for they might be able to spare the people much suffering and waiting, and might spare Latin America a great deal of disorder, if they would dare to swim against the current, reject prejudice, approach the people, and impel other nonoligarchic groups to follow their lead. To understand the gravity of this abandonment of responsibility, it is necessary to take into account the fact that political action in Latin America has always been stimulated by some previous intellectual movement. History abounds in examples. The Mexican Revolution of 1910–17 was preceded by the struggle of Antonio Caso and the "generation of the Atheneum" against the positivism justifying the dictatorship of General Díaz. University reform in Peru was advocated by the literary review *Colonida* as long ago as 1915. The "1922 Movement" in Brazil was, according to one of its founders, the poet Mario Andrade (1893–1945), "the harbinger of the nascent revolutionary attitude toward the country's problems."

Latin American literature and art reflected for a time the characteristics of the populists' positive nationalism. The clamor of social protest after World War I found expression in a new, vigorous, nonconformist realism. But, significantly, Latin America was then preoccupied with the fate of the individual, rather than with the abstract collective concept of a nation.

At that time, intellectuals generally avoided Communist influence. True, many had admired some of the achievements of the Bolshevik Revolution, but nearly all were repelled by Moscow's rigid dogmatism. Besides, as I have said, the Latin American intellectual, quite the opposite of the European, did not suffer from a guilt complex about his less privileged countrymen and, hence, was not inclined to sublimate his anxiety through the Party.

But, as this intellectual middle class improved its living conditions, increased in number, and adopted a bourgeois style of living, it began to feel twinges of conscience, which it soothed with an adulterated form, actually a schematic falsification, of

Marxism. Thus, while they abandoned all concern about the
results of negative nationalism, they yielded joyously to the de-
lights of conformity with it. In a way, it might be said that the
popularity of North American automobiles, refrigerators, alco-
holic beverages, and gadgets was the cause of the intellectuals'
anti-Yankeeism. In their efforts to obtain these things, they
shirked their responsibilities, and to divert blame from themselves, they cried out against the very people who had offered
them the technological means of arriving at their state of well-
being.

The Latin American artist has always had to confront dilem-
mas. Spanish or French influence? Russia or America? Foreign
or traditional native culture? He seems never to have found in
his public the stimulus necessary for original creation—or, rather,
his public has never seemed to ask for original concepts, forms,
or themes. Romanticism and naturalism, modernism and proletarian art, Joyceanism and social realism have successively appeared in literature, painting, the cinema, music, and even ballet.
And folklore has often been substituted for culture because of
the confusion of "native" with "national" art. A Mexican wrote:

For our mustachioed grandfathers and our haughty grandmothers of
the Porfiriate, culture and good taste could find a precise and refined
expression only in French. Anything Mexican was simply coarse or at
best tolerable. Among other contributions of greater or lesser importance, the revolutionaries rediscovered Mexico for the Mexicans. The
pendulum swung to the other extreme, and the elegance of Paris, London, and Washington became symbols of triteness, of bourgeois mediocrity. We have seen ladies worth millions startle their guests with sets
of the most Mexican earthenware dishes and decorate the walls of their
mansions with the incendiary paintings of Siqueiros, Diego [Rivera],
and Orozco. David Alfaro [Sigueiros] was shouting arrogantly and chal-
lengingly that in the graphic arts there was no way but ours! And the
fashionable intellectuals were screaming that there could not be two
Mexicos. Today, we are witnessing a mad, unsteady swing of the pendulum. Some intellectuals are beginning to discover that the elegant
and distinguished thing to do is to dispose of that foam of nationalism
by turning back to the trodden paths of our grandparents—that is, to
renounce, in words soft or harsh, everything Mexican: to deny that
pulque has quality, or that there is an old wisdom, or that a highly
developed culture is expressed in the bright-red *moles* of Oaxaca; to
affirm that not even our Revolution was worth taking seriously. Still,

there are loyal and persistent devotees of the nationalist vertigo and sickness of the second quarter of our century. They are the people who insist that our beer, our Revolution, our bullfights, and our police, to cite only a few examples, are all the better for being Mexican, as a slogan of the period puts it.[5]

The artist could have found a meaning for his activity and might even have discovered his true needs if he had approached the people. The resulting challenge would have provided him with the stimulation indispensable for original creation. But he felt he was drawing near the people when his wife, wearing a necklace of Aztec stones or a poncho, attended a cocktail party and sang folk songs learned not in the villages but from records.

In truth, Latin American artists and intellectuals are isolated from their own country and know nothing of its problems. They spend their lives in a world of their own making, built of their protests and their excuses for inaction. That is why, as the Uruguayan Mario Benedetti said, "A sincere presentation of national problems has been passé for some time. Hypocrisy is the word for it: The more one declares that he is thinking of his country's good, the more he is thinking of his own pocketbook, or at least of his personal advancement."[6]

This lack of roots inevitably produces ideological disorientation. The Latin American intellectual believes, however, that he has found a compass in ideologies, a substitute for roots. Instead of going to the people, he turns to dogmas. Naturally, the dogmas that attract him are those that provide answers to his questions but do not demand self-doubt or further searchings. Consequently, the Latin American intellectual of today feels that he is very left-wing, by which he means that he is at once anti-Yankee and pro-Soviet. We find this in a Chilean Christian Democrat like Carlos Naudon, who fancies himself a leftist and has been able to bring himself to write such obvious falsehoods as this: "Soviet imperialism, which recognizes without equivocation that bread is more important than elections to the hungry, has offered them [the hungry] a formula containing economic justice for the price of totalitarian control. This has permitted the creation of an order that is dictatorial but capable of producing a perceptible rise in the standard of living."[7] And we find it also in a moderate like the Chilean Radical Alberto Baltra (1912–), who made this inspired statement:

> In the Soviet Union, the People's Republic of China, and the other nations of the socialist world, the ideal of development is conceived by an elite, which guides the masses and imbues them with fervor within a discipline that combines authentic opportunities for education with the realization of all aptitudes and talents. Moreover, the sense of effective participation in the constructive work of a developed and independent economy is impressed on the people.[8]

These two examples are Chilean, but an infinite number like them can be found in every country. It might almost be said, too, that the more moderate an intellectual is on domestic social questions, the more pro-Russian or pro-Chinese (or pro-Cuban) he becomes in international affairs. That is his way of protecting himself against his unending fear that he may be.called anti-Communist, pro-Yankee, or pro-imperialist. One day, Haya de la Torre, having been released from his five-year confinement in the Colombian embassy at Lima, visited Jesús Silva Herzog (1892–), editor of the magazine *Cuadernos Americanos,* in Mexico City. Silva remarked to him, "You see, they say I'm a Communist. But being called a Communist does not frighten me." Haya answered softly, "No, no. What would frighten you would be if they called you a reactionary."

The Latin American intellectual of this type, who is afraid of being called a reactionary and who, if he does not belong to the majority, undoubtedly does belong to the noisiest and most influential minority, feels no obligation whatsoever to live according to the convictions he expresses. One among many examples of this schizophrenia shows up in the de luxe cultural publications put out by oil companies in Latin America. Almost all Venezuelan intellectuals who sign pro-Castro, pro-North Vietnam, or pro-Soviet documents have written for, or illustrated, *El Farol, Tópicos Shell,* and *Revista Shell,* all of which pay very well. In these publications, we find, for example, the Castroist Alejo Carpentier (1904–), the Communist Brazilian painter Candido Portinari (1903–62), and dozens of others.[9] No wonder, then, that some of the great battles between realistic and abstract painters —in Mexico, for example—have been fought not over theory or even over the social significance of the two schools but over prizes (offered by a United States oil company) and commissions.

The chief client and virtually the only Maecenas of the intellectual in Latin America is the state. "[No country] can aspire to be a great nation without a national literature; yet our writers have been abandoned and are unable to devote themselves to their art," says the headline of an article by Henrique González Casanova, a Mexican "Marxist."[10] Precisely because the intellectuals' comfort depends on state patronage, they always take a look at the official attitude before they speak. No Mexican writer dared to publish a single manifesto protesting the landing of U.S. Marines in the Dominican Republic until nine days after the event—in other words, until they knew the position the government had taken.[11]

On the other hand, when they have a chance to support official policy, like a demand for higher prices for raw materials, they gallop away, bit in teeth, into the realms of the imagination. Here is an example of how far the lyricism of an economist, Manuel Germán Parra, of Mexico, can go:

How is it possible that an economist like Professor Tannenbaum can be unaware that a great difference exists between the very low prices at which industrial nations purchase raw materials in bulk from the agricultural countries and the very high prices at which they sell manufactured articles, frequently made from those same raw materials? Shall we exchange the cotton from La Laguna for tractors, Guasave's tomato crop for automatic seeders, Yucatán's sisal for machines that will remove fibers, or the chicle of Quintana Roo for threshers? Are we going to buy internal-combustion engines with chocolate cups from Uruapan? Electric generators with the green glass toys of Atzopan, turbines with brooches from Durango, or pumps with the woolens of Santa Ana Chautempan? And, from the viewpoint of "high culture," how many necklaces of Puebla's colored alabaster will we have to give in exchange for a subscription to *Time*?[12]

But such things can be discovered not only by reading the work of such writers but also as a part of day-to-day experience. When a speaker before an American or West European audience expounds a point of view that disturbs or runs counter to its convictions, the audience will, by and large, assume that the facts he uses are trustworthy, and it will not see any use in "right thinking" that is supported by false data. But a Latin American audience, especially one made up of young people, refuses to believe facts if they run counter to its prejudices and convictions. Rather, it will think that the speaker is lying.

There are, undoubtedly, many psychological and cultural reasons for these differences in attitude. But, basically, Latin American audiences have never been exposed to honest facts, and, when they had been told that they were being given facts, reality has later proved that the "facts" were snares—that is, false or distorted statements. Thus, little by little, generation after generation has fallen into the habit of rejecting as false the data used to support any opinion, and so, when they are actually told the truth, they suppose it to be false. Consequently, facts have lost their validity, and it becomes easy to live on two distinct planes, one of the word and one of reality.

The Isolation of the Students

If the intellectual has become bourgeois and joined the oligarchic system, and if he disguises his allegiance behind his nationalistic protests, are things, by any chance, different among the students because they are young, more demanding, and more forthright?

In principle, the students of Latin America are not bound to the existing social order. Their freedom from commitment may make them a force for renewal or, equally, a force for regression. (The latter happened under Hitler and is happening now in Bolivia.)

Youth can play an active and useful role in society. At the moment, they have not given themselves to the mission they should be fulfilling—that of vitalizing, clarifying, enlightening consciences, and removing obstacles to the liberation of the masses. There are almost no students in any organization, movement, or activity in which the masses participate. Students take part only in activities of the ruling classes. Most of them are isolated from the historical process through which Latin America is passing and are insensitive to it. Their social awareness has no depth.

The Latin American educational institution is extraordinarily conformist, in spite of the many teachers who consider themselves revolutionaries. The teaching is poor, and no one is taught about the motives for rebellion or the possibility that rebellion might resolve social problems. For this reason, whenever the young can manage to understand a little about actualities, they rebel against them, but without being able to decide which of the many programs they are offered would serve the interests of the people and which would reduce the people to tools of other interests.

As a student approaches the end of his scholastic career and faces the need to climb the social pyramid, to make of himself a respectable person, to marry and have children, he forgets his convictions. Only 1 per cent of the youth of Latin America attend universities. This figure reveals how great is the privilege of being a student: It ought to give students chills and fever to think of the responsibilities they alone are educationally qualified to assume.

Only 1 per cent of the young people who do attend universities come from the working class, and less than 1 per cent from the peasantry. This, of course, also indicates that university students are not necessarily the most gifted in each country, but only those who have the necessary means. The universities select young people not according to their capacities to serve their country, or their consciences, or their minds but according to the wealth of their families. It is, therefore, not surprising that the characteristics of Latin American student organizations are ineffectiveness, purely verbal revolutionism, superficiality, and an incredible tendency to use commonplaces.*

* In 1964, a comparative study was made of various Latin American student organizations. According to it, student life in Latin America could be divided into the following groups:

1. Haiti, Honduras, Paraguay, Nicaragua, and Ecuador. Institutionalization of students is virtually nonexistent, ideological content is very scarce and on an extremely low level, so that it carries no significant political weight—particularly in Honduras, Paraguay, and Ecuador. Trade-union activity is almost nil.

2. Panama, the Dominican Republic, Mexico, and Colombia. Institutionalization is modest, although somewhat better in Mexico and Colombia because the student population in those countries is large. The ideological content is generally modest; it is somewhat better in the Dominican Republic, because cer-

Very often the university is a focal point of nationalist agitation. Newspapers tell us constantly of demonstrations, rock fights with the police, declarations by student groups. In some places, students have shown that they are capable of self-sacrifice, as in Venezuela, where they fought in guerrilla bands, or in Cuba, where they bore the full brunt of urban terrorism in the days before Castro. It matters little that the cause they serve is of no real value to the people, as long as they believe that it is fruitful. If their endeavor is vain, the fault lies not with the students but with their professors (often fonder of demagoguery than of objective documentation) and with the popular movements that have not learned how to endow the young with a sense of mission. In certain places, the students have tried to approach the people, albeit through fashionable paternalistic procedures: defense of poor prisoners, campaigns for sanitation, literacy classes, organization of cooperatives, etc. Not infrequently, their governments may view these activities with unfriendly eyes because they know that however paternalistic the students may be, they are contributing to an awakening of the people (though perhaps only a very small nucleus of them).

But, by and large, the Latin American student population lives today in a state of apathy and indifference. Nothing has emerged that is comparable to the splendid movement for peoples' uni-

---

tain groups have been stimulated by recent events. Union activity is low in Panama and the Dominican Republic, slightly greater in Mexico and Colombia. The political weight of the students is almost nil. In the Dominican Republic it is growing; in Mexico and Colombia the influence of the students is not very strong.

3. El Salvador, Peru, Guatemala, Venezuela, and Bolivia. Institutionalization is increasing, though it may be somewhat unstable. The ideological content is still inadequate, except in Peru. Union activity is scarce, except in Bolivia. The students' political influence varies; in Venezuela it is quite considerable.

4. Argentina and Costa Rica. Institutionalization is greater than in any of the preceding groups. The ideological content in Costa Rica is low, in Argentina quite high. Union activity is intense in both countries. Student political influence is lower than in the countries of the third group.

5. Chile, Brazil, and Uruguay. Institutionalization is more nearly complete. The ideological content is quite high. Union activity is also intense. And the students' political influence is by no means insignificant. See V. Blanc, "La juventud aislada," in which the findings of a survey by the Italian magazine *Il Paradosso* are analyzed.

versities and the struggles that led to university reform after World War I. Students then demanded the opportunity

to acquire in the university the knowledge by which to discover and know ourselves as a nation. The student in a complete and national South American university ought to be nourished by his people. His ideal should be to nourish, in its turn, his people. . . . The university ought to contribute also to the identification of the political, economic, and cultural stumbling-blocks that wound the people's dignity and prevent or invalidate their authentic expression; it should point out also what they must depend on for their emancipation.[13]

Most Latin American professors belong to the groups that try to soothe their bad consciences with nationalism. And however poorly they may live, they are doing splendidly by comparison with the people. They sacrifice nothing, not even their time, for the people—using the university as an instrumentality that will permit them to have a clear conscience, making the young their accomplices in their verbal radicalism. Only the students, instead of talking, throw stones. This slight distinction is purely fortuitous and vanishes when the student graduates.

The universities are sometimes competent enough to train professionals able to compete on even terms with their counterparts in Europe or the United States. But "the university—we are not speaking of self-deception by a few courses or series of lectures— has not been able to bring the South American face to face with his problems, his immense social dramas, his desperate spiritual conflict."[14]

At times nationalism sterilizes student action, when the latter occurs. In Quito, student demonstrations against the dictatorship —demonstrations in which students have lost their lives—have become commonplace. But what can be hoped from them if a student leader makes statements like those of Artemidoro Zevallos, president of the Federation of University Students (considered a leftist organization)? "Ecuador was conquered and betrayed in her conflict over boundaries with Peru by the oligarchies encysted in power. That was a tragic hour for Ecuador, weakened by the treason of military cabals."[15]

The typical student is not of the people. And though he may criticize the bourgeoisie, he would not care to be mistaken for a peasant or laborer. He believes he has been called to lead the people, but he will make no effort to go to them. In his heart he fears them. Nationalistic activism, under the veneer of leftism, not only gives him a sense of mission but also grants him the "means to satisfy at once his resentments and his need to rise and win social recognition; on the other hand, it calms his fear of being submerged in a mass with which he does not wish to be confused if indeed he is disposed to be identified with it at all."[16]

The "Jacobins"

The most active of the students and those best trained in ideology very often form the nucleus of groups and parties which we can call Jacobin. The adjective has been applied by Robert Alexander to movements that view themselves as leftist, are partisans of violent action, and are well disposed toward a more or less popular dictatorship (pro-Castro, pro-Peking, at times Trotskyist movements and their like). As a description of the psychology of their proponents and even their ideological ingredients, the adjective is appropriate.

But there is one important difference: The original Jacobins believed in what they preached, fought a revolution, and died for it. The "Jacobins" of Latin America preach in order to avoid fighting a revolution. Although it is rarely admitted by anyone, membership in a leftist movement in Latin America is a way to move upward, to become popular, to get certain jobs (in universities, publishing houses, newspapers, the entertainment world, radio and television, even business). And it entails no risk whatsoever. There is no known case of persecution to the death of elements of the Jacobin "left." The populists have suffered much more implacable persecution at the hands of the oligarchy than have the present-day "Jacobins." (It goes without saying that the socialists, unionists, and anarchists suffered them too, in the days before World War I.)

The "Jacobin" movements are not to be confused with Communist-front organizations or fellow-travelers. Often they are anti-Communist in their plans and internal policies, but they try to attract Communists and they support Party members who take pro-Italian or pro-Chinese positions and, sometimes, when the latter break with the Party, gather them in. They are more sympathetic to the Chinese position than to the Russian; they are pro-Castro (though on occasion they may be critical of Castro's policies or consider him a moderate). And they play the Communist game by taking a systematically anti-Yankee position. I must insist on the adverb "systematically," because this feature of the "Jacobin" program, which they share with all groups of this type, bears no relation to U.S. policy; it simply opposes the very existence of the United States. The "Jacobins" are just as anti-Yankee when an Eisenhower holds office as they are when a Kennedy does—and even when the State Department's Latin American policy takes its inspiration from a Goldwater mentality that dares not show itself as such. This anti-Yankeeism may lead to grotesque consequences, as when it deifies a madman like Pedro Albizu Campos (1893–1965) merely because he is anti-Yankee, echoes his paranoid denunciations of "long-distance torture by rays," and forgets that Albizu was pro-Franco and had championed a Fascist regime and a Catholic theocracy for Puerto Rico. Or the "Jacobins" sponsor the oligarchies' campaigns to obtain higher prices for raw materials without bothering to ask for guarantees that such prices shall benefit the people. And because Cheddi Jagan (1918–) is anti-Yankee, they support him in Guyana and forget his racism, even while they condemn racism in the southern United States; yet they give no indication of a willingness to imitate American students by running risks to fight racism in their own countries.

As this is a matter of small movements, of cabals surrounding a sectarian newspaper or person with a bent for dialectic, the "Jacobin" movement reflects faithfully the psychology of its membership, almost entirely middle-class. Only when a movement of this kind can count upon politically trained leaders, usually with a Trotskyist or populist background, does theory turn into action. The Venezuelan guerrilla fighters and terrorists were, and still are, young people led astray by the unfulfilled slogans of Acción Democrática rather than Communists. In Colombia, the guerrilla fighters are exasperated liberals rather than Communists. In Peru, the only people who attempted to fight along with

the peasants belonged to some groups headed by the Trotskyist
Hugo Blanco.

A writer who is sympathetic to the "Jacobins" has characterized
them as people showing

> . . . an ultra-leftism impenetrable to the masses, a tendency to rise too
> far above actuality, and a proclivity for solving socio-economic prob-
> lems without modifying the underlying structures. This tends in-
> evitably toward the loss of the working class and a kind of irrational
> fascination with the horrible that is obsessed by foreign events: the
> Chinese Revolution, the conflict between the U.S.S.R. and the United
> States, and, recently, the revolution in Cuba; their formula for reach-
> ing power is long-range subversion or Castroism. Their groups with
> revolutionary convictions try to destroy the active and operative left
> and, in the face of the impossibility of achieving that (because in real-
> ity they are outside the revolutionary process), become disillusioned
> little by little about their responsibilities, turn bitter, and isolate
> themselves.[17]

Although the "Jacobins" follow a certain tradition in Latin
America, there is a variant form of recent origin. I refer to the
Christian Democrats who follow a "Jacobin" orientation. Ac-
tually, there are Christian Democrats from all classes in Latin
America, ranging from the Chileans, who have adopted many
populist concepts, to those in Mexico who belong to National
Action, a conservative bourgeois party, and to those smaller,
slightly demagogic groups allied with the oligarchy, as in Peru.

The church, which during the colonial period tried to protect
the Indians without ceasing to serve the crown, showed itself
after independence to be a fervent defender of the oligarchic
order. Few were the priests who showed any understanding of
social problems until the twentieth century. In 1893, the Archbishop of Santiago, Mariano Casanova, stated in a pastoral letter
that "poverty is a treasure for the future life, a fertile seed for
the harvest of eternity"; hence the workers should remember that
"they have nothing in this world, but they may have the treasures
of heaven in the next if they bear the privations of their poverty
with Christian resignation."[18] This was the attitude of the church
in Spain, which sent forth a fair number of priests to perform
their office in Latin America. An American Catholic has admitted
that "non-Catholics and even the anti-Catholic forces have proved

more effective in encouraging natural morality during the past hundred years than the Catholic Church."[19]

When, after World War II, the Catholic movements (peasant brotherhoods, labor, etc.) began to gain a certain influence and to found some Catholic parties, and when later they began to receive material support from their German co-religionists and moral support through the encyclicals and policies of Pope John XXIII, the Christian Democrats, especially those of "Jacobin" tendency in the trade unions, had to concentrate on two objectives: to wipe out the memory of the church's past pro-oligarchic attitude (the church itself helped to do this in some countries, such as Peru and Chile, and in certain provinces of Ecuador and Brazil by apportioning out part of its lands), and to attract people who were not already in the populist or democratic union movements into the labor movement. Both objectives induced the Christian Democratic movement to adopt radical, sharply defined attitudes. The Latin American Federation of Christian Trade Unionists became more "leftist" than the Communists and Castroists, and more anti-Yankee than the traditional "Jacobins."* This had a certain logic, and probably the attitude will pass. Meanwhile, it is natural that the Christian Democratic government of Eduardo Frei in Chile should make decisions like the one to resume relations and sign trade agreements with the Sovietized countries, the first being Czechoslovakia.[20] The Christian Democrats have shown in this way that they are as neutral as a socialist-Communist alliance would have been and are proving that they are not "tools of imperialism," as the Communists have called them.

Now, Latin American Catholics have had very little experience in social matters and in organizing for any social struggle. Although they have founded some staff schools, like the Centro Intercultural de Documentación in Cuernavaca, Mexico, and Petropolis, Brazil, and though they have profited from the experience of other countries, they have not succeeded in rising above certain notions that have a leftist ring, actually the prod-

---

* To say that the Federation (Confederación Latinoamericana de Sindicalistas Cristianos or CLASC) *is* Communist is tantamount to abandoning the search for adequate means of countering its "Jacobinism."

ucts of "Jacobin" demagoguery. In a talk over Radio Inca, the Jesuit priest Romeo Luna Victorio advocated holding a plebiscite (an extra-Constitutional measure) to oppose Congress if the latter approved an agrarian-reform law not in conformity with "the canons of the Church."[21] The Archbishop of Lima, Monsignor Leonardo Ballón, proposed a five-point program for immediate social reform: nationalization of big business; producers' cooperatives; high inheritance taxes; reform of business and control for the purpose of coordinating production; and expropriation and distribution of the land.[22] Properly speaking, this program is not a "Jacobin" one; any populist could subscribe to it.

The Christian Democratic movement in Latin America is, in short, still too young, too uncertain of its personality and its ideology to be judged correctly. However, we may say that:

Today the objective of many Latin American intellectuals, among them many of the clerical and lay champions of Catholic social justice, is to solve all problems simply by changing the economic system. . . . In their preoccupation with economic betterment, many of the Peruvian clergy act from basic beliefs that are generally accepted as valid in the United States: that Communism prospers on misery; that if misery were to be made to vanish, Communism would disappear. In Peru, that presumption, broadly based on concepts of economic determinism, is most debatable.[23]

Another characteristic of the "Jacobin" movements is their facility for compromise—a trait found throughout Latin American politics, to be sure, but which has reached its peak with the "Jacobins." The attitude of the Argentine "Jacobins" in accepting the Oganía coup of 1966 is a case in point. At other times, in Brazil, for example, the "Jacobins" cling to their phrases and nationalist slogans but make compromises with the oligarchy that take the form of the most unbridled administrative corruption. An investigatory commission established after the Brazilian military coup in 1964 stated that "proofs of subversion were relatively minor by comparison with those of widespread corruption."[24]

A sad example of this type of Jacobinism is the case of the Colombian socialist Antonio García, one of the most brilliant thinkers of the left, whose new theory of imperialism was at once anti-Communist and anti-oligarchical.[25]

[Imperialism exists] wherever there is the will to annex—whether militarily, financially, or politically—and a consequent replacement of the people's right to self-determination with the right of might. Starting from this elemental and objective idea, we can locate imperialism wherever it may be, without any tactical commitment to any great power; we are seeking the solidarity and support of the people, but especially of all American peoples, beginning with those of the United States. . . . Imperialism is not only a system for conquest or subordination abroad, it is also an internal power system that serves as its base of operations: the springboard for that power system always has been a military or financial oligarchy.

Communist theories on imperialism, García said, have been formulated for the purpose of absolving the Soviet Union of that sin. An understanding of this is necessary to the struggle against imperialism, as is also awareness that it is "stupid to try to know American imperialism through the Russian Communist version of it or to involve the people of the United States in the policy of imperialist subordination." Actual world revolution would entail the "taking up of the nationalist case by the people."

García was using the Latin American political experience, Marxist teachings, and populist concepts to forge an interpretation of Latin America that might have renovated the doctrinal base of nationalism. But, in impatience, he let himself be seduced, as many other "Jacobins" have done, and came to believe that a general, Gustavo Rojas Pinilla (1900–   ), could bring about a social revolution in Colombia. Rojas fell, having done nothing, and García lost his entire following in the country.*

Marxists Without a Proletariat

Except for the aforementioned Justo, Mariátegui, and Aníbal Ponce (1898–1938), Latin America has produced no important Marxist theorists. But never until now has the outlook for their cause seemed so desolate and sterile. There is a swarm of Ph.D. Marxists, to be sure, each the center of his cenacle, little maga-

* Such a mistake is not a special privilege of the "Jacobins." Certain Marxists have also made it, among them the dissident socialists in Argentina who believed in Perón as a revolutionary and the Chilean socialists who expected the former dictator, Carlos Ibáñez, to carry out changes after he had won election by democratic methods. In each case, these Marxists' anti-Marxist hopes were frustrated.

zine, or even party. The Argentine Socialist Party has broken up into six groups; the Uruguayan into four; the Chilean into three. Communist partisans are split into Chinese, Russian, Italian, and even autochthonous factions. Even the Trotskyists are fragmented into rival groups.

Marxism nonetheless saturates Latin American intellectual life. Economists are a mixture of Marxists and Keynesians; sociologists are a mixture of Marxists and behaviorists; politicians, of Marxists and Carlylists (since each of them would like to be the prototype of the hero). Marxism has had a genuine influence on populism, still affects the Christian Democrats, and I suspect that more Marxists can be found among the radicals, conservatives, and Peronists than among the groups that call themselves Marxists. For the latter, pedantry is a substitute for militant action. If verbal Jacobinism provides the "Jacobins" with an excuse to avoid risks which the genuine Jacobins ran, Marxism serves the Marxists as an excuse for avoiding action. Lenin said there is no revolutionary action without revolutionary theory, but for the Latin American Marxists, theory obviates the need for revolutionary action. For the rest, the only difference between the "Jacobins" and Marxists is one of vocabulary: the former's expression of nationalism is taken from the populist lexicon, the latter's from the Marxist.

Monteforte said of this type of Marxism that

Its nationalist focus is upon the progress of society within geopolitical limits. . . . It recognizes that no Ibero-American country possesses the natural and human resources sufficient and ready to leap over stages [of development], especially if their situation within the orbit of the most powerful imperialism that ever existed on earth is taken into account. . . . In greater or lesser degree, nationalist Marxism is influenced by the policy of the so-called neutral bloc.[26]

Of course those "Marxists" never quote what Marx himself said about Bolívar being a reactionary, or justifying the war over Texas, or the conquest of Algiers by the French, or of India by the English, and they have the major handicap of not being able to find even one sentence by Lenin referring to Latin America. Indeed, a "Letter from Lenin to the Mexican Workers," circulated in 1919 as written by Lenin about Mexico, was really a paraphrase, or falsification, put out by the first Mexican Communists of the "Letter from Lenin to the [North] American Workers."[27]

Most of the "Marxists" are young people from the middle class; they do not know the labor movement or the proletariat and have no personal contact with it. Yet their behavior is more dynamic, impassioned, and dogmatic than that of the "Jacobins." Possibly some of them might be ready to drop their pedantry and take up arms if the hour for action should strike.

A young Argentinian thus explained how he discovered "Marxism":

When September 16 [the date of Perón's downfall] came around, I had just turned twenty. The Peronist "process" was something I had lived through by indirect experience—my parents' experience. A typical petit bourgeois liberal home which had profited objectively from Perón's political economy, but which had rejected it absolutely on the ideological level. . . . So, as a large portion of the university youth, or those simply from the middle class, had embarked upon conspiracies against the "dictatorship," I, like the rest of that youth, nourished myself on the motheaten sterility of treatises on law or on the far-off profundity of Greek philosophy. While General Lonardi [leader of the forces that ousted Perón] delivered his address, I was in the Plaza de Mayo with the girl who was then my fiancée and is now my wife, listening to the [speech]. . . . There, as I waved a little Argentine flag, I took the first active position of my own in politics. . . . A surprising uneasiness stirred in me. I decided to take a good look at those who were in the plaza. It was not difficult to sort them out. They were fat ladies, my parents' friends, and students. It was useless to look for the workers. They were not there. In the afternoon as we were leaving the center of the city and going through the rich north district, we were aware of dark, suspicious, angry looks. The people, the authentic people, were enduring their defeat.

As usual, my reaction was intellectual. I decided to read, "to soak myself" in revolutionary thought. Simultaneously, I kept drawing nearer to the Radical Party groups pledged to Frondizi. There were many like me. The experience was short-lived but it went deep. That was a party without a revolutionary potential, and we wanted to accomplish an authentic revolution. In those days we attended at least six "foundings" of potential "parties," each more "revolutionary" than the last. We quarreled learnedly over the Russian and Chinese revolutions and believed that insurrection was a task for professional specialists.

We decided, on that account, to join the Communist Party. We were not unaware of the criticisms made of its obtuse and antinational trajectory. We knew about its internal life through reports by "expelled" members. But in spite of all that, we joined. Perhaps our motivations differed. I recall my own exactly. It was one of total "rebellion" against the world of my education; it was "sacrifice" for the "revolution." I signed my membership card in a well-known confectionery in the northern quarter, curiously decorated by a grotesque print of Don Bernardino Rivadavia. When we signed up, we felt that we were "Leninist" enough to be able to change the Party's orientation "from within," to convert it effectively into a revolutionary party. The experience was brief and instructive. In my case, the one positive lesson was that the crushing apparatus of the little parlor-pink party could not work. It never performed the usual "oedipal" and "deforming" function.[28]

This not exceptional case reveals the great ideological void that existed in Latin America. The young man's confession appears as a prologue to an edition of the book he mentions by Hernández Arregui, one of the theorists of a "national left," a form of Latin American Marxism he defines thus:

The expression "national left" applied in a dependent country should be understood in a broad sense as the general theory applied to a concrete national case that is analyzed in the light of Marxism. Meanwhile, it is a method for interpreting reality, bearing in mind the peculiarities and the development of each country: the economy, history, and culture of its national, defensive and revolutionary entity. Also, it coordinates such a technical analysis with the practical struggle of the masses against imperialism on a three-fold level: the national, the Latin American, and the world, in this order.

Another exponent of this "Marxist" nationalism is Jorge Abelardo Ramos. He is beyond a doubt one of the few thinkers who took Marxism seriously, but he reveals even more plainly the theoretical malnutrition of a "Marxism" which, though it strives to be so national, does no more than mix imported formulas with outworn ones:

The hour has struck for restoring the maimed tradition . . . of democratic, revolutionary nationalism. . . . The present favorable juncture derives not from our capitalistic development but from the world crisis of the capitalist system, which pre-sets an authentic occasion for the national revolution, which has been deprived since May 1, 1810, of its fullest Bolivarian expression, which served only to hasten the dispersion and Balkanization of Spanish America under the pressure of the great industrial powers that have reduced us to reserve trading-posts and purveyors of raw materials.[29]

Clichés have such great force among the "Marxists" that they can sterilize any Marxist effort to find Latin American solutions to Latin American problems. Consider the unrealistic statements of Silvio Frondizi:

It is no longer a question of carrying out the democratic-bourgeois revolution as a self-contained stage, but [a question] of accomplishing bourgeois-democratic tasks in the course of socialist revolution. . . . Although the agrarian revolution is of vital importance, it is not important in its own function but in the struggle against imperialism and in our industrialization; this makes the participation of the peasantry in the Argentine revolution of much less significance than in Czarist Russia.[30]

Revolution, to Silvio Frondizi, has a basically nationalistic objective: "Let us look particularly at what will be the tasks of the new society. First and foremost, the struggle against imperialism. . . . In conjunction with the anti-imperialist struggle, and as one of its manifestations, it will be necessary to solve the grave problems that hinder the industrial and agrarian development of the country."

It is significant that the Marxism I have described has flourished best in Argentina, a country with a socialist tradition that is going through a far-reaching political crisis it inherited from a demagogic dictatorship, a crisis aggravated by the intellectual inadequacies of an uncompromising oligarchy and the conversion of the greater part of the armed forces into a police force. But we find it in Chile too, both within and without the Socialist Party. Oscar Waiss, a socialist who left his party, explains his nationalistic conception of socialism thus: "The Communists and the Yankees play the same dirty game of waiting for their chance to win the game and to be left alone to gobble up the continent without interference. . . . Socialism's mission in Latin America is not just to emancipate the laboring and farming classes, but also to win national and continental independence from imperialist control."[31]

The present theorists of Chilean socialism are in fact the only Marxist groups with a certain political strength, although it is not certain whether it is their own or whether they have gained it through alliance with the Communists. One Chilean socialist admitted that they had been unable to infiltrate the working class: "The electoral stagnation among workers and slum-dwellers reflects, in our judgment, a structural and evaluational situation which thus far has not been made clearly manifest. It might be defined as a basic condition of depoliticalization." [32] But if the Chilean working class is "depoliticized," it is because the "Marxists" have been unable to find words to win them over or slogans and programs to keep alive its interest in politics. In addition, the Marxists have made another implicit admission: "We socialists must oppose another concept of nationalism to the chauvinistic and reactionary one the right has used. We must manage to build a dynamic vision of nationalism and transform it, if the facts so demand, into the nucleus of a global strategy." Evidently, they have not known how to set their own concept of nationalism against the nationalism of the right. Or perhaps the problem is that their "dynamic vision"—which, in fact, separated them from the Chilean workers—was really the same as the rightists'. But the lesson has not been learned.

As I have said, this kind of Marxism creates a situation in which clichés obscure reality. For instance, a "Marxist" has argued that when Salvador Allende, in his political campaign of 1964 (supported by socialists and Communists), came out for the nationalization of copper, he alienated the vote of the miners who did not want nationalization because "foreign companies give them special wages and loan services." Now, to atone for such a daringly realistic remark, the writer hastened to add, "After all, simple 'nationalization' is a bourgeois program"—as if that would matter to the miners if they thought that nationalization would benefit them! And this cliché-ridden "Marxism" can become so far removed from reality that it begets major errors, like this one, admitted by the same writer quoted above: "It is very interesting to note that for the first time in Chilean history, since the beginning of the century, a president could rise [to office] by an absolute majority and do so when the people of the left believed they were going to win. This mistake seems unexpected, and it reveals that we know very little about what is going to happen, that we make incredible mistakes." [33]

The Chilean case gave some of the Marxists cause to ponder.

A Mexican Marxist says that Allende "carried out his campaign within the general plan of tropical Latin American leftists"; that is, the campaign was "an encounter between the two ways of conceiving national development and its revolutionary acceleration: one [that of Frei] sees revolutionary elements in the realities themselves; the other [Allende's] denies reality, condemns it, and demands a change in it whenever there is room [for change]."[34] Another Marxist put it this way after the defeat of Castroism in the Venezuelan elections of 1964:

[To achieve] the supreme objectives of structural change, the leaders, in addition to being ideologically inconsistent and lacking in sincerity, have not succeeded in measuring the full extent of the enemy forces: the latifundists, the bosses, foreign investors, Creole capitalists, the Army, the foreign-affairs ministry, the clergy, and various other sectors that resist them or threaten to endanger their illusory security. If one stops to think about such things, he reaches the conclusion that among the many enemies that have brought about the wreck or postponement of structural changes in the country, either by way of peace or armed might, are the ideological inconsistency and the consequent insincerity of many of the leaders who have preached such changes.[35]

The Schizophrenia of the Bourgeoisie

Industry came to Latin America thirty to fifty years later than it did to Europe, and capital development in Latin America occurred very slowly, as a marginal aspect of latifundism. The high bourgeoisie either submitted to the oligarchy or became its ally, though on occasion during boom times it showed flickers of independence. Meanwhile, as was logical, a middle class, which tried to assert its independence, was beginning to take shape. With time, as we have seen, improvement in its living conditions led this middle class to accept the existing social structure and to try only gently to change it instead of, as before, to alter it more radically. Nowadays, in some countries, it has achieved a certain degree of participation in government. But to participate in power is not the same thing as to have power. The time came when the middle class, and the bourgeoisie in general, faced a dilemma: either it must arouse the submerged masses in order, with them, to destroy the power of the oligarchy and create a capitalist society; or it must make an effort, from within the oligarchic society, to win control of the government. The old, traditional bourgeoisie preferred the latter way. But the new, young bourgeoisie, educated abroad, the product of a speeded-up industrialization, favored planning and social reform and had not resigned itself to sharing control with the oligarchy: it wanted power for itself. But that young bourgeoisie believed that democracy had failed to accelerate development and create stability. They had so often heard the myth of Latin America's vocation for freedom, the oligarchic governments had so thoroughly "sold" them on the idea that they were democratic governments, that they could not but conclude, since Latin American development has been deficient under this free democratic system, that they must now turn to other than democratic means to achieve success. Amid the general political hypocrisy, no one pointed out to them that Latin America has vainly tried everything—paternalism, demagoguery, statism, private initiative, and so on—*but* genuine democracy.

This young bourgeoisie, influenced somewhat by the "Jacobins" and "Marxists," is growing impatient. It needs efficiency to shape it; for stimulation, it requires social reforms that will provide markets for its industry; and, intellectually, it wants to use "energetic" methods to achieve its ends. As an Arab nationalist, Albert Hourani, has said, "Our fathers would have stressed the 'superiority of European [political] institutions and morale' as a standard to measure up to if they wished to achieve independence, whereas the present generation . . . think[s] of this problem first of all in terms of 'heavy industry, technology, and the scientific aptitudes that make these possible.' "[36]

The old bourgeoisie viewed anything that might tend to transform society as "exotic," "foreign to the environment." The new bourgeoisie, on the other hand, regards as pernicious anything that does not imitate foreign methods, although that does not keep them from professing an intense economic nationalism. (They share this with many Europeans, Asians, even Americans who live and work in Latin America. Not infrequently the fiercest anti-Yankees are upper-middle-class Americans who have settled in Latin America, own a small or medium-sized company, and do not intend to return to the United States.) At times, this nationalism assumes bizarre forms. In Mexico, for instance, long arguments took place over the choice of cycle in the national electric system. One engineer remarked that, as things were, the following equations seemed to have been established: "American imperialism, 60 cycles per second; European imperialism and the Soviet countries, 50 cycles per second. For Mexico, which follows the politics of neither, probably the most suitable choice would be 55 cycles, or 50 *and* 60 cycles."[37]

As I have said, the new bourgeoisie is in a schizophrenic situation, torn between the people and the oligarchy, between social reform and profit-making. We find an expression of this division in the attitude taken on prices for raw materials. The new bourgeoisie insists on obtaining trade terms favorable to the oligarchy's products because a portion of the profit goes into their pockets. Yet they realize that as the profits do not reach the people, their own profit is less than it would be if a mechanism could be set up by means of which higher prices would result in greater buying power for peasants and laborers, bureaucrats, and white-collar workers. For example, the United States buys 90 per cent of Latin America's coffee crop. If Americans had to pay ten cents more per pound, coffee would cost the American consumer less than an additional $3 a year, but the Latin American coffee producers would receive $350 million more a year. Of that, a bare $50 million would trickle back to potential Latin American consumers. The new bourgeoisie wants a higher price—that is, the extra $350 million—but it also wants *all* the money to reach potential domestic buyers.[38] As it happened, "toward 1959–60, it seems that a period intervened when prices fell sharply; in 1960, a measure of stability began to be evident, which turned into a rise in prices of most Latin American export products for 1961–63, especially in the second half of 1963, although the price of sugar already had risen before that."[39] The U.N. Economic Commission for Latin America, which for years had hammered away insistently on business problems but had not worried about Latin America's social structure, even though its technical experts had a clear social consciousness, now reflected the contradictory views of the new bourgeoisie and began to deal with social questions. This may well (if unintentionally) reflect the bourgeoisie's increasing inclination to look for clear-cut solutions that would emancipate it from the oligarchy and at the same time not force it to turn the government over to the people.

The new bourgeoisie is divided on another question, that of foreign investment. Despite its realization that, to create new industries of any importance, foreign capital is essential (since the local exporters of raw materials also export a large share of their earnings), the new bourgeoisie mistrusts foreign investments, especially if they come from the United States, because they fear being squeezed out. They are intensely protectionist, too, in opposition to Washington's over-all trade policy; but the stoutest ally it can find here is the *American* investor—who, having put his money into foreign enterprise, is eager for tariff protection that will help him to make a rapid profit. In Venezuela, when on March 25, 1965, the Chamber of Deputies passed a law requiring 51 per cent of the capital of all insurance firms to be Venezuelan—a kind of measure, in force for decades in Mexico, which has been spreading gradually throughout Latin America— it was opposed by a strongly protectionist group of businessmen called "Pro Venezuela"!

A cause of major distrust concerning North American investments is not so much the fear that foreign investors will intervene directly in domestic politics, as the fear that they will exert pressure in Washington and make the United States Government, in turn, bring pressure to bear in favor of certain Latin American measures. The time has passed when United Fruit, Grace, and other American firms can make and unmake Latin American governments. But the time has not passed when they can enlist the aid of an Attorney General and send him to Brazil to extract the "indemnification due" a telephone company affiliated with International Telephone and Telegraph for the expropriation of its holdings. (After all these pressures, and a savage campaign in the United States, payment of the indemnity was effected. Hubert Humphrey, then a Senator, remarked on the Senate floor that so much money had been squeezed out of the Brazilians that even the company felt "embarrassed."[40])

It is because of things like this that each time American intervention on behalf of a U.S. enterprise gets out of bounds, *all* U.S.

investments in Latin America are endangered. Suspicion increases when a veritable civil war is unleashed, as in the Dominican Republic, to serve the interests of a few investors or would-be investors. There, real estate left by Trujillo, which his sons and daughters had been unable to carry off—sugar mills, plantations, factories, etc.—accounted for approximately one-third of the country's entire economy. The oligarchy, which served Trujillo but did not share in his rule, had expected to be able to divide up these properties, but the PRD won the elections after Trujillo's downfall, and Juan Bosch (1909–   ), the new president, announced that the property would be placed under state ownership. In September, 1963, a *coup d'état* took place with the hidden motive of seizing these properties and distributing them among the oligarchy, putting the latter in control of the government. But Donald Reid Cabral, who eventually set up a dictatorial regime, proposed instead to sell them at low prices to Dominican-American companies. A protest arose. He did not dare to make any sales immediately, but he hoped to become president and do it "legally." When in April, 1965, a coup to overthrow him in turn became, under pressure from the people, a movement to restore the constitution, the groups who had been negotiating with Reid Cabral over the Trujillo properties realized their opportunity would vanish if the PRD should return to office. Accordingly, they arranged it so that American press agencies would spread exaggerated or twisted reports of a supposed Communist influence behind the constitutionalist movement. Thanks to those reports, which kept snowballing, they succeeded in invoking U.S. intervention "to prevent a Communist take-over." The result has been that there are more Communists than ever in the Dominican Republic, that the United States has jeopardized its entire Latin American policy and has spent more money on the intervention than the aspirants who wanted the Trujillo properties stood to gain. And it cost several American soldiers and hundreds of Dominicans their lives.

In the face of such occurrences, the uneasiness of the Latin American bourgeoisie is understandable. One of their best known figures, Carlos Trouyet of Mexico, advisor to two banks and five of the country's major firms, said:

We are totally opposed to direct foreign investments. Let financial aid come [as] foreign investment in companies with Mexican capital. Direct investment, no. The time has passed when colonialist and feudal capital could damage our economy with impunity. . . . Of what interest is it to an English investor, for example, to put his money into Mexico for the purpose of contributing to her development? The Englishman invests, then he collects his dividends and goes off to spend them—where? In England. No, we need capital associated with our own capital, which will be reinvested in Mexico. For only continuous reinvestment is favorable to a country's effective economic development.[41]

It may be safely said that what Mexico is doing today in the matter of investment, the other Latin American countries will be doing tomorrow. Mexico's stability offers an example that many of them are trying to imitate—albeit without taking into account that there was a revolution in Mexico, a basic land reform and abolition of the old oligarchy, and a move to save the country from militarism. To be sure, Mexico has used other means by which to obtain attractive foreign capital. These have been summed up by the Secretary of the Treasury, Antonio Ortiz Mena, in the following terms:

1. We are a country still in a very primitive stage of development. We must import a great part of what we need in order to grow more rapidly—especially machinery. We are not a country that can produce [it], and the new industries have a basic need of it.

2. In order to pay for machinery abroad, as well as for the industrial equipment that rapid economic development requires, it is not enough to sell abroad part of our production of goods and services; capital in flow is needed, too—that is to say, direct investments and foreign credits.

3. This foreign capital has to be paid for in installments, like the utilities and similar interests. In order to do this, the importation of more capital from abroad would suffice. The amounts obtained should be greater than that which has to be paid so that the rest of it may be used to import machinery and other investment bonds.

4. This financial policy means a constantly growing foreign debt owed by our country. But that does not imply any danger, because the nation will keep growing, economically, and will always be able to keep up its payments on the loans.

5. This means that if Mexico owes $1,000 million while growing at the rate and in the way we are [now,] she soon will be able to owe $2,000 million, and it would be stupid of us to be content with $1,000

million when we can use $2,000 million. . . . To believe that the public debt should decline in a developing country would be tantamount to believing that brakes should be put on development. . . . Debt not only does no damage, it is very healthy when used well.

6. This financial policy has another great advantage in that it eliminates the possibility that the Mexican currency might be devalued, for even though the level of the balance of trade may drop, even though the tourist trade and other service [industries] may not be enough to restore the balance, and even though the cost of amortization and interest on small business firms may increase constantly, still the total of new foreign credits will be great enough to keep the payments in balance.[42]

In the United States, there is frequent talk of the fear that the Latin American countries may nationalize American industries. Actually, Washington's "new" Latin American policy, adopted by Washington in 1965, seems to be directed by a negative tropism to nationalization and to measures that might constrict free enterprise and private initiative, although this is hidden behind various forms of anti-Communism, none of which accords with the present realities. The nationalization of industries in Latin America has none of the earmarks of revolution; actually, it comes in the context of a long tradition, inherited from the colonial period, of state interventionism and management, and it has meant only state control. The Latin American economy, whether under the Incas and Aztecs, the Spaniards and Portuguese, or later (and now) the oligarchy, has always been directed, limited, and controlled—sometimes by the state, sometimes by the oligarchy, or sometimes (in the smaller countries) even by foreign investors. Pressure from the State Department cannot change this tradition, nor can a Marine landing.

The semantic confusion that surrounds nationalism has two sources. The first is the prestige of the term, derived from socialist literature, especially from the nationalization of industries in France by Léon Blum in 1936 and by the Labour Party in England between 1945 and 1951. The second is the fact that, when a nation is not authentic and complete, the state is taken for the nation and hence what is really *state* seizure is called *nation*alization. All this has meant that only a narrow margin exists between economic absurdities like Perón's "nationalization" of the Argentine telephone service, and such moves as Mexico's nationaliza-

tion of the oil and electrical industries, which were of great benefit to the country.

The important point, in fact, is not whether a company is
owned by national or foreign capital, but whether it is owned by
private or public capital. Thus, to "nationalize" a company
should mean to place it in the service of the national society, to
make it legally the property of society, through a process that
varies for each country. Nationalization of industry, in the traditional meaning of the term, consists of turning over to society the
ownership of certain companies, whether they are national or
foreign. In the view of false Latin American nationalists, however, nationalization of industry has meant turning over to the
capitalists of a country the ownership of companies previously
under foreign ownership.

This leads to the conclusion that what is called nationalization
of industry in Latin America is devoid of any tinge of revolution
—that is, of opposition to the oligarchies—so long as it is not preceded by nationalization of the land, by the granting of land
directly to the country's citizens. The oligarchies are not ad-
versely affected if the mines, the oil industry, the electrical or
railroad companies are nationalized, since such nationalization
is merely a change of ownership; indeed, through manipulation
of state machinery, the oligarchs may even become the new
owners. The screams of indignation that echo all over the United
States each time American companies in Latin America are
nationalized may come from people whose purses are affected,
but they cannot express any ideological uneasiness, for the property remains as sacred as it was before.

What happened after the landing of American Marines in the
Dominican Republic in April, 1965, demonstrates that the incor-
rectly labelled nationalizations of industry are empty of revolutionary content. The very Latin American governments that
are always ready to appease their bogus leftists by nationalizing
everything but the land had at their disposal a sure-fire means to
force the Marines to withdraw. They had only to announce that
if the troops did not leave within twenty-four hours after foreigners were evacuated, American-owned property in the country
would be seized. But the oligarchic governments' action was lim-

ited to a resolution by the Organization of American States that did not even demand withdrawal of the Marines or restoration of the invaded Dominican Republic's poor representative democracy.[43] The nonoligarchic governments refused to vote for that shameful resolution, but by themselves they could not put effective pressure on Washington. Nationalization of industry was thus not used at a time when it would really have made sense. It is kept simply as a means of obtaining some small advantages for the oligarchy or to soothe the "leftists." It is not used to protect the people.

It is logical, and need surprise no one, that the bourgeoisie, especially the younger bourgeoisie, are anti-Yankee and believe that that is the way to be nationalistic. On the one hand, in American industry and investment they see competitors with the advantage over them. On the other, they see the difference between what the big American companies preach and what they practice—indeed, those companies that in the United States often finance extreme right-wing anti-Communist campaigns, prefer, as I have said, to deal in Latin America with trade unions dominated by Communists because such unions are less demanding than the free ones.*

The "new" U.S. policy in Latin America has recreated a situation, absent for several years, that breeds new worries among the younger management levels who had known their elders' anxieties only by hearsay and never by personal experience. Ever since a few months after President Kennedy's assassination, American capital has been conducting a general offensive in Latin America, its strategy being either to acquire stock and thus force a partnership with American capital, or to obtain tariff exemptions and other advantages for more American companies. The result has been doubly catastrophic: there will be much more private American capital in Latin America than ever before, and, often, it will

---

* This attitude on the part of certain American companies has its imitators. The Association of Metallurgical Industrialists in Chile called upon its members to subscribe to aid for the victims of an earthquake, and published the list of contributors in the Communist newspaper *El Siglo* of Santiago.[44] No doubt the steel executives thought they would earn the good will of the Communists when the time came to renew their work contracts, and perhaps they were not mistaken.

be privileged capital. This means that there will be more companies to "nationalize," hence more grounds for friction and conflict, more possibilties of discovering crypto-Communists. Furthermore, the Latin American bourgeoisie, never before aggressive,
is beginning to be angry. It is turning into what the Communists
call a "national bourgeoisie," and regards foreign capital as its
chief enemy.

The "new" American policy-makers are confident, no doubt,
that in countries where the expanse of territory is too great to
make a Marine landing practicable, they can count on some local
generals being willing to protect American investment if it is
threatened by the anger of the "national bourgeoisie." But that,
as we shall see, becomes less likely every day. For though the
"Jacobins" and Marxists have not succeeded in reaching the people, and the anti-Yankee bourgeoisie does not want to, yet all
these groups are ready to turn to the army to give effect to a
policy ridding them of their competitors. And the army grows
more willing by the day to be seduced by them.

Leninist Military Men

Latin American armies have a two-fold history: one of efficiency in policing the interests of the oligarchies, and of occupying their own countries when needed; and one of total ineptitude
as an instrument for the defense of their nations' territories.

Each time that a populist movement seems to be gaining
strength, each time that it succeeds in having socially progressive
legislation passed, the army stages a coup under the pretext of
defending public order, or "civilization," and sets up a dictatorship. This kind of militarism gave way, immediately after World
War II, to a demagogic militarism, inspired by European Fascist
techniques, that seized power under the pretext of serving the
public interest (viz., Vargas and Perón).[45] But these demagogic
military regimes, although they may have granted some concessions to the trade unions, failed to modify the Latin American
social structure. (It is precisely because they never had any serious
intention of modifying it that they merit the adjective demagogic.) They have been succeeded by a new generation of officers,

better trained, better educated, and more oriented to technology and organization; these young officers may be the germinus of a new, still more dangerous type of militarism.[46]

The Latin American armies, as they stand today, do not perform their basic and unique function of defending the nation's territory: first of all, the nation's territory is not being threatened; and second, the armies are not equipped to carry on a defensive continental war. They have never drawn up plans for the evacuation of the big cities or for the protection of the civil population in case of an attack on the continent. But today we are entering upon a new stage. In Colombia, the Minister of War, Major General Alberto Ruiz Novoa, had to be removed from his command in 1965 because he was making demagogic promises, even as he was slowing up the army's action against the guerrillas, in the hope of acquiring a halo as a leftist or perhaps of using the guerrillas for his own ends. In Bolivia, another general, René Barrientos, when he was vice president, headed a coup in 1964 "to restore the revolution" and, after liquidating his allies, had himself elected president. In Brazil, some old-style generals arranged a coup, also in 1964, to do away with the "Jacobins" who had served the oligarchy when the latter had gone to such extremes that it seemed impossible to avoid the passage of social legislation. These coups, like those in Peru in 1962 and Ecuador in 1963, show signs of the new militarism. Only the coups in Honduras and the Dominican Republic (1963) were accompanied by barracks-style pronouncements. The Argentine coup of 1966 was in large measure prodded by the business world, and one of its first acts was to give the private banks control of the public credit unions.

Still, the armies are divided, their morale undermined. Whereas the old soldiers believe in the mailed fist, the stiff back, and the "virtues" of the club, the younger ones realize that the army has lost all social prestige and that its officers have lost respect. They realize that the army must represent something else besides the oligarchy if it is to be effective, and they would like to reclaim it.

The young soldiers admire most the efficiency of modern business techniques. But at the same time they have learned other lessons. They have studied Leninism and learned from it techniques of propaganda and organizing the move to power. They admire Nasser and other army men who have emerged in developing countries, and they believe that they spell progress. (Theories involving the need to seize power in order to bring about a "revolution from above" keep appearing in nearly all the Latin American armies; their proponents call it Nasserism. Some groups feel a great admiration for the U.S.S.R.) They are on the side of social reform—since they realize that without it they cannot win prestige or succeed in fulfilling a function that would socially justify their existence—but they have no faith in the ability of democratic movements to achieve it, believing that democracy has been a failure in Latin America and that other means must be sought to accelerate development. And there is a consistent anti-Yankeeism among the young men in arms, even though many were trained in the United States and abetted in their ambitions by the Pentagon.*

Perhaps the best summary of the disparate theoretical elements in this new militarism—which I call technocratic militarism— has been given by the Argentine "Jacobin" Rogelio García Lupo.[47] He has reproached Washington for looking askance at Argentina's neutrality in both world wars, and argued that the reason the Argentine bourgeoisie supported Perón and wanted a resumption of diplomatic relations with the U.S.S.R. was that it was unfriendly to its opposite number in the United States. The Argentine industrial bourgeoisie was interested in directing its business toward the East and away from Washington. Therefore the army was in duty bound to implement this trend and to carry out social reforms that would give the upper middle class the capability of making the country great.

Since the new armies' objectives coincide with those of the younger members of the bourgeoisie, the joining of the two forces is almost inevitable. It is also logical to suppose that the

---

* Anti-Yankeeism is not exclusive with any one shade of public opinion. A Central American military man, a member of a government strongly supported by the United States, said to a specialist a short time ago: "I am opposed to birth control in spite of the fact that my country is overpopulated. The good thing about [overpopulation] is that by the year 2000 there will be two Latin Americans for every Gringo." Merely an anecdote? Yes, but told me by a "friend of the United States" who has a government job.

frustrated intellectuals will join them—the "Jacobins" and "Marxists" who are ready to support the military if they can prove their dynamic qualities—as they earlier supported Perón.

The real "Communist threat" in Latin America no longer means the threat of a Communist seizure of power. It comes, rather, from the new technocratic militarism, as few except the Communists themselves, of course, seem to realize. The new militarists may try to impose reforms from above, paternalistically, and without the collaboration of the people. Impelled by their nationalism, they will want to capitalize in the Soviet manner, and then will need Communist aid to organize and "propagandize" the masses for the purpose of persuading them to make the necessary sacrifices (since the Communists are really the only people in Latin America who have mastered totalitarian techniques of organization and propaganda; they have already proved their effectiveness at this job in Cuba). The middle class, the intellectuals, and the students, who consider themselves very revolutionary today, would support them, knowing that they would not be the ones who would have to work harder, earn less, and "capitalize" their own toil.

Communist "National Democracy"

The theory of national democracy adopted by the Communists for colonial and semi-colonial countries does not seem to have been very effective in the past. But now it is finding an attentive audience in Latin America because it is saying what people there want to hear. The audience is composed of the militarist-technocrats and technocratic-militarists whom I have just described, and a not inconsiderable number of "Jacobins" and Marxists as well. They are offered a theoretical justification for their self-interest and at the same time a pretext for ignoring the people.

In a "Declaration of the Eighty-one Communist and Labor Parties" (Moscow, November, 1960), a new strategy was adopted that now figures in the program of the CPSU and of most Latin American Communist parties. It bids the Communists struggle for the "establishment of national democratic states"—in other words, for regimes, whatever their grade of real or pretended democracy, that not only permit all kinds of Communist activity but also give the Communists a decisive voice in the government, in anticipation of the moment at which, to suit the purposes of the U.S.S.R., they would move on to "popular democracy en route to socialism," etc.

But who is going to set up this "national democracy"? The Communists, of course, not through the proletariat or the workers' and peasants' leagues, as anyone would have said forty years ago, but through the middle classes, as they did in Cuba, according to a Soviet writer:

In the persistent ideological struggle, the advanced forces of the Cuban people have defeated the right compromising wing of the petty bourgeoisie, which had attempted to paralyze the revolutionary movement and to impede the anti-imperialist policy of nationalization and the creation of an independent economy. At present even broader strata of the petty bourgeoisie and the intelligentsia are becoming convinced that only in a free independent Cuba do they have full opportunities for utilizing their creative forces and knowledge.[48]

The Communist attitude to this *petite bourgeoisie* has been well described by Ramón López, of the Communist Party in Colombia:

The petty bourgeoisie is an intermediate class between the bourgeoisie and the proletariat. Its ideology is not and cannot be neatly differentiated from that of the bourgeoisie. In semi-colonial and dependent countries, the petty bourgeoisie has the peculiarity of being more radical, because in addition to being exploited by the bourgeoisie, it bears on its shoulders the exploitation of the monopolistic great landholders, and imperialist oppression. This explains its desperation, its impatience for a change in the social structure. But it may be stated categorically that it is not a class in process of development, it is not a class on the rise. On the contrary, it is politically unstable owing to its ideological closeness to the bourgeoisie. Only that sector of it that comes under the influence of the working class and its ideology is capable of cutting its mooring lines to the bourgeoisie and of allying itself more solidly with the cause of the proletariat.[49]

Lombardo Toledano lay the cards on the table when he said: "The elements of the petty bourgeoisie are faced with the dilemma of joining the cause of the working class or that of the bourgeoisie and imperialism. The Communists refuse to give the middle class the initiative because they intend to use the middle class as a ladder to power, after which they will eliminate it as

a class by making it a part of the proletariat. The petty bourgeoisie is not the class that has been summoned to play the role
of leadership in the revolution."[50]

On the slogan "National Democratic State," there is little difference between Moscow and Peking. The difference rests, most
of all, on the Soviet and Chinese appraisals of Latin America
actuality. To those in Moscow, this is a field for a legalistic
struggle; to those in Peking, it is not. The former show a dis-
position to negotiate and bargain with Washington over Communist advances in Latin America in order to obtain concessions
elsewhere and establish a state of co-existence. The latter do not
accept this possibility—for the time being.

To sum up, then, the nationalism that certain bourgeois groups
use as an opium for their conscience leads, by more or less tor-
tuous courses, to those groups being used by the Communists,
and to conditions that permit them to keep their privileges and
even add to them.

8

Great Nation or Little Countries?

Six Propositions

Let us recapitulate my thesis:

A. Why did Spanish America, richer and better organized in 1810 than the poorer and more backward United States, fail to maintain its strength *vis-à-vis* the northern country? Because in Latin America there was an oligarchy that prevented the countries there from evolving into nations. This is still true, although isolated instances may tell of progress and change.

B. Latin American society is composed of an "upper" layer, which I call that of public opinion, composed of the oligarchs and their lackeys, the bourgeoisie, the middle class, the professional people, the intellectuals and specialized workers, who are growing in number and whose standard of living is constantly rising; and a great submerged mass, on the fringe of political life and, to some degree, on the fringe of the commercial economy. So long as the latter is not incorporated into the social and political life of Latin America, so long as it does not really participate in government, the Latin American countries will not be nations.

C. The landholding oligarchy hinders this integration of the submerged mass and, at the same time, continues to attract to itself the other sectors of public opinion, as their living conditions improve, and to draw them away from their essential mission of arousing the submerged mass, organizing it, and making it a participant in politics. The oligarchy, then, is the great obstacle to the Latin American countries' conversion to nationhood.

D. A collective schizophrenia afflicts public opinion. The *modus vivendi* bears no relation to the *modus scribendi* of the intellectuals or the *modus operandi* of the bourgeoisie, professionals, or organized proletariat. Public opinion turns to nationalism to offset the effects of this schizophrenia. The various forms of nationalism have in common anti-Yankee sentiment and the fact that they constitute an excuse for doing nothing to help the people. The populist movements, the trade unions related to them, and the Christian Democrats (in certain countries) are the only exceptions to this general rule. But they, too, keep moving further from the people, because the middle class and a part of the laboring class, from which they draw their strength, conform more closely every day to the oligarchic system and find consolation for their conformity in nationalistic attitudes.

E. This negative type of nationalism, together with the obsession with efficiency shown by the younger bourgeoisie and certain military groups, could lead to a new type of technocratic militarism that would ask ultimately for Communist collaboration, and this situation constitutes the most serious form of the "Communist threat."

F. In sum, so long as the people have neither voice nor vote, so long as the oligarchy is not abolished (by means of land reform and other equally *political* measures), it will be impossible to establish authentic democracy in Latin America—economic, social, *or* political—and Latin America will have neither stability nor general progress. The current brand of nationalism in Latin America is an obstacle to progress, for there can be no true progress unless the people produce it. This nationalism is harmful to the Latin American people because it has abandoned them, and harmful to the United States because it is systematically anti-Yankee regardless of what policy the United States may adopt. Accordingly, it would be as much to the advantage of the Latin American peoples as it would be to the United States as a nation (though not to certain American business interests) if the Latin American countries were to become true nations.

Where Is the Revolution?

At first glance, it might seem that such a situation, rife with social tensions and psychological contrarieties, ought to lead to what the journalists and instant experts call the "coming revolution in Latin America." But is that the case? It is humiliating that, in order to convince Americans—and their legislators—that their country should collaborate in Latin America's social transformation, one must use the blackmail of a "Communist threat" and say that if there is not a peaceful revolution there will be a violent one. And it is shameful that the oligarchies, in order to obtain loans, aid, and higher prices for their raw materials, use a plea they know to be false, and argue that revolution will surely occur unless they are aided to become richer and richer at the expense of their own countrymen and the people of the United States.

The oligarchies know there is no such threat; if there were, they would already have yielded to it and a series of land reforms would be under way in Latin America. Those who wanted a revolution in the past have renounced all thought of it (though they go on talking about it). The common people themselves have not the faintest notion of the possibility of revolution; they have no idea that they have any rights and do not even imagine that during the Kennedy administration the United States was their potential ally. (Not even the Kennedy administration dared to go directly to the people.) Only the people of the United States believed in the possibility with any conviction, and only during the Kennedy administration.

Lenin said that a revolution requires three prior conditions: that the dominant class be in a state of decay, that the people be aware that they can improve their lot by revolution, and that there be an organization capable of directing it. None of those conditions prevails in Latin America today. The landholding oligarchy is not in a state of decay. The people live on the verge of social unrest, but no one has preached revolution to them (not even the Castroists, except in small isolated centers). And there are no strong groups yearning for revolutions.

One conclusive proof of the falsity of the threat of revolution —or, better, the hope of revolution—lies in the events of April, 1965, in the Dominican Republic.[1] There is no question but that if there had been the will to revolution or even a sincere anti-imperialist sentiment or an honest anti-Yankee obsession, this would have necessitated adoption of measures strong enough to make Washington halt the occupation of the Dominican Republic. To be sure, there were protests at the landing of Marines, but the protests came only from those who were organized to save face. People stoned the American embassy; they hissed at Johnson in the newsreels. But there are more effective methods of exerting pressure. If they had honestly wanted to help the Dominicans or to express an effective solidarity with them, they had only to take a page from the history of the labor movement —and stage demonstrations, put pressure on the legislatures, sign petitions, sponsor press campaigns. And, besides that, they could have boycotted American films and products and taken other classic and perfectly legal steps. Trade unions could have ordered their members who worked for companies with American capital to decrease their production and could have requested the same action all over the world. But not even the Christian Democratic unions suggested such steps, in spite of their protestations of being anti-imperialist and leftist. The "Jacobins" and Marxists never dreamed of it.

Compare the words of any Latin American leader of today with those of the Nicaraguan Augusto César Sandino (1893–1934), while he was fighting at the head of a handful of men against the American Marines who had landed at Las Segovias. Compare his conduct—the cause of his assassination by the father of the present-day Somozas—with that of Juan Bosch, who did not risk going to the aid of his people, dying for his cause, but remained instead in San Juan. Sandino said, in 1927, "The oligarchs will say that I am a plebeian. Thàt doesn't matter: It is my greatest honor that I came from the bosom of the oppressed, who are the soul and nervous system of the race, those we have survived."[2] He did not permit himself the ignoble policy of finding a scapegoat. He acted, and he risked his life; he did not need excuses. Thus, while he resisted the Marines, he pointed to those who were really responsible for the situation: "Who are they who have bound my country to the post of ignomiy? Díaz and Chamorro and their lackeys, who still want to have the right to govern this hapless fatherland of ours with the help of the invader's bayonets and Springfield rifles."

Thirty years ago, Sandino had to learn the lesson that has again been assigned to the men of today: that oligarchical governments will never defend the people.

For fifteen months, the Army for the Defense of Nicaragua's National Sovereignty, in the face of the cold indifference of the Latin American governments and thrown back on its own resources and strength, has been able to confront with honor and brilliance the terrible blond beasts and the renegade pack of Nicaraguan traitors who have lent aid to the invader's sinister designs. During this time, *Señores Presidentes,* you have not responded by doing your duty—for as representatives of free and sovereign peoples, which you are, you are under obligation to protest through diplomatic channels or with arms that the people have entrusted to you, if need be, against the nameless crimes that the government in the White House has ordered consummated in cold blood in our unfortunate Nicaragua, without any right to do so and through no fault of our country other than its refusal to kiss the whip with which it is lashed, or the fist of the Yankee who beats it.

More recent events in the Dominican Republic prove that the objective conditions for a Latin American revolution do not exist. The consequences of this will be far-reaching, but not because of what is usually mentioned by those with no political vision—"the creation of unfavorable popular opinion." Kennedy and Johnson knew that, in international matters, public opinion has less weight than actual power does, and that the latter modifies the former. The serious thing is that the United States—by having put the Marines in the service of the oligarchic forces—had abandoned the Kennedy concept that relations between the United States and Latin America could be made meaningful if the United States were to defend the Latin American people against the oligarchies and against overly greedy North American companies. This idea perished in the Dominican Republic, and it may be a very long time before American diplomacy can revive it —and then only with great difficulty. Destroyed as it was just as it was beginning to take root, its replanting would call for a personality or group with great imagination, great political boldness, and a new vision of the United States' world role; with a feeling not so much for politics as for history, who can see that the United States, as it is today, constitutes a force for revolution by its very existence and that this implies a policy that will support, and be supported by, revolutionary forces.

There were certain aspects of the Dominican affair that discretion forbade American commentators to point out, but which we Latin Americans must emphasize. The responsibility was not Washington's alone, although its responsibility was crushing and it will weigh on American administrations for many years. Other elements were equally responsible:

1. President Juan Bosch of the Dominican Republic, who failed to go to Santo Domingo within forty-eight hours of the outbreak of the trouble, before there was talk of landing the Marines and when his presence at the side of men who were fighting and dying to defend the constitutionalist cause might have turned events to a clearer course and made the landing impossible. Once more, intellectuals proved that they are poor politicians.

2. The Latin American governments, which failed to take the initiative without waiting for a decision by the White House, which failed to send a commission for the defense of democracy to the Dominican Republic to learn the facts quickly and advise on the only step that could be taken with decorum: immediate recognition of the constitutionalist government and the sending of elements to support it. This would also have prevented the landing of the Marines.

3. The Latin American populist movements, which did noth-

ing but sign declarations. That the Castroists and Communists and the bogus intellectual left should content themselves with statements was natural and habitual. But that the populist parties did no more seems sad and almost incredible.

Dream and Nightmare

Spain saw her Indies as one unit, even though she named them in the plural. She created a system of overseas and overland communications and introduced two important factors that would make for unity: the Castilian language and Catholicism. She required that the viceroyalties and captaincies general recognize the Spanish Crown as the political, cultural, and administrative focal point of all important matters.

In many documents drawn up by the forerunners of Latin America's independence, the word "America" prevails over the names of individual countries. "All America exists in the nation," said a verse of a Caracan song that later became Venezuela's national anthem. The Peruvian Juan Pablo Vizcardo y Guzmán wrote at the end of the eighteenth century, "The New World is our fatherland."

Before the war against Spain, the aspiration to independence created what was described by Alfonso Reyes (1899–1959) as a "walking Americanery" among the Creoles residing in Europe. Agitation for independence emerged later in Latin America, not at one fixed point but everywhere, and war broke out everywhere. San Martín went to Chile; Bolívar went to Colombia, Ecuador, and Bolivia; O'Higgins used all Chile's resources in the naval expedition that moved on Peru; Madariaga, a Chilean, was the important figure in the movement in Caracas; and the Guatemalan Antonio José Irisarri (1786–1866) played an important role in Chile.

The old empire might easily have served as the basis for a new federation. Indeed, the minutes of the 1810 Congress of Tucumán opened with these words: "We, the representatives of the United Provinces of South America. . . ." Hidalgo, in Mexico, gave himself the title of "Generalissimo of the Americas" and so signed the decree emancipating the slaves in Mexico. José Cecilio del Valle (1780–1834) proclaimed Central America a single nation. The Argentine Bernardo de Monteagudo (1785–1825) wrote an *Essay on the Need for a General Federation Among the Spanish American States and a Plan for Their Organization* published in Lima and reprinted in Chile and Guatemala. In 1810, Juan Martínez de Rozas (1759–1813) published in Argentina a *Political-Christian Catechism* in which he recommended confederation of the Spanish colonies for the purpose of repelling foreign domination. And, as Mexican delegate to the Cortes and during its reunion (held in Madrid in 1821), Lucas Alamán joined other deputies in presenting a plan for a "federation composed of the various American states and Spain, under the name of the Spanish American Federation."

Bolívar was the leader who went furthest in his efforts to create a federation of the old Spanish colonies. He took the initiative by convoking the Panama meeting of 1826, where he proclaimed two very broad guidelines: "The New World will be constituted of independent nations, all bound by a common law that establishes their foreign relations and offers them the power, through a general and permanent Congress, to abide by it"; and, "Differences in origin and color will lose their influence and power."

But great expanse of territory, jurisdictional divisions, and local interests all operated against plans for a Latin American confederation. No measure of unity was achieved, even within regions. A plan for a federation in Upper Peru was strangled by national conflicts. The separation of Paraguay from Río de la Plata had historical precedents, and in the new era it was impossible to bring about a reunification on the basis of the network of rivers in that area. The Union of Greater Colombia collapsed. Other unsuccessful efforts were the annexation of Central America by the Empire of Mexico and attempts to unite the Central American people in a federal republic. Later plans for a federation of the Antilles did not thrive either.[3]

After the Panama project of 1826 had broken down, any further plans for union were agreed on out of concern for the need for self-defense against a feared aggression. Mexico made unsuccessful proposals to revive the Congress of Panama in 1831, 1838, and 1840. In 1848, delegates from Colombia, Ecuador, Peru,

Chile, and Bolivia met to discuss the creation of an assembly with the power to arbitrate disputes. In 1856, a defensive Treaty of Continental Union was drawn up and signed in Santiago de Chile. Another like it was signed that same year by the United States, Mexico, Guatemala, El Salvador, Costa Rica, Venezuela, and New Granada. None of these agreements was ever enforced. In 1864, while a Spanish squadron was anchored off the coast of Peru, representatives from El Salvador, Venezuela, Ecuador, Colombia, Peru, Chile, and Bolivia met in Lima; and in 1883, in Caracas, those of Mexico, El Salvador, Venezuela, Colombia, Peru, Bolivia, and Argentina assembled. Except for the Congress of Panama, the United States took no part in those meetings until 1889, when the first Pan-American Congress met in Washington and the future heavy machinery for Pan-American (then called Inter-American) affairs was assembled. It had nothing to do with any aspirations toward union.

Ideals of Latin American unity were in fact invoked only during times of international crisis and were forgotten once the danger had passed. But certain concepts kept appearing: union among the states; a peaceful solution of controversies and differences among the federated states or with foreign states by means of arbitration or mediation (Lima, 1848; Santiago, 1856; Lima, 1856); the use of land and naval contingents to defend any member state under attack (Lima, 1848); and the principle of nonintervention (Lima, 1848, and Santiago, 1856).[4]

None of the ideas for a strong Latin American union ever jelled, owing to political instability, the lack of economic ties among the states, and each oligarchy's interest in keeping apart from all the others. This tendency was sometimes manifest in dictatorships, and:

. . . the dictatorships and tyrannical regimes that prevailed and still prevail in several Spanish American states created conflicts with a neighbor nation or kept alive the specter of possible wars as a means of evading domestic political anxieties. This made them vulnerable to easy infection by [the germ of] patrioteering to prevent an outbreak of internal irritation against the tyrant. The little Talleyrands who sometimes headed our chancelleries also cultivated secret diplomacy and practiced the maneuvers and intrigues that they copied on a minuscule scale from the European nations. Although international congresses, meetings of experts, economic and financial agreements may have served to overcome many prejudices and to make for better mutual understanding, the Spanish American union is, above all, a great historic undertaking that calls for enthusiasm and faith on the part of the respective peoples; one that must penetrate not alone the hermetically sealed policy of the chancelleries, but also the everyday policy of the street.[5]

And this the oligarchies have never permitted.

The Paraguayan war of 1865–70 and the War of the Pacific of 1879–83 killed any possible tentatives toward union. Both were wars without quarter, in which "the principles that formed the very structure of our nervous system, such as arbitration and the prohibition of conquest, were forgotten by the victor."[6]

In the twentieth century, the chancelleries no longer held the initiative; they conformed to the framework of the Pan-American Union. But the populist movements asked for more than that. The trade unions united across national lines with other organizations—sometimes hemispheric, sometimes Latin American. Anarchist groups and populist and democratic parties also took tentative steps toward international coordination.[7] After World War I there emerged, particularly among intellectuals, a state of mind that found expression in a famous proclamation by the Mexican Alfonso Reyes: "We have come of age." Therefore, he demanded recognition of "the right to universal citizenship, which we have won," and added that "our mind is naturally internationalist."[8] At about the same time, Romain Rolland wrote: "I believe in the mission of your peoples. . . . Federate! Unite! Get to work without delay! Not a single day must be wasted. Young men of Spanish America, I envy you; you have the most beautiful and most heroic cause for which to sacrifice yourselves!"[9]

Rolland expressed well the growing urgency. Haya de la Torre —possibly the greatest generator of political ideas that Latin America has had in our era—had proposed in concrete form a unity of Indo-America, as he called it, by founding APRA as a continental organization. Despite its later dwindling down to a Peruvian party, the Aprista ideal of Latin American unity had taken root among the populists.

For Haya de la Torre, Latin America was one great nation. No effective social or political solution to its problems could be narrowly national.

Latin American or Indo-American socio-economic problems overflow our political and administrative boundaries. The union of our peoples must stand as Point No. 1 [on the agenda] of all truly revolutionary democratic parties. . . . The present political boundaries between our countries are economic frontiers, but they belong to a feudal stage. The Creole feudal class drew them up when they won freedom from Spain, but they do not belong in a modern anti-feudal delimitation, much less to a revolutionary and scientific one.[10]

Forty years later, Haya was still affirming:

In Latin America, we feel that we are becoming more and more interdependent. This continent-wide economic nationalism assumes that it is impossible for small or subdivided and isolated economies to subsist. Hence, it may be said today that the New World is divided between the United States of the North and the disunited States of the South. But behind this division, which stems the flow of our progress, the obvious reality of our *inter*dependence appears. . . . The old nineteenth-century idea, publicly approved by some of our statists, of making our states into so many autarkies that would produce whatever they consume, or the fancy that Latin American economic unity will be possible only when each national economy becomes "solid," has been offset by a new and realistic concept: A strong economy will be attained in each Latin American state when a [Latin American] economic community is established.[11]

Like many others, then, Haya believed that there are urgent and basic reasons for Latin American unity. Duties on Argentine cattle, for example, prevent Chileans from enjoying low-priced meat; the West Indies have a serious food shortage, yet Venezuela could develop a cattle-raising industry that would satisfy the domestic market and the Caribbean areas, too. Economic unity would help to raise the standard of living in other ways also. For example, certain shipping cartels have charged as much for moving cargo from New York to La Guaira as for a voyage to South Africa, and a Greater Colombian Fleet has been proposed, to be operated jointly by Venezuela, Colombia, and Ecuador, which would lower cargo costs and so keep down the cost of imported goods.[12] Years ago, Manuel Ugarte said something worth repeating today: "It is not enough for this [country] to exist; it is necessary that it be able to live. . . . An independent Cuba with 2 million inhabitants, only a few hours away from Florida, would have been an [improbable] phenomenon. The autonomy of Panama is a pipedream. . . . Can Nicaragua possibly subsist for long, given the circumstances surrounding it? . . . Are not some of our homelands obvious historical impossibilities?"[13]

José Ingenieros, who drew up a program for the Latin American Union founded in 1925 in Buenos Aires, argued that

. . . our nationalities are facing a clear dilemma: either to surrender submissively and praise the Pan-American Union (America for the North Americans), or to prepare to defend their shared independence by laying the foundations for a Latin American Union (Latin America for the Latin Americans). We know that it will prove long and difficult to accomplish the second task, for already there exist very great interests created by the shadow of powerful financial syndicates.

To achieve its purpose, the Union adopted the following principles:

Political solidarity for the Latin American people and joint action on all questions of world-wide interest. Repudiation of official Pan-Americanism and abolition of secret diplomacy. Solution by arbitration of any dispute that may arise among the nations of Latin America over exclusively Latin American jurisdictions, and reduction of national armaments to the minimum compatible with the maintenance of internal order. Opposition to any financial policy that might compromise the national sovereignty, particularly to the contracting of loans that may consent to or justify coercive intervention of foreign capitalistic states. Reaffirmation of democratic postulates in harmony with the most recent conclusions of political science. Nationalization of the sources of wealth and abolition of economic privilege.[14]

These principles were to serve as the guidelines for action. The Union's immediate objectives were to be "a Latin American high tribunal to rule on political problems pending among the contracting parties; a Supreme Economic Council to regulate cooperation in production and commerce; collective resistance to anything that might imply a right to intervention by foreign powers; gradual amortization of the loans that mortgage the peoples' independence." After forty years, all these goals are still only aspirations.

Some believe that Latin American union should be approached by stages:

The integration of Ibero-America ought perhaps to go first through a stage of forming great blocs of nations, such as the Central American Federation, the Federation of Greater Colombia, that of Peru and Bolivia, and so on. The assignment of a preponderant role to culture, living together in justice, freeing the worker and the peon from the latifundio, frequency and consistency in political interchange would give the great blocs of nations the opportunity to accelerate the formation of the Great Spanish American Confederation.[15]

World War II provided the advocates of union with new arguments:

If any lesson can be drawn . . . from the present conflict, it is that there are no national solutions, that there exists so close an economic and social interdependence that there cannot be progress, peace, tranquility, or happiness for one people so long as other peoples are fighting in the narrow confines of an economic dead-end or against an oppression that impedes alike the free course of national life and the most precious individual freedoms, considered almost until yesterday as the elemental victories of civilization.[16]

And when a country went through a revolution, it tried to push forward, verbally at least, the cause of unity: "The Bolivian Revolution, working for its own fatherland, believes it is doing its part in the process of American integration, which is vital to our peoples. In this era of industrial civilization, it is possible to find an adequate framework for the full development of collectivities only within continental boundaries."[17]

When the Christian Democrats appeared on the political scene, they, too, declared themselves unionists: "We have to have economic unity so that the spiritual unity and the political unity of our people of Latin America may be cemented onto the economic unity."[18] By 1958, the slogan of unity was heard everywhere. The following were the words of writers, politicians, economists— from conservative to socialist—meeting in Caracas to celebrate the fall of the Pérez Jiménez dictatorship.

With the triumph of the democratic movements, the union of our America will enter upon a new era, more worthy of honor in hemispheric negotiations, more significant in projecting outside the hemisphere the spirit that guides us. . . . We cannot continue with the building of American unity simply on the negative and systematic basis of rejecting Communism. We reject it, yes, but we wish the unity accepted and longed for by every one to arise from a clear, effective affirmation of our own free personality.[19]

It is no secret that Washington has always looked askance on attempts to achieve Latin American unity—that what was a dream in Latin America was a nightmare for American diplomats. The reasons for Latin Americans desiring unity were the same for Washington fearing it, during the long period in which its Latin American policy consisted chiefly in defending the interests of American business, since Latin American unity signified a threat to the privileges obtained by North American enterprises from the oligarchic governments. Still, it was not a bad nightmare, for the Americans had the means to keep it from coming true; indeed, they often did not have to use their own resources, since the oligarchic governments themselves would take on the job of thwarting any effort with a chance of succeeding.

Little by little, experience showed Washington that the nightmare could be a means of salvation. A united, contented, and democratic Latin America could better defend itself against the "Communist threat" than a disunited, frustrated, and oligarchic one. This idea was dimly descried at the onset of the Kennedy administration; and the inevitability of Latin American union was understood. The United States accepted this and considered that it would accord with its own national interests. The Alliance for Progress—as it was originally conceived, not as it was falsified by the Latin American oligarchies—took a major step toward one form of unity.

Before Bolívar had ever thought of the Congress of Panama, a Chilean, Juan Egaña (1769–1836), drafted a constitution for his country. In it, he called Chile a *people,* and the union of Chile with other American peoples, which he predicted and favored, he called a *nation.*[20] Today for the first time, Latin America has reached a point at which it is possible to succeed in forming that kind of Latin American *nation* composed of specific *peoples.* But this goal has again become a nightmare for Washington.

Efforts Toward Unity

Two achievements in the cause of Latin American unity have won support, for better or for worse, because they pose no threat to the oligarchies.[21] One is the Central American Common Market, formed in 1960 by Costa Rica, El Salvador, Guatemala, Honduras, and Nicaragua. The groundwork for this common market had been laid as early as 1951, when the national ministers of economy began to meet together regularly. (Later, the ministers of education followed suit.) An Organization of Central American States (ODECA), with headquarters in San Salvador, was founded, and then finally the common market, complete with a Central American Development Bank. In 1950, inter–Central American trade had amounted to only $8.3 million; in 1964, it passed the $80-million mark. Moreover, industries that would not otherwise have been established are now ready to produce on a relatively economical scale for a market of 12 million people.

The success of the Central American Common Market is predicated on the understanding that it will not jeopardize the local oligarchies. This has been possible as a result of the decision to go ahead with economic integration and forget for the moment anything having to do with union as a political issue; once the decision to establish the common market was taken, the politicians left the field to civil servants and technocrats. Also, there is no great disparity in the development of the five Central American republics, all of whom have a fundamentally agrarian economy. In short, there were not many vested interests demanding national protection.

But, some experts have pointed out, "the region's capacity to import will not grow enough to permit an improvement in the standard of living, which is the goal of the Alliance for Progress, through increasing importation of consumer goods produced outside the region. If the required growth is to occur, it will have to be as the result of internal structural changes."[22] In other words, the Central American Common Market has so far meant nothing, in the social sense, to the people.

The other attempt cannot have a much better result, since it has not even succeeded in being a common market but is only a timid and hesitant step toward one. This is the Latin American Free Trade Association (LAFTA), whose technocrats do not even make passing reference to social questions.

About midway through 1958, Raúl Prebisch (1901–   ), then secretary-general of the U.N. Economic Commission for Latin America (ECLA) and a firm champion of economic integration, established contact with the Argentine, Brazilian and Chilean governments and suggested that they set up a multilateral trade system within their region. Argentina proposed a broadening of Prebisch's proposal to include all Latin America. Two meetings were held in Montevideo, the second of which, in February, 1960, brought forth the treaty that regulates LAFTA. It was ratified by seven countries in June, 1961: Argentina, Brazil, Chile, Mexico, Paraguay, Peru, and Uruguay. Later in the same year, Colombia and Ecuador joined.

The nine nations in LAFTA cover 76.5 per cent of the surface of Latin America and have a population of approximately 180 million. Their combined GNP is equivalent to three-quarters of the total GNP of Latin America. In the LAFTA zone, annual negotiations have lowered the tariff barriers on more than 5,000 products; trade within the zone has risen by 75 per cent over what it was in 1960 to about $1,200 million.

The first years of LAFTA brought no complications because each member country could meet its commitment to ease the importation of goods it did not produce (getting in exchange an advantage in the placement of its own goods in categories not produced by any of the others). Trouble started at the Conference of Mexico, in 1963, when the lowering of tariffs on industrial products came up for discussion. All the countries, in autarkic fashion, had been developing independent industries, all of which managed to get along only because they were protected. The industrialists objected to running the risk of foreign competition; moreover, it was by then apparent that the countries with more advanced industries, like Argentina, Brazil, and Mexico, had in general benefited most from LAFTA, and the medium-sized countries—Colombia, Chile, Peru, and Uruguay—feared that, as LAFTA's relaxation of trade barriers advanced, their chances of gaining more benefits would be thwarted. Their protests led to a decision to provide special treatment for "countries with insufficient markets," but nothing specific was decided on. On the other hand, the complaints also led to an acceptance of the idea of coordinating national development plans. Joint committees from ECLA, the Inter-American Development Bank, and the Institute for Planning are studying the *regional* aspects of the iron-and-steel, petrochemical, and fertilizer industries. But the coordination of individual plans would be tantamount to accepting the principle of an international division of labor and hence will provoke resistance when the question of putting it into practice arises.

We are now in a situation where the need for Latin American unity is great, the realization that this is so is small, and the men who ought to fit the realization to the need are very few indeed. The Bank of Foreign Trade of Mexico recognized this when it stated:

The politicians have been unable or have not wished to make the major decisions that are needed to carry forward the process of integration. They have not done this, sometimes because they have not dared to oppose various domestic interests; sometimes because they have yielded meekly to the pressure of certain economic groups and have shown timidity when national and regional objectives could be reconciled only by firmness and boldness. The road to integration is not an easy one; it will be necessary in each country to make adjustments in the economy. . . . To make such adjustments, to direct them adequately, it is necessary that the politicians be disposed to run the risks that all decisions affecting such interests imply. How many have demonstrated that readiness of spirit until now? How capable are they of taking and maintaining an attitude that may make them powerful enemies? . . . The company presidents have thus far been unable to make the great promotional effort that LAFTA calls for. At times, their failure to make it has been owing to a lack of initiative . . . for they have not yet developed the awareness of export possibilities that would impel them to reach outside their small internal markets, and often because they have not fulfilled their primary economic function, which is to take risks. If LAFTA has lacked anything, it is that effort on the part of the enterprises. . . .

Neither have there been experts of the high caliber required if they are to meet the demand that they put their conclusions to the test, if they are to be asked to exert pressure on their political and company

chiefs on the one hand, and on the public on the other, or to consider that they have met their responsibility only when they have seen
, their plans submitted to the acid test of facts.[23]

It is clear that people talk about governments, heads of companies, and experts—the elements that form a part of public
opinion. But no one ever mentions the *people,* not even that
portion which is organized into trade unions, cooperatives, and
the few existing brotherhoods of farm workers. Not once has
there been any talk in the Central American Common Market or
in LAFTA of land reform.

But administrative and technological solutions *are* being sought.
New meetings have been announced, products discussed one by
one, more offices created. Yet both LAFTA and the common
market are beginning to suffer the same fate as the Alliance for
Progress: with the latter soon as it became evident that it had
become an agreement between a capitalistic (albeit democratic)
government and a number of oligarchic governments, instead of
a search for an alliance *between peoples,* another body was set up,
the Inter-American Committee of the Alliance for Progress, which
has done absolutely nothing and has solved none of the existing
problems. There seems to be an absolute impermeability to experience. In the OAS, too, each time there is talk of a crisis—and
this is a charitable euphemism for what, since the events in the
Dominican Republic, has been the putrefaction of the OAS's
cadaver—instead of looking to the people for a solution, the OAS
keeps talking about ministerial conferences, new agencies, de-
centralization, etc. But dismemberment cannot possibly bring a
cadaver back to life.

Let us not deceive ourselves. It is not a question of the inability to profit from experience. (That inability is possibly more
prevalent among American diplomats, who go on deluding themselves that a decision adopted with the votes of Haiti, Nicaragua,
or Paraguay is valid.) For the Latin American governments are
profiting nicely from past experience. They know that nothing
will change while new organizations are set up, decrepit ones
overhauled, committees and commissions appointed, and meetings held. As they are oligarchic governments whose basic desire

is that there shall be no change, they are always ready to play the bureaucratic game and, moreover, let the United States pick up the tab. The few nonoligarchic governments would like to see genuine solutions, but they are paralyzed by the fear that, since they are outnumbered by the dictators and oligarchic governments, any useful and constructive proposal will be reversed. To believe that passing a measure forbidding military coups or giving the OAS a greater political role will resolve anything, is to believe that human problems can be solved by spirits from another world. Would measures against military coups be observed by the oligarchic governments, which foment coups? And would those governments expand the OAS' political role, when such expansion would jeopardize the Latin American oligarchic system?

Economics or Politics?

All efforts to achieve Latin American unity, until now, have been made exclusively in the economic field—almost, one might say, in the commercial field. And all have been carried forward without any popular participation. Unionist aspirations, basically political, have found an outlet in selling more products and lowering tariffs. But in the opinion of many people, even that represents progress. Little by little, the industrial segment of society will grow stronger and the oligarchic segment will thereby grow weaker.

But the oligarchy does not see the matter in this light. If the oligarchs had thought that LAFTA or the Central American Common Market might ultimately bring about that result, they would have opposed both experiments from the beginning and would have caused them to fail. But the landowning oligarchs believe that reinforcement of the bourgeoisie, of the middle class, even of organized labor, in a society where the real power is in their hands, is no danger, because it is possible to allow these other groups a limited degree of participation in government and thereby convert them from potential enemies into *de facto allies* or accomplices. Further, any form of unity that is not political and that debars the people is a weapon to brandish before the United States for the purpose of demanding higher prices for raw materials or preferential treatment. Besides, unity is a beautiful slogan that will divert attention and help to conceal the true nature of the society that takes these unionist steps.

Three new steps were taken in 1965. Felipe Herrera, President of the Inter-American Development Bank, had suggested in 1963 that it would be advisable to create a Latin American parliament and an inter-American high court.[24] These proposals were also made in a study prepared by Herrera and other experts at the Bank. Published in April, 1965, it contained a time-table for the formation of a Latin American Community, including, by the year 1980, some form of political union, a central bank, and a common market. From the beginning, this plan set political and social objectives; it also looked ahead to the establishment of a regional information agency, a regional insurance system, and a supranational development plan.[25]

The plan was to go through three stages in application. In the first, six-year stage, the following objectives would be pursued: the signing of a general treaty for a Latin American Community, the setting up of its working parts, and approval of the first regional development plan; integration in the most strategic fields, beginning with the iron-and-steel and other heavy industries, by establishing coordinating councils; reactivation of LAFTA by gradually standardizing tariffs and eliminating the intra-zonal tariffs on strategic products; coordination of a regional system of central banks and insurance schemes; establishment of intra-regional machinery for payments; issuance of a sound region-wide agency, by mobilizing reserves and gradually bringing monetary and foreign-exchange policies into harmony; the establishment of a central university council and a Latin American information agency; and taking the first step in a vast regional campaign for universal literacy.

During the second stage, from 1971 to 1975, the system established by the general treaty would be consolidated and the second development plan approved; the efforts of the strategic sectors would be defined; the LAFTA program for free trade and a customs union for strategic industries would be completed; regional operations of the central bank and insurance companies would be broadened; convertible regional money would be strengthened; the literacy campaign would end.

In the third and final stage, efforts would be made to lift the Community to the political level; the third development plan would be approved; integration would be extended to nonstrategic sectors; the work of establishing a Latin American common market would be completed; the monetary systems and financial policies would be further integrated and regional convertibility would be achieved, together with an integrated capital market for the entire area; a program for obligatory secondary education in all the urban areas of Latin America would start.

Not long before the formulation of this plan, the Peruvian parliament, on the initiative of the Aprista minority, called a constitutional convention for a Latin American parliament (Lima, December 6–11, 1964). Delegates from various parties in thirteen national legislatures—Argentina, Brazil, Colombia, Costa Rica, Chile, El Salvador, Guatemala, Nicaragua, Panama, Paraguay, Peru, Uruguay, and Venezuela—were present. They agreed to create a unicameral regional body whose function would be "to become acquainted with, debate, and resolve by recommendations any matter, motion, or plan that may have a relation to the political, economic, social, and cultural integration of Latin America, or to problems of common interest to Latin America." The Latin American Parliament was to be composed of delegations from each nation, each with an equal number of votes, who would meet once a year in the capitals of member countries in rotation.

It is significant that whereas the previous Latin American parliamentary meetings inevitably degenerated into empty oratorical contests, the delegations that met in Lima showed much more realism. Most of the debates and recommendations dealt with serious domestic and foreign problems confronting Latin America, and [the delegates] forebore, perhaps for the first time in the history of such meetings, to divide their time between panegyrics to the continent's great historical figures and a search for scapegoats to blame for all their ills.[26]

Andrés Townsend, the prime mover behind efforts to put into practice the old Aprista aspirations, and Secretary of the Latin American Parliament, pointed out that:

It will be a permanent institution, democratic in character and representative of all existing political trends, and the proper organ for channeling and promoting the movement toward integration. The will to found regularly functioning executive bodies, which will reconcile the Latin American points of view before the world and coordinate and plan for development, is clearly recognized, as is also a Latin American court of justice. The Declaration affirms [Latin America's] faith in democracy, its rejection of imperialism, dictatorship, oligarchy, and colonialism, and its solidarity with the underdeveloped countries in the world struggle to defend the interests and aspirations of their majorities.[27]

The questions discussed in Lima did not reach the common man, to be sure, for few Latin American parliaments actually represent the popular will and few are able to attract the attention of the man in the street, or merit his trust. Few of the dictators, who had their own "parliaments," failed to attend the Lima meeting, but this was inevitable and should not have been a reason for wasting the opportunity to take the step.

Neither did the delegates waste the opportunity offered them by the Christian Democratic President of Chile, Eduardo Frei, in asking four economists (José Antonio Mayobre, Felipe Herrera, Raúl Prebisch, and Carlos Sanz de Santamaria) to draw a plan for economic integration. Each of the four acted in an individual capacity, but it is significant that all were directors of international bodies—ECLA, the Inter-American Development Bank, the United Nations Conference on Trade and Development, and the Inter-American Committee, respectively. The bank study was the starting point; at least two, possibly three, of the four men agreed with it. But they were under heavy pressure to drop three of its basic features: the Latin American-oriented development plan, the political objectives, and the timetable. The end result was a new plan that set only general objectives, emphasizing commercial aspects (of primary interest to the oligarchy) and with a good deal of water in the wine as far as political aspects were concerned.[28] A Latin American parliament, consultative in function, and a council of ministers composed mainly of representatives of the oligarchic governments were proposed in the plan. Only an executive board of experts chosen on their merits regardless of nationality would be (theoretically) beyond the oligarchy's reach. But that board would have no better guarantees than the Council of "Nine Wise Men" or the Inter-American Committee of the Alliance for Progress that it would be immune to diplomatic and governmental pressure.*

In any event, it is worth pointing out that, in the matter of integration, the risks are the same as they were in the case of the Alliance for Progress. The very fact that there is a need to use the word "integration," which has technical connotations, instead of "unity," which connotes a political tradition and affirmation, is a warning. I regret having to repeat this so often, but each time the same problems arise, and one tends to forget that everything in Latin America must be shaped on the fringe of government or even in opposition to government. (The fact that two or three governments are excepted from this general condemnation is unfortunately not enough to change the picture.)

The Alliance for Progress was self-defeating because it tried to help the people to change their social structure and elected to work to that end through the existing governments. It was felt that under the three-fold pressure of populist movements, the need for American aid, and fear of Castro, the oligarchies would give ground. But the oligarchies were more realistic. They had no fear of Castro because they knew that Castroism was essentially a middle-class movement that would tend to settle down and turn bourgeois (and that is happening); on the matter of American aid, the oligarchies skillfully invoked the obsessive "Communist threat" to obtain aid without effecting social reforms; and the oligarchy could easily handle the populist movements by "softening them up" with military coups that Washington was helpless to prevent.

After President Kennedy's death, the oligarchs reversed the roles, and used *Washington's* fear of Castro and of populist move-

---

* This does not imply that the board would have to renounce doing whatever it could for unity on the pretext that this would be to work through oligarchic governments. That would be tantamount to adopting the all-or-nothing position of the "Jacobins" and Marxists who, as they "know" they cannot achieve everything they want, use this as an excuse for sitting at home and resigning themselves to doing nothing.

ments to liquidate the Alliance for Progress. Thus, the Latin American oligarchic system has never before seemed as solid and self-assured as it does now. It can even indulge in the luxury of talking constantly about revolution and allowing guerrilla skirmishes to occur, continuing, in this way, to impress Washington and oppose the people.[29]

During the Kennedy era, Latin Americans had the support of the United States but lacked experience. To put the matter in terms a Communist might use, we Latin Americans made mistakes on the left (overestimating the masses) and on the right (underestimating the adversary). Today, we cannot count on official support from the United States (although I believe we can count on more support from the American people than before), but, in exchange, we have had the experience of our mistakes and can avoid repeating them. Yet, today, everything is much more difficult than it was a few years ago. Militarism is stronger and more openly daring. And the social groups that fought for social change earlier are now going along with the status quo, while many of those who still desire change would like to turn their backs on the people and accomplish their reforms paternalistically. The people, for their part, are no more awake and no more conscious of their potential than they were before. Those among them who had begun to awaken are suffering terrible disillusionment now, which may lead them into indifference or turn them into willing accomplices of the "paternalistic revolutionaries" or technocratic militarists.

The course of the Latin American economy demands change. We have reached a moment when the oligarchy's perdurability is beginning to injure (not merely to irritate, anger, or morally offend, but actually to do economic damage to) major segments of society. The problem is to convince those sectors that their interest is identical with that of the submerged masses.

This is not simple, but it is not impossible. And, besides, the task is inspiring. To fulfill it, the people must first be taught who are the friends and who are the enemies of Latin American unity.

The Enemies of Unity

Lenin wrote: "Marxism cannot coexist with nationalism, however just, pure, noble, and civilizing it may be. Marxism supports internationalism as opposed to nationalism, the fusion of all the peoples into a greater unity."[30]

But in practice, from Stalin's time until now, the Soviet Union has opposed any attempts at international unity, including those made by its satellites. Remember that in 1945, Dimitrov and Tito talked about a Balkan alliance but suddenly fell silent when Moscow called the idea "premature." Communists have displayed hostility to all forms of European union (until, some time ago, the Italian Communist Party disagreed). Why should their position be any different in Latin America? Some instances will show that Communist opposition to attempts at unity is not a mere matter of propaganda but that it assumes active forms. When the Organization of Central American States was founded early in the 1950's, Guatemala was a member; all the Guatemalan political parties came out in favor of Central American unity but one—the Labor Party (Communist). Guatemala seceded from ODECA in 1953, when the Communists were exerting a determining influence on the regime of Colonel Arbenz. Again, the CTAL, affiliated with the Communist World Federation of Trade Unions, did not have in its program any point that would support continental unity; this objective was also conspicuously absent from the programs of all the Communist parties in Latin America.

Moscow has had something to gain by dealing separately with each of Latin America's twenty countries, but would have no chance if she dealt with an over-all Latin American organization. Soviet literature offers, therefore, a theoretical justification for Communist opposition to Latin American unity: "The countries of the Western Hemisphere are now in a state of 'interdependence' under the aegis of American imperialism. But there are powerful forces of national liberation coming into action—Cuba is a prime example—which are undermining this 'interdependence' and opposing it with a struggle to strengthen national sovereignty and achieve economic liberation."[31]

This position was immediately echoed in Latin American Communist literature, as one might expect. In a bulletin of a so-called Permanent Congress for Syndical Unity of the Workers of Latin America, published in Santiago de Chile (the fourth attempt by the CTAL to create a broader Latin American labor organization), we read as follows about Latin American integration:

Economic integration seems to many Latin American bourgeois statists and capitalists a historic option for the consolidation and defense of national capitalist interests, a means for creating a new market zone and for co-existing with American imperialism within the present system. Of course that is an idyllic conception of reality, for which reason, American imperialism supports and stimulates integration; but at the same time it is using every means to become lord and master within that integration—that is, it moves unremittingly to gain the greatest advantage from it.[32]

In addition, as Professor José María Traibel, a Uruguayan delegate to ECLA, made clear when he argued for the abolition of preferential trade regulations, "The demand for bilateralism (I'll buy from you if you'll buy from me) made by the socialist countries would, if accepted, prevent the Latin American countries from accumulating surpluses to set aside for export to member countries of the Latin American Common Market."[33] In short, Latin American unity would not suit the U.S.S.R. or the Communist countries of Eastern Europe, even if it only appeared in the form of a common market obstructing Russia's trade policy. This is of more immediate importance than the long-range objectives and doctrinal rationalizations expounded by Lenin:

Capitalism in development recognizes two historical trends in the national problem. First: the awakening of national life and national movements, the struggle against the national yoke, the creation of national states. Second: the development and repetition of every kind of relations among nations, tearing down national barriers, creating an international unity of capital, of economic life in general, of politics, science, and so on. Both trends are the basic law of capitalism. The first prevails at the beginning of its evolution; the second characterizes a mature capitalism on the way toward its transformation into a socialist society.[34]

From the point of view of the oligarchy or upper bourgeoisie, this could be the best possible argument for opposing unity, but neither has used it, preferring to use many of the arguments that modern Communists advance.

The oligarchic elements support a shabby nationalism that expresses their habitual turn of mind—

a series of petty prejudices that rise up under the cloak of patriotism like false spiritual demarcations between one nation and another. By a curious psychological process of transference the technical or economic feeling of inferiority in each country seeks to sublimate itself by pointing up or inventing certain collective myths. Courage in war, what is called *machismo* in Mexico, was one of those regional myths. Country A scorns Country B because A's men are the best and most virile soldiers in America. Even purely natural factors such as climate become the object of arbitrary idealization. The countries in the temperate zone of South America—Chile, Argentina, Uruguay—have spoken for some time with scorn of the countries in the tropical zone, attributing to them a certain predestined inferiority.[35]

Opposition to unity is more active in Argentina, for there it can profit by the widespread belief that the Argentines are more European than Latin American (currently heard in Buenos Aires but much less frequently outside it). *La Prensa,* the newspaper to which Peronist persecution restored a kind of ideological virginity, in its issue of December 27, 1964, called the convocation of the "so-called first Latin American Parliament" an "attempt to open the door to Castroist infiltration in America." It called the plan drawn up by the four experts "a leap into the abyss" and stated that if it "should win assent, . . . we would find that all of a sudden we have been incorporated, at least in principle, into a strictly political supranational organization [that is] incompatible with our constitutional system."[36]

One argument against Latin American integration, used by economists and businessmen, consists in saying that they favor "national economic integration" (a phrase much in fashion). The Argentine minister of economics, Juan Carlos Pugliese, made some astonishing remarks on the subject: "I have not had an opportunity to analyze the subject in depth, but my first impression is that national integration must precede the regional," he said. Arturo Frondizi was even more vigorous: "We completely oppose letting regional integration be postulated as a substitute for national integration for each of our countries that already has begun industrialization. In these countries, the plans for actuarial complementation would act as a brake on new developments and explorations."[37]

The "Jacobins" and Marxists, in addition to shuffling around the arguments used by Communists, oligarchs, and businessmen, have added still another. They say that local industries, in order to produce surpluses for export within Latin America, will avoid satisfying the domestic markets. And, citing the example of the European Common Market, they demand that "equal pay" and other measures only beginning to be applied in Western Europe be applied instantly in the future Latin American Common Market—the object being obviously to frighten the industrialists and set them against it.

The most dangerous anti-unionist force is, however, the land-holding oligarchy, Already it is readying its weapons. At a meeting of the Inter-American Economic and Social Council of the OAS, in December, 1964, it was decided to form a common front of governments (most of them oligarchic, naturally) under the name of the Special Commission for Latin American Coordination. As the Uruguayan delegate Héctor Lorenzo Ríos said, it was a matter of "setting up a guild of the countries producing raw materials in order to have a dialogue of peers with the industrialized countries."[38] It is easy to see that the Commission will either be one of the bargaining agents to bring about the death of plans for unity, or a tool the oligarchies will use to bring about a unity they can control.

Purchase or Sterilization?

United States diplomacy in Latin America was shaped by the Monroe Doctrine. This doctrine has now become a cherished myth, something untouchable, even though events have proved again and again that it is an anachronistic doctrine which Washington cannot apply without more risk than advantage, and that its results have been minimal or negative.

President Monroe originally made three points: Europe must not plant future colonies in the Americas; intervention in the Americas by European powers would be considered a hostile act against the United States; the United States, in turn, would not intervene in European colonies already existing in America. But only a year after the doctrine was proclaimed, Secretary of State Henry Clay declared that the danger to which Monroe alluded had ceased to exist. Later, there was a new definition of the Monroe Doctrine (with the formulation of which, it should be remembered, the Latin American countries to which it applied had nothing to do). The *Diario Oficial* of the Republic of El Salvador published on March 6, 1920, a note from the United States Government to the effect that that government's opinion with regard to the Monroe Doctrine was contained in a speech by President Wilson to the delegates to the Second Pan-American Scientific Congress in January, 1916, in which the following principles were explicitly stated: (1) a warning to the European powers against establishing new colonies in America; (2) a statement that this warning did not imply any political or moral protectorate by the United States over other countries on the American continent; (3) guarantees to each of the American states of its absolute political independence and territorial integrity; (4) dedication to the principle of arbitration in order to maintain the international and internal peace of the Americas; (5) mutual respect among the American states for the rights of all; and (6) absolute political equality and equality of rights.

But Wilson's six points became a dead letter when the United States intervened in Nicaragua, Haiti, the Dominican Republic, etc. Many experts considered that the Monroe Doctrine had ceased to function and sought a new guideline on Washington's Latin American policy. Several—Bryce, Coolidge, and Kirkpatrick among them—pointed out that the promotion of a certain degree of union among the Latin American countries would serve the interests of the United States. They did not believe it was good for Washington to have to deal with so many weak countries. They did not go so far as to conceive of a Latin American union, but they did propose unity within zones.[39]

Events forced Washington to go further. Under Eisenhower, measures to unify Latin America began to win acceptance. Secretary of the Treasury George Humphrey opposed the creation of the Inter-American Bank, but his successor had to announce that the United States would not only support such an enterprise, but even supply a large part of its capital. President Kennedy sought to apply the unifying concept of the Alliance for Progress through bodies that would themselves make for unity—the Bank and the OAS—and resigned himself to acceptance of his country's role as *de facto* guardian of the OAS only because he realized that under oligarchic governments none of the benefits offered by the Alliance would reach the people. It is not presumptuous to believe that if Kennedy were alive today he would be an open partisan of Latin American unity and would understand the importance of making integration a political instrument instead of an economic agency.

But Washington's policy has changed. Now it is held that it is not necessary for the people to receive a share of the benefits of aid offered under the Alliance (in the concrete case of peons on coffee plantations), or of the profits from higher coffee prices. Washington now hopes that any profits not sent abroad on deposit will be used to reinvest in plant and that, when the new industries using this plant need labor, they will employ rural workers—so that, in the long run and indirectly, the people will receive the benefits of aid and of the best prices for raw materials.[40]

The authors of this "new" policy do not openly oppose plans for economic integration. Why should they revive old disputes or provoke protest when, with a few exceptions, the Latin American governments are lukewarm about integration and will support it only as a bargaining point? Washington knows that each time a plan for union is under discussion or there is talk of reforming the OAS, a moment of truth always arrives when the Latin American delegates will offer some high-sounding resolution leaving the matter of integration for the future, and will settle for more agencies in which the oligarchs' relatives are allowed to make "studies on integration." This is the moment when, in exchange for the vague generalities, the U.S. delegates offer some treaty or other (similar to the one already approved by Congress pledging itself to abide by the world agreements on coffee prices) or agree to give preferential treatment to Latin American raw materials (a step they have always refused to take until now).

The "new" policy, however, will have a consequence its authors have not foreseen. It will permit the oligarchies to capitalize on the people's discontent and indignation, which they will use, along with the concomitant anti-Yankeeism, to continue to pressure the United States for higher prices, etc. The people will not benefit, and Washington, thanks to the nearsightedness of a few high officials, will find itself alienated from the Latin American people.

In this way a vicious circle is established: Officials in Washington with iron fists and closed minds say, "We can do whatever suits us, and there won't be anything but verbal protests"; the "nationalists" in Latin America content themselves with verbal protests that entail no risk, a passivity that seems to prove that the Washington officials are right. But the people of Latin America and the people of the United States have to pay.

Which Way Does the Wind Blow?

Most of the advocates of Latin American unity are found in that sector of public opinion which refuses to believe that democracy has failed; they believe there has never been any democracy in Latin America and consider that democracy is precisely what needs to be tried. Such people are to be found mainly in the populist movements and in some governments headed by populists or strongly influenced by them.

Besides the basic motive—Latin American unity will make possible the first changes that will turn the countries into true nations in a supranational framework (or, more precisely, in a broader nationality)—diverse other reasons influence the partisans of unity. Some of them should be highlighted in order to demonstrate how necessary and urgent unity has become and how multiple its effects would be.

What are the chief obstacles to industrialization in Latin America? The lack of markets and national capital—that is to say, the absence of coordination among the various Latin American countries. Now land reform is indispensable if industrialized countries are to find large stable markets. But what are the obstacles to land reform? On one hand, the threat that it might provoke military coups, on the other, the fear of active discontent among the people unfavorably affected by it. No national land-reform plan has succeeded to this day in overcoming both these obstacles. The threat of the military coup has been averted in some cases. Up to now no one has found a solution to the problem of compensation for expropriated estates that has not evoked loud protest. Yet if a continental plan of land reform could be set up—a Latin American scheme that would take into account the present situation in each nation and the various degrees of agricultural development, that would coordinate production, that would use varied methods of reforms in accordance with each local situation—in other words, a very flexible plan—the possibility of a continental coup would be inconceivable. And, if it were financed with international public funds, the solution of the problem of indemnities would be in sight. They could be paid with international public funds on the condition that the money be invested in the country containing the expropriated land. Industrialization would then receive an enormous injection of national investment; the landholding oligarchy would perforce become a scattered and incohesive element.

This is not Utopia or "the individual notion of a genius." It is a course already suggested by many people, economically valid and in accordance with the new character of capitalism all over the world.*

There are still other reasons for favoring Latin American unity. One that is seldom mentioned, for fear of arousing the opposition of the militarists, derives from the very existence of Latin American militarism. National defense in Latin America really means continental defense. Would it not be logical to entrust that defense to a continental army? The most natural, effective, direct, and uncomplicated solution to the problem of militarism would be on a continental scale: to adopt a blend of methods

---

* Delegates from Chile and Peru proposed that land reform be financed by means of aid from international bodies that would guarantee the bonds issued as indemnification for the expropriations of land (AP dispatch, March 25, 1965). The author may be allowed the vanity of pointing out that he formulated this same proposal in 1957, in an essay entitled *"La integración vertical,"* which was reprinted with other articles early in 1964 in *Los subamericanos* (pp. 70 ff.).

common to all the Latin American countries, apply them gradually to all, and establish *one* Latin American army. Such a Latin American army would have a technical efficiency impossible for any national army, and at much lower cost.[41] And it would be improbable that a *Latin American* army could stage a coup.

It seems that the hidden, unconfessable reasons for Latin American unity are the most important ones. Not only would union make land reform possible without the risk of military coups and do away with militarism by establishing a Latin American army as a truly effective defense of the continent against foreign aggression, but it would provide the only possible way to prevent big nations from crushing medium-sized and small ones. The Latin Americans never say so, but the fact is that the three or four largest countries—in size and resources—tend to take the lion's share of all Latin American profit from aid agreements, treaties, and the like. This became very clear at the Punta del Este conference where the rough plan of the Alliance for Progress was approved. Argentina, reeling from military coups and countercoups and with its government bouncing like a ball from one barracks to another, proposed nothing less than this: that the United States (or the Alliance) aid the development of three or four key countries and that these countries, in turn, aid other countries on their respective boundaries: Mexico would aid Central America and the Caribbean; Brazil would aid Venezuela and Colombia; Argentina would aid Chile; Uruguay would aid Paraguay; Peru would aid Bolivia and Ecuador. . . . Naturally, the peripheral countries took a poor view of the proposal. A compromise was reached: the Argentine plan would not come up for debate, but neither would the conference approve the small countries' idea that the Alliance lay out a general plan for Latin America—a step that would have given the Alliance valuable prestige as having taken the first step toward organizing unification. The medium-sized countries, always ready to compromise, are unlikely to stand beside the big ones when the chips are down. But if genuine Latin American unity existed, that is, unity based not on economic factors alone, these inequalities would not loom as large as they do now.

On the other hand, the small countries, many of which are

ruled by dictators, constitute a political threat to both the medium-sized and large countries, where, from time to time, attempts are made to introduce more democracy into the life of the people and in at least three of which (Mexico, Venezuela, and Chile) the beginnings of democracy seem more or less guaranteed. The latter's insistence on nonintervention and their refusal to accept the idea of a Latin American army arise not so much from their traditional principles as from their fear of a majority of dictatorships in the Organization of American States. What would happen if, on some not far distant day, fifteen countries in the OAS were governed by dictators? If the people of any of those countries rose up, an inter-American army would be sent to support the regime. And if there was a military coup in a non-dictatorial state, the same Latin American army would be sent to support the insurgent. An inter-American army, under these circumstances, would be an army at the service of dictators and would not protect the people against extra-continental attack or against a true Communist threat.

In politics, it is futile to believe in the possibility of deceiving the adversary. The adversary may be conquered, but he cannot be fooled. To present the unity movement as a simple economic mechanism to expedite the formation of a common market will not deceive the oligarchy. The oligarchy will accept a common market only so long as it feels sure that it will not become something more. Never will the oligarchy willingly accept an integration plan that has for its immediate object making possible an authentic land reform. Neither will it ever accept an integration plan whose ultimate purpose is to change the Latin American countries into nations and make the latter the basis of a new Latin American supranationality.

The dilemma, then, is clear: either to content oneself with an integration that has no objective beyond that of establishing a common market—the least common possible—with the support of the oligarchic governments and the authors of the United States' "new" policy; or to search for pressure points where integration can be oriented toward political phase. For what is needed is *political* unity, the making of twenty countries into a single nation. That does not seem possible as things stand, but something may be achieved. A Latin American parliament with delegates from both the more or less authentic and the more or less bogus legislatures; economic integration among mixed, semi-capitalistic, and oligarchic economies. . . .

I do not mean that it was not a good thing to seize upon certain favorable circumstances to raise the problem of unity. Better a fictitious parliament that may make people believe in the possibility of its becoming real than no parliament at all. Better economic integration that habituates businessmen, labor, and consumers to react in Latin American terms than no integration at all.

Political integration is as desirable for Latin America as for the United States. No one can shrug off the problems of Latin America by saying, "If things don't go as I want them to, I'll stay home." The reality is before us; we can see that there are roadblocks on the path to unity, but we can also see the necessity for unity and the presence of forces that could make unity possible. The proper course, then, is not to be resigned to the obstacles but to find and mobilize the forces that can overcome them.

The wind is blowing toward unity. The sails are tattered, but somewhere new sails must be hidden away, ready to catch the wind and carry the ship into a fair harbor. The task is to find the sails and hoist them.

Notes

Publication data on cited works may be found in the Bibliography, pages 233–42.

1. DEFINITION AND CONFUSION

1. Adam Smith, *An Inquiry into the Nature and Causes of the Wealth of Nations,* p. 532.
2. Carter Goodrich, "Argentina as a New Country," p. 72.
3. *Comercio Exterior* (Mexico City), January, 1965, p. 53.
4. Hans Kohn, *The Idea of Nationalism: A Study in Its Origins and Background,* p. 6.
5. Carlton J. H. Hayes, *The Historical Evolution of Modern Nationalism, passim.*
6. Citations of Szechenyi, Arnold, and Veblen in Boyd C. Shafer, *Nationalism: Myth and Reality,* p. 180.
7. Henri Lefebvre, *Le nationalisme contre les nations,* p. 8.
8. *Ibid.*
9. Ernest Renan, *Qu'est-ce qu'une nation?*
10. Cited in Federico Chabod, *L'idea di nazione,* p. 61.
11. Joseph Stalin, *Marxism and the National Question,* p. 15.
12. Cited in Antonio G. Birlán, *El Estado, la patria y la nación,* p. 135.
13. Kohn, *op. cit.,* p. 23.
14. Cited in Leonard W. Doob, *Patriotism and Nationalism: The Psychological Foundations,* pp. 4–5.
15. Cited in Arthur P. Whitaker, *Nationalism in Latin America, Past and Present,* pp. 4–5.
16. Kohn, *op. cit.,* p. 12.
17. Doob, *op. cit.,* p. 6.
18. Alexander Manor, *Apuntes sobre la cuestión nacional,* pp. 74–75.
19. Cited in Rudolf Rocker, *Nationalism and Culture,* p. 203.

20. Kohn, *op. cit.,* p. 3.
21. Cited in Birlán, *op. cit.,* p. 130.
22. Kohn, *op. cit.,* p. 9.
23. Cited in Luis Alberto Sánchez, *Examen espectral de América Latina,* pp. 84–85.
24. See Pedro Henríquez Ureña, "El descontento y la promesa."
25. Cited in Roberto Fabregat Cúneo, *Caracteres sudamericanos,* p. 171.
26. Henríquez Ureña, *op. cit.,* pp. 32-33.
27. José Martí, "Nuestra América," p. 118.
28. Leopoldo Zea, *Dos etapas del pensamiento en Hispanoamérica,* pp. 9, 17–18.
29. Antonio Carrillo Flores, *El nacionalismo de los países latinoamericanos en la postguerra,* p. 17.
30. Fabregat Cúneo, *op. cit.,* p. 50.
31. Manuel Ugarte, *El porvenir de la América Latina,* p. 309.
32. Carrrillo Flores, *op. cit.,* p. 16.
33. K. H. Silvert, "Les valeurs nationales, le développement, les leaders et leurs troupes," p. 601.

2. INDEPENDENCE WITHOUT NATIONALISM

1. Both this and the following quotation are from Miguel Aguilera, "Lo típicamente español de la emancipación americana," pp. 95, 125.
2. As cited in Bernabé Navarro, "El pensamiento moderno de los jesuitas mexicanos del siglo XVIII," pp. 32–33.
3. See Jaime Jaramillo Uribe, "Influencias del pensamiento español y del pensamiento escolástico en la educación política de la generación precursora de la independencia de la Nueva Granada," pp. 398 ff.
4. Cited in Carlos Felice Cardot, "Rebeliones, motines y movimientos de masas en el siglo XVIII venezolano," p. 217.
5. Cited in Jaramillo Uribe, *op. cit.,* p. 405.
6. Cecil Jane, *Liberty and Despotism in Spanish America,* p. 133.
7. Manuel Pérez Vila, "Consideraciones sobre una posible síntesis de la historia de la independencia hispanoamericana," p. 243.
8. Julio César Jobet, "La revolución de la independencia," p. 8.
9. Jane, *op. cit.,* p. 144.
10. Cited in Ezequiel Martínez Estrada, *Diferencias y semejanzas entre los países de América Latina,* p. 412.
11. Cited in Jaramillo Uribe, *op. cit.,* p. 402.
12. On the persistence of racism in Latin America, see Víctor Alba, *Alliance Without Allies: The Mythology of Progress in Latin America,* pp. 82–83, and "Hipocresía y discriminación raciales."
13. Pérez Vila, *op. cit.,* p. 246.

14. Víctor Paz Estenssoro, "La revolución boliviana," pp. 152–53.
15. Pérez Vila, *op. cit.*, pp. 247–48.
16. Rómulo Betancourt, "Las posibilidades históricas de Venezuela," pp. 139 ff.
17. Jane, *op. cit.*, p. 118.
18. Cited in Rudolf Rocker, *Nationalism and Culture*, p. 274.
19. Cited in Martínez Estrada, *op. cit.*, p. 364.

3. The Colony Lives on in the Republic

1. Cited in Roberto Fabregat Cúneo, *Caracteres sudamericanos*, p. 11.
2. José Martí, "Nuestra América," p. 119.
3. Juan Bautista Alberdi, "Conveniencia y objeto de un Congreso General Americano."
4. Cited in Fabregat Cúneo, *op. cit.*, p. 31.
5. *Ibid.*, p. 112.
6. Ezequiel Martínez Estrada, *Diferencias y semejanzas entre los países de América Latina*, p. 403.
7. Julio Ycaza Tigerino, "Las formas políticas: Anarquía y dictadura," p. 103.
8. Martínez Estrada, *op. cit.*, pp. 470 ff.
9. Ycaza Tigerino, *op. cit.*, p. 102.
10. Martínez Estrada, *op. cit.*, p. 466.
11. Cited in Joaquín Gabaldón Márquez, "El municipio, raíz de la República," p. 365.
12. See Víctor Alba, *Alliance Without Allies: The Mythology of Progress in Latin America*, pp. 82–83.
13. Raúl Carrancá y Trujillo, *Panorama crítico de nuestra América*, pp. 160 ff.
14. Rómulo Betancourt, "Las posibilidades históricas de Venezuela," p. 141.
15. Fabregat Cúneo, *op. cit.*, pp. 114 ff.
16. See Víctor Alba, *Las ideas sociales contemporáneas en México*, pp. 49 ff.
17. Cited in Leopoldo Zea, *Dos etapas del pensamiento en Hispanoamérica*, p. 74.
18. Cited in Martínez Estrada, *op. cit.*, p. 483.
19. Agence France-Presse dispatch, February 27, 1965.
20. Zea, *op. cit.*, p. 34.
21. Cited in Mariano Picón Salas, "Unidad y nacionalismo en la historia hispanoamericana," pp. 327 ff.
22. Arthur P. Whitaker, *Nationalism in Latin America, Past and Present*, pp. 35–36.
23. This and following quotations from Zea, *op. cit.*, pp. 106 ff.
24. *Ibid.*, pp. 348, 46–47. This book offers excellent documentation on

positivism in Latin America. As to Mexico, see also Alba, *Las ideas sociales contemporáneas en México,* chap. iii. All the quotations from the positivists can be found in these two volumes.

25. Whitaker, *op. cit.,* pp. 26, 34.
26. Picón Salas, *op. cit.,* p. 331.
27. Martínez Estrada, *op. cit.,* p. 373.
28. Cited in Dardo Cúneo, "El pensamiento económico de José Hernández," p. 159.
29. Arturo Frondizi, *Breve historia de un yanqui que proyectó industrializar la Patagonia (1911–1914),* *passim.*
30. Charles A. Gauld, *The Last Titan: Percival Farquhar, American Entrepreneur in Latin America,* p. 240.
31. This and the following quotations from Manuel González Prada, "Nuestros indios," *passim.*
32. Alfredo Pareja Diezcanseco, "Un poco de geografía espiritual ecuatoriana," p. 64.
33. Cited in Cúneo, *loc. cit.*
34. Martínez Estrada, *op. cit.,* p. 418.
35. *Ibid.,* pp. 547 ff.
36. Cited in Manuel Ugarte, *El porvenir de la América Latina,* p. 312.
37. Julián Gorkín, in *Mondo latinoamericano e responsabilità della cultura europea,* p. 148.
38. Academy of Sciences of the U.S.S.R., *Nueva historia de los países coloniales y dependientes: América Latina,* p. 97.
39. Whitaker, *op. cit.,* p. 21.
40. Picón Salas, *op. cit.,* p. 333.
41. Cited in Zea, *op. cit.,* p. 167.
42. Cited in Martínez Estrada, *op. cit.,* pp. 382–83.

4. ATTEMPTS AT A POSITIVE NATIONALISM

1. Mario Monteforte Toledo, *Partidos políticos de Iberoamérica,* p. 136.
2. Zea, *op. cit.,* p. 297.
3. Cited in *ibid.,* p. 292.
4. José Ingenieros: "La formación de una raza argentina."
5. Leopoldo Zea, *Dos etapas del pensamiento en Hispanoamérica,* pp. 301 ff.
6. Manuel González Prada, "Nuestros indios," p. 51.
7. Manuel González Prada, *Los partidos y la Unión Nacional, passim.*
8. For more detail on the populist movements, see Víctor Alba, *Politics and the Labor Movement in Latin America,* chap. 7 (or the Spanish edition of the same, cited—in cases where the material is not exactly similar in the American edition—by its Spanish title), from which I have taken all the quotations in this section. Here, I shall speak only of the general ideological tendencies of populism

and of what they signify in relation to Latin American nationalism. I shall not give the history of each of these movements.

9. Venustiano Carranza, speech delivered at Hermosillo Sonora, September 24, 1913.
10. Rómulo Betancourt, "Las posibilidades históricas de Venezuela," p. 142.
11. Víctor Paz Estenssoro, "La revolución boliviana," pp. 162, 171–73.
12. Víctor Raúl Haya de la Torre, in *Mondo latinoamericano e responsabilità della cultura europea,* pp. 125 ff.
13. *Inter-American Conference for Democracy and Freedom,* pp. 195 ff.
14. *Report of the Second Inter-American Conference for Democracy and Freedom,* pp. 250 ff.
15. *Latinoamérica más allá de sus fronteras,* pp. 109 ff.
16. For data on the Latin American trade-union movement, see the second part of Alba, *op. cit.,* where its evolution is set forth in sufficient detail to make unnecessary an extended account here.
17. On the opposing concepts in the Mexican Revolution and its orienting forces, see Víctor Alba, *Las ideas sociales contemporáneas en México, passim.*
18. Bert F. Hoselitz, "Desarrollo económico de la América Latina," p. 354.
19. Cited in Eliseo Rangel Gaspar, "Los golpes de Estado y la revolución."
20. UPI dispatch, October 18, 1964.
21. Víctor Alba, *Esquema histórico del movimiento obrero en América Latina,* p. 79.
22. Manuel Germán Parra, "La doctrina de la Revolución Mexicana."
23. Agence France-Presse dispatch, October 28, 1964.
24. *Excélsior* (Mexico City), December 27, 1964.
25. *Ibid.,* January 30, 1965.
26. AP dispatch, September 10, 1964.
27. Irving Kristol, "The Poverty of Equality."

5. THE NATIONALISM OF THE EMPEROR'S CLOTHES

1. Roberto Fabregat Cúneo, *Caracteres sudamericanos,* p. 164.
2. *Ibid.,* p. 125.
3. Lucio Mansilla, *Una excursión a los indios ranqueles,* p. 252.
4. Víctor Paz Estenssoro, "La revolución boliviana," p. 161.
5. Corporación de Fomento, *Resumen del programa general de desarrollo económico para el próximo decenio (1959–1968),* pp. 4–16.
6. "Chile's Christian Democrats."
7. Jorge Luis Recavarren, "Notas sobre la burguesía peruana."
8. Agence France-Presse dispatch, April 3, 1965.
9. Mario Verdú, in "Por una reforma agraria," demonstrates the existence of an acute agrarian problem and suggests solutions.

10. Arturo Frondizi, *La Argentina, ¿es un país subdesarrollado?* pp. 19–20.
11. *Panoramas* (Mexico City), No. 14, March–April, 1965, p. 29.
12. Cited in Luis Guillermo Piazza, "Entretelones del deterioro financiero de Argentina."
13. Agence France-Presse dispatch, March 26, 1965.
14. Elmer von Feldt, "Se investiga expulsión de sacerdote." Further documentation of this case, worthy of a book in itself, may be found in the following Guatemalan publications: *Prensa Libre*, July 27, 1964, and *La Hora*, July 30 and 31, 1964.
15. *Hanson's Latin American Letter* (Washington, D.C.), November 14, 1964, and February 20, 1965.
16. UPI dispatch, February 17, 1965.
17. Bert F. Hoselitz, "Desarrollo económico de la América Latina," p. 354.
18. Cited in Ezequiel Martínez Estrada, *Diferencias y semejanzas entre los países de América Latina,* p. 437. On Brazilian militarism, see also Stenio de Eviao, "Un militarismo especial."
19. *Hanson's Latin American Letter,* December 19, 1964, and March 20, 1965.
20. Cited in Leopoldo Zea: *América como conciencia,* pp. 141 ff.
21. Arthur P. Whitaker, *Nationalism in Latin America, Past and Present,* pp. 34 ff., and Ricardo Rojas, *El profeta de la pampa, passim.*
22. José Vasconcelos, in *Integración política de Iberoamérica,* pp. 45–46.
23. Ycaza Tigerino, "Las formas políticas, Anarquía y dictadura," pp. 106–7.
24. Ycaza Tigerino, *Sociología de la política hispanoamericana,* pp. 288, 32, 127.
25. Fabregat Cúneo, *op. cit.,* p. 169.
26. Cited in *ibid.,* p. 172.
27. *Ibid.,* p. 112.
28. Whitaker, *op. cit.,* p. 52.
29. Alberto Baeza Flores, "Los reflejos condicionados de la cultura."
30. Carlos Pellegrini, *Discursos y escritos,* p. 107.
31. Whitaker, *op. cit.,* pp. 37–38.
32. See "Los nazis argentinos," *Panoramas,* No. 2, March–April, 1963, and "Nazis de Chile," *Panoramas,* No. 11, September–October, 1964. See also John J. Kennedy, *Catholicism, Nationalism, and Democracy in Argentina, passim.*
33. Agence France-Presse dispatch, January 27, 1965.
34. UPI dispatch, February 12, 1965.
35. UPI dispatch, August 27, 1964.
36. AP dispatch, September 10, 1964.
37. UPI dispatch, November 17, 1964.

38. A. González Hernández, "La distribución de la renta en Ibero-américa."
39. Agence France-Presse dispatch, March 12, 1965.
40. The two following tables, compiled by Carlos A. Tello, appear in his "El sector agrícola y el desarrollo económico en los países latinoamericanos." The figures shown are those most recently available.
41. Agence France-Presse dispatch, March 13, 1965.
42. Antonio J. Posada, "La coyuntura económica de América Latina."
43. Fabregat Cúneo, *op. cit.,* pp. 60, 56.
44. *Ibid.,* p. 59.
45. *Ibid.,* p. 56.
46. Alfredo Pareja Diezcanseco, "Un poco de geografía espiritual ecuatoriana," p. 61.
47. *Comentarios* (Buenos Aires), March 25, 1964, pp. 7–8.
48. *Panoramas,* No. 11, September–October, 1964, pp. 121–22.
49. ECLA Report, in *Comercio Exterior* (Mexico City), November, 1963, p. 785.
50. *Ibid.*
51. AP dispatch on a conference sponsored by the United Nations at Viña del Mar, Chile, March 27, 1965.

6. NEGATIVE NATIONALISM

1. Parts of this chapter have appeared previously in the form of articles published in *Problems of Communism* (Washington, D.C.).
2. For a more detailed study, see Robert J. Alexander, *Communism in Latin America,* and Víctor Alba, *Historia del Frente Popular.*
3. See Víctor Alba, *Esquema histórico del comunismo en Iberoamérica,* pp. 81 ff.
4. A. Losovsky, *El movimiento sindical latinoamericano, sus virtudes y sus defectos,* p. 5.
5. Rodolfo Piña Soria, "Viaje por suscripción popular."
6. *La Correspondencia Internacional* (Paris), March and August, 1940.
7. Cited in Luis Chávez Orozco, "Por qué renuncié al cargo de secretario general del Sindicato de Trabajadores de la Educación."
8. Cited in Alba, *Esquema histórico del comunismo en Iberoamérica,* p. 102.
9. See Alba, *Politics and the Labor Movement in Latin America,* pp. 142 ff.
10. Alexander, *op. cit.,* pp. 194 ff.
11. Vicente Lombardo Toledano, *El nuevo programa del sector revolucionario de México,* p. 15.
12. Cited in A. López Aparicio, *El movimiento obrero en México,* p. 230.

13. See Alba, *Esquema histórico del comunismo en Iberoamérica*, pp. 148 ff.
14. Víctor Alba, *Alliance Without Allies: The Mythology of Progress in Latin America*, pp. 67–74.
15. Alexander, *op. cit.*, pp. 22–23.
16. Víctor Alba, "Triunfo comunista en Guatemala."
17. José Carlos Mariátegui, set forth in *Siete ensayos de interpretación de la realidad peruana.*
18. *Bajo la bandera de la CSLA*, pp. 15 ff., 46 ff., 65 ff., 147 ff.
19. *El movimiento revolucionario latinoamericano*, pp. 233, 266.
20. Julio Cuadro Caldas, *Las trágicas payasadas de los comunistas criollos*, pp. 60 ff.
21. *Ibid.*, pp. 146 ff.
22. Victorio Codovila, *Nuestro camino desemboca en la victoria*, pp. 203–4.
23. *Los socialistas y la realidad cubana*, pp. 300 ff.
24. José Boglich, *La cuestión agraria*, pp. 196 ff.
25. This and following quotations from Víctor Alba, *Las ideas sociales contemporáneas en México*, pp. 307–12.
26. Ronald M. Schneider: *Communism in Guatemala, 1944–1954*, pp. 47, 76, 77, 205–8.
27. *Revista Internacional* (Prague), March, 1961.
28. Robert J. Alexander, *The Bolivian National Revolution*, pp. 62 ff.
29. *Informe al IV Congresso do Partido communista do Brasil.*
30. *Por una paz duradera* (Bucharest), February 25, 1955.
31. These opinions appeared in *Revista Internacional* (Prague), January–March, 1961.
32. Gilberto Vieira: "Las luchas en el campo colombiano y el Partido Comunista."
33. See the contributions by Jorge Prado and Pedro Saad in the exchange of opinions printed in *Revista Internacional*, March, 1961.
34. Blas Roca, *The Cuban Revolution*, p. 99.
35. Alba, *Historia del movimiento obrero en América Latina*, pp. 203–4, 212–13.

7. Nationalism as an Opium of the Conscience

1. Manuel Ugarte, *El porvenir de la América Latina*, p. 84.
2. *Ibid.*, p. 78.
3. Cited in Leopoldo Zea, *América como conciencia*, p. 142.
4. *Ibid.*, p. 145.
5. "Nacionalismo y patriotería."
6. Cited in Luis Guillermo Piazza, "Desesperanza de Benedetti."
7. Carlos Naudón, *América impaciente*, p. 196.
8. Alberto Baltra, *Crecimiento económico de América Latina*, p. 71.
9. Juan Liscano, "Objetividad crítica y revistas petroleras."

10. *Siempre* (Mexico City) October 14, 1964.
11. "El ataque norteamericano a la Dominicana es una amenaza a todos los hogares de América," *El Día* (Mexico City), May 6, 1965.
12. *Problemas agrícolas e industriales de México,* IV, No. 3, 282.
13. Gabriel del Mazo, "De la universidad medieval europea a la universidad argentina y sudamericana," pp. 195–96.
14. Roberto Fabregat Cúneo, *Caracteres sudamericanos,* p. 88.
15. AP dispatch, January 29, 1965.
16. Georges Goriély, "Université, démocratie et notion d'élite."
17. Mario Monteforte Toledo, *Partidos políticos de Iberoamérica,* p. 123.
18. Víctor Alba, *Politics and the Labor Movement in Latin America,* p. 89.
19. Frederick B. Pike, "The Modernized Church in Peru: Two Aspects," p. 314.
20. UPI dispatch, March 25, 1965.
21. *Ibid.,* p. 318, quoting *La Prensa* (Lima), April 13, 1964.
22. David Kirk, "The Catholic Church and Social Revolution."
23. Pike, *op. cit.,* p. 316.
24. "Brazil: Progress Report."
25. The following quotations are from Antonio García, *La rebelión de los pueblos débiles,* pp. 58, 76, 79, 97, 142.
26. Monteforte Toledo, *op. cit.,* pp. 128–29.
27. Rodrigo García Treviño, *La ingerencia rusa en México,* p. 60.
28. Rodolfo Ortega Peña, Introduction to Juan José Hernández Arregui, *Imperialismo y cultura,* pp. 7–9.
29. This and the following quotations from Jorge Medina, "La 'izquierda nacional.'"
30. Silvio Frondizi, *La realidad argentina,* I, 230, 237, 238.
31. Oscar Waiss, *Nacionalismo y socialismo en América Latina,* pp. 138, 144.
32. This and following quotation from Hugo Zemelman Merino, "Problemas ideológicos de la izquierda."
33. Cited in Angel Guerra, "Carta sobre las elecciones en Chile."
34. Carlos Rojas Juanco, "El programa de Allende y la izquierda latinoamericana."
35. Juan Ignacio Prieto, "Venezuela: ¿una revolución frustrada?"
36. Cited in Arthur P. Whitaker, *Nationalism in Latin America, Past and Present,* p. 16.
37. Glicerio González López, "Aportes al análisis del problema del ciclaje."
38. Jacobo Zabludovsky, "Decir la verdad."
39. ECLA Report in *Comercio Exterior* (Mexico City), November, 1964, p. 786.
40. *Hanson's Latin American Letter,* May 1, 1965.
41. *Política* (Mexico City), September 15, 1964.

42. Manuel Germán Parra, "Una nueva teoría económica."
43. AP dispatch, May 1, 1965.
44. *El Siglo* (Santiago), April 9, 1965.
45. On Latin American militarism, see Edwin Lieuwen, *Arms and Politics in Latin America,* and *Generals vs. Presidents: Neomilitarism in Latin America;* John J. Johnson, *The Military and Society in Latin America* (very optimistic on the evolution of the military); and Víctor Alba, *El militarismo: Ensayo sobre un fenómeno político-social iberoamericano.*
46. See Víctor Alba, *El ascenso de militarismo tecnocrático,* and *Alliance Without Allies: The Mythology of Progress in Latin America,* pp. 119 ff.
47. Regelio García Lupo, *Historia de unas malas relaciones.*
48. A. Shul'govskiy, "Imperialism and the Ideology of National Reformism in Latin America," p. 325.
49. Cited in Víctor Alba, *Politics and the Labor Movement in Latin America,* pp. 165–66.
50. Cited in *Historia del movimiento obrero en América Latina,* p. 272.

8. Great Nation or Little Countries?

1. The best analyses of the events in the Dominican Republic are those written by Theodore Draper. For the situation which preceded it, see also Juan Bosch, *Trujillo: Causas de una tiranía sin ejemplo,* and *Crisis de la democracia de América en la República Dominicana.*
2. This and following quotations appear in Augusto C. Sandino, "Primer manifiesto político," and "Carta circular."
3. Silvio Zavala, "El fin de los imperios europeos en America," and Antonio Gómez Robledo, *Idea y experiencia de América,* chap. iii–v.
4. Mario Hernández Sánchez-Barba, *Las tensiones históricas hispanoamericanas en el siglo XX,* pp. 188–89.
5. Mariano Picón Salas, in *Integración política de Iberoamérica,* p. 33.
6. Gómez Robledo, *op. cit.,* p. 162.
7. Víctor Alba, *Politics and the Labor Movement in Latin America,* pp. 57–59, 114–17, 166–67.
8. Cited in Leopoldo Zea, *América como conciencia,* p. 62.
9. Romain Rolland, "Carta a Alfredo L. Palacios."
10. Peruvian Aprista Party, *Cuarenta años de lucha por la unidad de América Latina, 1924–1964,* p. 8.
11. Víctor Raúl Haya de la Torre, in *Mondo latinoamericano e responsabilità della cultura europea,* pp. 138–39.
12. Mariano Picón Salas, "Unidad y nacionalismo en la historia hispanoamericana," pp. 340–41.
13. Manuel Ugarte, *El porvenir de la América Latina,* pp. xiv–xv.

14. This and the following quotation from José Ingenieros, "Por la unión latinoamericana."
15. Alfredo Pareja Diezcanseco, in *Integración política de Iberoamérica,* p. 25.
16. Antonio Carrillo Flores, *El nacionalismo de los países latinoamericanos en la postguerra,* p. 16.
17. Víctor Paz Estenssoro, "La revolución boliviana," p. 177.
18. Rafael Caldera, "La batalla que estamos librando."
19. "A la conciencia de América."
20. Arthur P. Whitaker, *Nationalism in Latin America, Past and Present,* p. 57.
21. For a view on the integration of the Latin American economy, see Victor L. Urquidi, *The Challenge of Development in Latin America,* and *Trayectoria del Mercado Común Latinoamericano,* for a history and analysis of the Latin American Common Market. See also Miguel S. Wionczek (ed.), *Latin American Economic Integration: Experiences and Prospects.*
22. José A. Guerra and Enrique Lerdau, "Planeación e integración en América Central," p. 355.
23. "La ALALC en la encrucijada."
24. Felipe Herrera, "Tres propuestas de un 'visionario.' "
25. "La integración de la América Latina."
26. "Nuevo paso hacia la cooperación regional latinoamericana,"
27. Andrés Townsend, "Ya existe el parlamento latinoamericano."
28. For the economic aspects of Latin American integration, see Wionczek, *op. cit.* See also *Hacia la integración acelerada de América Latina,* which contains the plan drawn up by José Antonio Mayobre, Felipe Herrera, Carlos Sanz de Santamaría, and Raúl Prebisch. Some speeches by Felipe Herrera deal with the problem of political integration, as does much of the Aprista literature. Nothing is in print on social integration, even though that is the most fundamental aspect of the problem.
29. The causes of this situation are analyzed in Víctor Alba, *Alliance Without Allies: The Mythology of Progress in Latin America,* chap. iii.
30. Cited in Alexander Manor, *La question nationale,* p. 11.
31. A. Shul'govskiy, "Imperialism and the Ideology of National Reformism in Latin America," pp. 309, 316.
32. *Boletín Sindical Latinoamericano* (Santiago), No. 9, 1964.
33. "Crítica uruguaya a las exigencias socialistas."
34. Cited in Academy of Sciences of the U.S.S.R., *Nueva historia de los países coloniales y dependientes: América Latina,* p. 73.
35. Mariano Picón Salas, in *Integración política de Iberoamérica,* pp. 28–29.
36. Cited in *Visión* (Panama City), May 14, 1965, p. 38.
37. Cited in *ibid.*

38. Cited in Agence France-Presse dispatch, December 9, 1964.
39. Raúl Carranca y Trujillo, *Panorama crítico de nuestra América*, pp. 112–33.
40. *Hanson's Latin American Letter*, May 22, 1965.
41. This argument is set forth in greater detail in Víctor Alba, *El militarismo: Ensayo sobre un fenómeno político-social iberoamericano*, pp. 157 ff.

Bibliography

ACADEMY OF SCIENCES OF THE U.S.S.R. *Nueva historia de los países coloniales y dependientes: América Latina.* Havana: Ed. Páginas, 1943.

AGUILERA, MIGUEL. "Lo típicamente español de la emancipación americana," in *El movimiento emancipador de Hispanoamérica,* Vol. IV. Caracas: National Academy of History, 1961.

"La ALALC en la encrucijada," *Comercio Exterior* (Mexico City), September, 1964.

ALBA, VÍCTOR. *Alliance Without Allies: The Mythology of Progress in Latin America.* New York: Frederick A. Praeger, 1965.

————. *El ascenso del militarismo tecnocrático.* Mexico City: Centro de Estudios y Documentación Sociales, 1963.

————. *Esquema histórico del comunismo en Iberoamérica* (3d ed.). Mexico City: Ed. Occidentales, 1960.

————. *Esquema histórico del movimiento obrero en América Latina.* Mexico City: Costa Amic, 1957.

————. *Historia del Frente Popular.* Mexico City: Libro-Mex, 1959.

————. *Historia del movimiento obrero en América Latina.* Mexico City: Libreros Mexicanos Unidos, 1964.

————. *Las ideas sociales contemporáneas en México.* Mexico City: Fondo de Cultura Económica, 1960.

————. *El militarismo: Ensayo sobre un fenómeno político-social iberoamericano.* Mexico City: Instituto de Investigaciones Sociales, Universidad Nacional Autónoma de México, 1959.

————. *Politics and the Labor Movement in Latin America.* Stanford, Calif.: Stanford University Press, 1967.

233

————. *Los subamericanos.* Mexico City: Costa Amic, 1964.

————. "Triunfo comunista en Guatemala," *Resaca* (Mexico City), November, 1954.

ALBERDI, JUAN BAUTISTA. "Conveniencia y objeto de un Congreso General Americano," in *Hispanoamérica en lucha por su Independencia.* Mexico City: Cuadernos Americanos, 1962.

ALEXANDER, ROBERT J. *The Bolivian National Revolution.* New Brunswick, N.J.: Rutgers University Press, 1958.

————. *Communism in Latin America.* New Brunswick, N.J.: Rutgers University Press, 1957.

ARICÓ, JOSÉ M. "Examen y conciencia," *Pasado y Presente* (Córdoba, Argentina), January–March, 1964.

"El ataque norteamericano a la Dominicana es una amenaza a todos los hogares de América," *El Dia* (Mexico City), May 6, 1965.

BAEZA FLORES, ALBERTO. "Los reflejos condicionados de la cultura," *Panoramas* (Mexico City), No. 14 (March–April, 1965).

Bajo la bandera de la CSLA. Montevideo, 1929.

BALTRA, ALBERTO. *Crecimiento económica de América Latina.* Santiago: Ed. del Pacífico, 1960.

BETANCOURT, RÓMULO. "Las posibilidades históricas de Venezuela," in EUGENIO CHANG-RODRÍGUEZ and HARRY KANTOR (eds.), *La América Latina de hoy.* New York: Ronald Press, 1961.

BIRLÁN, ANTONIO G. (ed.). *El Estado, la patria y la nación.* Buenos Aires: Americalee, 1956.

BLANC, V. "La juventud aislada," *Panoramas* (Mexico City), No. 16 (July–August, 1965).

BOGLICH, JOSÉ: *La cuestión agraria.* Buenos Aires: Claridad, 1937.

BOSCH, JUAN. *Crisis de la democracia de América en la República Dominicana.* Mexico City: Centro de Estudios y Documentación Sociales, 1964.

————. *Trujillo: Causas de una tirania sin ejemplo.* Caracas, 1961.

"Brazil: Progress Report," *New Statesman* (London), December 25, 1964.

BULLRICH, SILVINA. *Los burgueses.* Buenos Aires: Sudamericana, 1964.

CALDERA, RAFAEL. "La batalla que estamos librando," in LINO RODRÍGUEZ ARIAS (ed.), *La democracia cristiana y América Latina.* Lima: Ed. Universitaria, 1961.

CARRANCA Y TRUJILLO, RAÚL. *Panorama crítico de nuestra América.* Mexico City: Imprenta Universitaria, 1950.

CARRANZA, VENUSTIANO. Speech delivered at Hermosillo, Sonora, September 24, 1913, in *Hispanoamérica en lucha por su independencia.* Mexico City: Cuadernos Americanos, 1962.

CARRILLO FLORES, ANTONIO. *El nacionalismo de los países latinoamericanos en la postguerra.* Mexico City: El Colegio de México, 1945.

CEPEDA, ALFREDO. Oposición en el ejército argentino," *El Dia* (Mexico City), May 20, 1964.

CHABOD, FEDERICO. *L'idea di nazione* (2d ed.). Bari, Italy: Laterza, 1962.

CHANG-RODRÍGUEZ, EUGENIO. *La literatura política de González Prada, Mariátegui y Haya de la Torre.* Mexico City: Studium, 1957.

———— and KANTOR, HARRY (eds.). *La América Latina de hoy.* New York: Ronald Press, 1961.

CHAVARRÍA, MANUEL F. In *Integración política de Iberoamérica.* Mexico City: El Colegio de México, no date.

CHÁVEZ OROZCO, LUIS. "Por qué renuncié al cargo de secretario general del Sindicato de Trabajadores de la Educación," *Acción Social* (Mexico City), September 15, 1945.

"Chile's Christian Democrats," *The New Republic* (Washington, D.C.), March 20, 1965.

CODOVILA, VICTORIO. *Nuestro camino desemboca en la victoria.* Buenos Aires, 1954.

"A la conciencia de América," in EUGENIO CHANG-RODRÍGUEZ and HARRY KANTOR (eds.), *La América Latina de hoy.* New York: Ronald Press, 1961.

"La Conférence Régionale de l'Agriculture de l'Amérique Latine à México." Supplement to *Mouvement Syndical Mondial* (Paris), 1951.

CORPORACIÓN DE FOMENTO. *Resumen del programa general de desarrollo económico para el próximo decenio (1959–1968).* Santiago: Corporación de Fomento, 1959.

"Crítica uruguaya a las exigencias socialistas," *Excélsior* (Mexico City), May 15, 1965.

CUADRO CALDAS, JULIO. *Las trágicas payasadas de los comunistas criollos.* Puebla de Zaragoza, Mexico: S. Loyo, 1934.

"La cuestión agraria y el movimiento de liberación nacional," *Revista Internacional* (Prague), January–March, 1961.

CÚNEO, DARDO. "El pensamiento económico de José Hernández," *Cuadernos Americanos* (Mexico City), Vols. XI–XII, 1964.

DOOB, LEONARD W. *Patriotism and Nationalism: The Psychological Foundations.* New Haven: Yale University Press, 1964.

DRAPER, THEODORE. "The Dominican Crisis," *Commentary* (New York), December, 1965.

————. "The Roots of the Dominican Crisis," *The New Leader* (New York), May 24, 1965.

EVIAO, STENIO DE. "Un militarismo especial," *Panoramas* (Mexico City), No. 10 (July–August, 1964).

FABREGAT CÚNEO, ROBERTO. *Caracteres sudamericanos*. Mexico City: Instituto de Investigaciones Sociales, Universidad Nacional Autónoma de México, 1950.

FELDT, ELMER VON. "Se investiga expulsión de sacerdote," *Boletín de la NA* (Lima), February 27, 1965.

FELICE CARDOT, CARLOS. "Rebeliones, motines y movimientos de masas en el siglo XVIII venezolano," in *El Movimiento emancipador de Hispanoamérica,* Vol. II. Caracas: Academia Nacional de la Historia, 1961.

FRONDIZI, ARTURO. *La Argentina ¿es un país subdesarrollado?* Buenos Aires: Ed. CEN, 1964.

————. *Breve historia de un yanqui que proyectó industrializar la Patagonia (1911–1914)*. Buenos Aires, n.d.

FRONDIZI, SILVIO. *La realidad argentina*. Buenos Aires, 1960.

GABALDÓN MÁRQUEZ, JOAQUIN. "El municipio, raíz de la República," in *El Movimiento emancipador de Hispanoamérica,* Vol. II. Caracas: Academia Nacional de la Historia, 1961.

GARCÍA, ANTONIO. *La rebelión de los pueblos débiles*. Bogotá: Fondo Socialista de Publicaciones, 1953.

GARCÍA LUPO, ROGELIO. *Historia de unas malas relaciones*. Buenos Aires: Jorge Alvarez ed., 1964.

GARCÍA TREVIÑO, RODRIGO. *La ingerencia rusa en México*. Mexico City: Ed. América, 1959.

GAULD, CHARLES A. *The Last Titan: Percival Farquhar, American Entrepreneur in Latin America. (Hispanic American Report)*. Stanford, Calif.: Institute of Hispanic American and Luso-Brazilian Studies, Stanford University, 1964.

GÓMEZ ROBLEDO, ANTONIO. *Idea y experiencia de América*. Mexico City: Fondo de Cultura Económica, 1958.

GONZÁLEZ CASANOVA, HENRIQUE. "No se puede aspirar a hacer una gran nación sin una literatura nacional," *Siempre* (Mexico City), October 14, 1964.

GONZÁLEZ HERNÁNDEZ, A. "La distribución de la renta en Iberoamérica," in *Cuadernos para el diálogo* (Madrid), December, 1964.

GONZÁLEZ LOPEZ, GLICERIO. "Aportes al análisis del problema del ciclaje," *El Día* (Mexico City), April 3, 1965.

GONZÁLEZ PRADA, MANUEL. "Nuestros indios," in EUGENIO CHANG-RODRIGUEZ and HARRY KANTOR (eds.), *La América Latina de hoy*. New York: Ronald Press, 1961.

————. *Los partidos y la Unión Nacional*. Lima, 1898.

GOODRICH, CARTER. "Argentina as a New Country," *Comparative Studies in Society and History* (The Hague), October, 1964.

GORIÉLY, GEORGES. "Université, démocratie et notion d'élite," *Etudes* (Brussels), No. 4 (1963).

GORKÍN, JULIÁN. In *Mondo latinoamericano e responsabilità della cultura europea.* Genoa, 1958.

GUERRA, ANGEL. "Carta sobre las elecciones en Chile," *El Día* (Mexico City), September 20, 1966.

GUERRA, JOSÉ A. and LERDAU, ENRIQUE. "Planeación e integración en América Central," *Economía Latinoamericana* (Pan-American Union, Washington, D.C.), July, 1964.

Hacia la integración acelerada de América Latina. Mexico City: Fondo de Cultura Económica, 1965.

HAYA DE LA TORRE, VÍCTOR RAÚL. In *Mondo latinoamericano e responsabilità della cultura europea.* Genoa, 1958.

———. *Pensamiento político.* Lima: Ed. Pueblo, 1961.

HAYES, CARLTON J. H. *The Historical Evolution of Modern Nationalism.* New York: Richard R. Smith, 1931.

HEGEL, GEORG WILHELM FRIEDRICH. *The Philosophy of History.* Translated by J. SIBREE. New York: Colonial Press, 1900.

HENRÍQUEZ UREÑA, PEDRO. "El descontento y la promesa," in EUGENIO CHANG-RODRÍGUEZ and HARRY KANTOR (eds.), *La América Latina de hoy.* New York: Ronald Press, 1961.

HERNÁNDEZ ARREGUI, JUAN JOSÉ. *Imperialismo y cultura.* Buenos Aires: Hachea, 1964.

HERNÁNDEZ SÁNCHEZ-BARBA, MARIO. *Las tensiones históricas hispanoamericanas en el siglo XX.* Madrid: Guadarrama, 1961.

HERRERA, FELIPE. "Tres propuestas de un 'visionario,'" *Panoramas* (Mexico City), No. 4 (July–August, 1963).

"Hipocresía y discriminación raciales," *Panoramas* (Mexico City), No. 16 (July–August, 1965).

Hispanoamérica en lucha por su independencia. Mexico City: Cuadernos Americanos, 1962.

HOSELITZ, BERT F. "Desarrollo económico de la América Latina," *Revista Interamericana de Ciencias Sociales* (Washington, D.C.), Vol. I, No. 3 (1962).

INGENIEROS, JOSÉ. "La formación de una raza argentina," *Revista de Filosofía* (Buenos Aires), Vol. I (1915).

———. "Por la unión latinoamericana," in *Hispanoamérica en lucha por su independencia.* Mexico City: Cuadernos Americanos, 1962.

"La Integración de la América Latina," *Comercio Exterior* (Mexico City), April, 1965.

Integración política de Iberoamérica. Mexico City: El Colegio de México, no date.

Inter-American Conference for Democracy and Freedom, Havana, 1950.

JANE, CECIL. *Liberty and Despotism in Spanish America.* New York and Oxford: Oxford University Press, 1929.

JARAMILLO URIBE, JAIME. "Influencias del pensamiento español y del pensamiento escolástico en la educación política de la generación precursora de la independencia de la Nueva Granada," in *El movimiento emancipador de Hispanoamérica,* Vol. IV. Caracas: Academia Nacional de la Historia, 1961.

JOBET, JULIO CÉSAR. "La revolución de la independencia," *Arauco* (Santiago), October, 1959.

JOHNSON, JOHN J. *The Military and Society in Latin America.* Stanford, Calif.: Stanford University Press, 1964.

KENNEDY, JOHN J. *Catholicism, Nationalism, and Democracy in Argentina.* Notre Dame, Ind.: University of Notre Dame Press, 1958.

KIRK, DAVID. "The Catholic Church and Social Revolution," *New America* (New York), November 30, 1964.

KOHN, HANS. *The Idea of Nationalism: A Study in Its Origins and Background.* New York: Macmillan, 1944.

KRISTOL, IRVING. "The Poverty of Equality," *The New Leader* (New York), March 1, 1965.

Latinoamérica más allá de sus fronteras. San José, Costa Rica: Ed. Combate, 1960.

LEFEBVRE, HENRI. *Le nationalisme contre les nations.* Paris: Ed. Sociales Internacionales, 1937.

LIEUWEN, EDWIN. *Arms and Politics in Latin America.* New York: Frederick A. Praeger, 1960.

———. *Generals vs. Presidents: Neomilitarism in Latin America.* New York: Frederick A. Praeger, 1964.

LISCANO, JUAN. "Objetividad crítica y revistas petroleras," *Zona Franca* (Caracas), November, 1964.

LOMBARDO TOLEDANO, VICENTE. *El nuevo programa del sector revolucionario de México.* Mexico City, 1944.

LÓPEZ APARICIO, A. *El movimiento obrero en México.* Mexico City: Ed. Jus., 1952.

LOSOVSKY, ANATOL. *El movimiento sindical latinoamericano, sus virtudes y sus defectos.* Montevideo, 1929.

MANOR, ALEXANDER. *La question nationale.* Tel Aviv: Bibliothèque Idéologique, 1957.

MANSILLA, LUCIO. *Una excursión a los indios ranqueles.* Buenos Aires: Anaconda, 1931.

MARIÁTEGUI, JOSÉ CARLOS. *Siete ensayos de interpretación de la realidad peruana.* Lima: Ed. Amauta, 1928.

MARTÍ, JOSÉ. "Nuestra América," in *Hispanoamérica en lucha por su independencia.* Mexico City: Cuadernos Americanos, 1962.

MARTÍNEZ ESTRADA, EZEQUIEL. *Diferencias y semejanzas entre los países de América Latina.* Mexico City: Universidad Nacional Autónoma de México, 1962.

MAZO, GABRIEL DEL. "De la universidad medieval europea a la universidad argentina y sudamericana," in EUGENIO CHANG-RODRÍGUEZ and HARRY KANTOR (eds.), *La América Latina de hoy.* New York: Ronald Press, 1961.

MEDINA, JORGE. "La 'izquierda nacional,'" *Panoramas* (Mexico City), No. 16 (July–August, 1965).

MENDOZA DIEZ, ALVARO. *La revolución de los profesionales e intelectuales en Latinoamérica.* Mexico City: Instituto de Investigaciones Sociales, Universidad Nacional Autónoma de México, 1962.

MONTEFORTE TOLEDO, MARIO. *Partidos políticos de Iberoamérica.* Mexico City: Instituto de Investigaciones Sociales, Universidad Nacional Autónoma de México, 1961.

El movimiento revolucionario latinoamericano. Buenos Aires, 1929.

"Nacionalismo y patriotería," *El Día* (Mexico City), March 5, 1965.

NAUDÓN, CARLOS. *América impaciente.* Santiago: Ed. del Pacífico, 1963.

NAVARRO, BERNABÉ. "El pensamiento moderno de los jesuitas mexicanos del siglo XVIII," *La Palabra y el Hombre* (Jalapa, Veracruz, Mexico), January–March, 1964.

"Los Nazis argentinos," *Panoramas* (Mexico City), No. 2 (March–April, 1963).

"Nazis de Chile," *Panoramas* (Mexico City), No. 11 (September–October, 1964).

"Nuevo paso hacia la cooperación regional latinoamericana," *Comercio Exterior* (Mexico City), December, 1964.

ORTEGA PEÑA, RODOLFO. Introduction to JUAN JOSÉ HERNÁNDEZ ARREGUI, *Imperialismo y cultura.* Buenos Aires: Hachea, 1964.

PAREJA DIEZCANSECO, ALFREDO. In *Integración política de Iberoamérica.* Mexico City: El Colegio de México, no date.

―――. "Un poco de geografía espiritual ecuatoriana," in EUGENIO CHANG-RODRÍGUEZ and HARRY KANTOR (eds.), *La América Latina de hoy.* New York: Ronald Press, 1961.

PARRA, MANUEL GERMÁN. Commentary on FRANK TANNENBAUM, "La lucha por la paz y por el pan," *Problemas agrícolas e industriales de México,* Vol. IV, No. 3.

————. "La doctrina de la Revolución Mexicana," *Excélsior* (Mexico City), March 11, 1965.

————. "Una nueva teoría económica," *Excélsior* (Mexico City), December, 31, 1964.

PARTIDO APRISTA PERUANO. *Cuarenta años de lucha por la unidad de América Latina, 1924–1964.* Lima, no date.

"Partidos," *Panoramas* (Mexico City), No. 11 (September–October, 1964).

PAZ ESTENSSORO, VÍCTOR. "La revolución boliviana," in EUGENIO CHANG-RODRÍGUEZ and HARRY KANTOR (eds.), *La América Latina de hoy.* New York: Ronald Press, 1961.

PELLEGRINI, CARLOS. *Discursos y escritos.* Buenos Aires: Ed. Estrada, 1959.

PÉREZ VILA, MANUEL. "Consideraciones sobre una posible síntesis de la historia de la independencia hispanoamericana," in *El movimiento emancipador de Hispanoamérica,* Vol. IV. Caracas: Academia Nacional de la Historia, 1961.

PIAZZA, LUIS GUILLERMO. "Desesperanza de Benedetti," *Excélsior* (Mexico City), December 16, 1964.

————. "Entretelones del deterioro financiero de Argentina," *Excélsior* (Mexico City), March 6, 1965.

PICÓN SALAS, MARIANO. In *Integración política de Iberoamérica.* Mexico City: El Colegio de México, no date.

————. "Unidad y nacionalismo en la historia hispanoamericana," in *Ensayos sobre la historia del Nuevo Mundo.* Mexico City: Instituto Panamericano de Geografía e Historia, 1951.

PIKE, FREDERICK B. "The Modernized Church in Peru: Two Aspects," *The Review of Politics.* (Notre Dame, Ind.), July, 1964.

PIÑA SORIA, RODOLFO. "Viaje por suscripción popular," *Acción social* (Mexico City), March 15, 1943.

POSADA, ANTONIO J. "La coyuntura económica de América Latina," *Boletín de la Academia de Historia del Valle del Cauca* (Cali, Colombia), January, 1965.

PRESTES, LUIS CARLOS, *Informe al IV Congreso do Partido Comunista do Brasil.* Rio de Janeiro, 1953.

PRIETO, JUAN IGNACIO. "Venezuela: ¿una revolución frustrada?" *El Día* (Mexico City), September 29, 1964.

RANGEL GASPAR, ELISEO. "Los golpes de Estado y la revolución," *El Día* (Mexico City), November 30, 1964.

RECAVARREN, JORGE LUIS. "Notas sobre la burguesía peruana," *El Mundo en Español* (Paris), March 6–13, 1965.

RENAN, ERNEST. Qu'est-ce qu'une nation? Paris: C. Levy, 1882.

Report of the Second Inter-American Conference for Democracy and Freedom, New York, 1961.

Roca, Blas. *The Cuban Revolution*. New York: New Century Publishers, 1961.

Rocker, Rudolf. *Nationalism and Culture*. Translated by Ray E. Chase. Los Angeles: Rocker Publications Committees, 1937.

Rodríguez Arias, Lino (ed.). *La democracia cristiana y América Latina*. Lima: Ed. Universitaria, 1961.

Rojas, Ricardo. *El profeta de la pampa*. Buenos Aires: Losada, 1945.

Rojas Juanco, Carlos. "El programa de Allende y la izquierda latinoamericana," *El Día* (Mexico City), November 24, 1964.

Rolland, Romain. "Carta a Alfredo L. Palacios," *La Nación* (Buenos Aires), June 25, 1925.

Sánchez, Luis Alberto. *Examen espectral de América Latina*. Buenos Aires: Losada, 1962.

Sandino, Augusto C. "Primer manifiesto político" and "Carta circular," in *Hispanoamérica en lucha por su independencia*. Mexico City: Cuadernos Americanos, 1962.

Schneider, Ronald M. *Communism in Guatemala, 1944–1954*. New York: Frederick A. Praeger, 1959.

"Se predica una revolución violenta," *Hoja de Información económica* (Mexico City), May 1, 1965.

Segovia, Rafael. Review of Juan José Sebreli, "Vida cotidiana y alienación," *Foro Internacional* (Mexico City), October–December, 1964.

Shafer, Boyd C. *Nationalism: Myth and Reality*. New York: Harcourt, Brace & World, 1955.

Shul'govskiy, A. "Imperialism and the Ideology of National Reformism in Latin America," in Thomas Perry Thornton (ed.), *The Third World in Soviet Perspective: Studies by Soviet Writers on the Developing Areas*. Princeton, N.J.: Princeton University Press, 1964.

Silvert, K. H. "Les valeurs nationales, le développement, les leaders et leurs troupes," *Revue Internationale des Sciences Sociales* (Paris), No. 4 (1963).

Smith, Adam. *An Inquiry into the Nature and Causes of the Wealth of Nations*. New York: Modern Library, 1937.

Los socialistas y la realidad cubana. Havana: Popular Socialist Party of Cuba, 1944.

Stalin, Joseph. *Marxism and the National Question*. Moscow: Foreign Languages Publishing House, 1947.

Tello, Carlos A. "El sector agrícola y el desarrollo económico en los países latinoamericanos," in *El Trimestre Económico* (Mexico City), January–March, 1965.

Townsend, Andrés. "Ya existe el parlamento latinoamericano," *El Mundo en Español* (Paris), February 6, 1965.

UGARTE, MANUEL. *El porvenir de la América Latina*. Valencia: Sampere, no date.

UNITED NATIONS ECONOMIC COMMISSION FOR LATIN AMERICA. *El desarrollo social de América Latina en la postguerra*. Santiago: The Commission, 1964.

―――. "Informe sobre las actividades económicas latinoamericanas de 1960 a 1963," *Comercio Exterior* (Mexico City), November, 1964.

URQUIDI, VICTOR L. *The Challenge of Development in Latin America*. Translated by MARJORY M. URQUIDI. New York: Frederick A. Praeger, 1964.

―――. *Trayectoria del Mercado Común latinoamericano*. Mexico City: Centro de Estudios Monetarios Latinoamericanos, 1960.

VASCONCELOS, JOSÉ. In *Integracion política de Iberoamérica*. Mexico City: El Colegio de México, no date.

VERDÚ, MARIO. "Por una reforma agraria," *Panoramas* (Mexico City), No. 14 (March–April, 1965).

VIEIRA, GILBERTO. "Las luchas en el campo colombiano y el Partido Comunista," *Revista International* (Prague), May, 1961.

WAISS, OSCAR. *Nacionalismo y socialismo en América Latina*. Santiago: Prensa Latinoamericana, [1954].

WHITAKER, ARTHUR P. *Nationalism in Latin America, Past and Present*. Gainesville: University of Florida Press, 1962.

WIONCZEK, MIGUEL S. (ed.). *Latin American Economic Integration: Experiences and Prospects*. New York: Frederick A. Praeger, 1966.

YCAZA TIGERINO, JULIO. "Las formas políticas. Anarquía y dictadura," in EUGENIO CHANG-RODRÍGUEZ and HARRY KANTOR (eds.), *La América Latina de hoy*. New York: Ronald Press, 1961.

―――. *Sociología de la política hispanoamericana* (2d. ed.). Madrid: Instituto de Estudios Politicos, 1962.

YUDELMAN, MONTAGUE. *The Inter-American Development Bank and Agricultural Development in Latin America*. Washington, D.C.: Inter-American Development Bank, 1966.

ZABLUDOVSKY, JACOBO. "Decir la verdad," *Siempre* (Mexico City), April 21, 1965.

ZAVALA, SILVIO. "El fin de los imperios europeos en América," in *El movimiento emancipador de Hispanoamérica*, Vol. IV. Caracas: Academia Nacional de la Historia, 1961.

ZEA, LEOPOLDO. *América como conciencia*. Mexico City: Cuadernos Americanos, 1953.

―――. *Dos etapas del pensamiento en Hispanoamérica*. Mexico City: El Colegio de México, 1949.

ZEMELMAN MERINO, HUGO. "Problemas ideológicos de la izquierda," *Arauco* (Santiago), November, 1964.

Index

SOUTHERN COLORADO STATE COLLEGE LIBRARY